The Lost Island of
Columbus
SOLVING THE MYSTERY OF GUANAHANI

Keith A. Pickering

SUNBURY
PRESS
Mechanicsburg, PA USA

Published by Sunbury Press, Inc.
Mechanicsburg, Pennsylvania

SUNBURY
PRESS

www.sunburypress.com

For information about special discounts for bulk purchases, please contact Sunbury Press Orders Dept. at (855) 338-8359 or orders@sunburypress.com.

To request one of our authors for speaking engagements or book signings, please contact Sunbury Press Publicity Dept. at publicity@sunburypress.com.

ISBN: 978-1-62006-712-3 (Trade paperback)
ISBN: 978-1-62006-713-0 (Mobipocket)

Library of Congress Control Number: 2017939364

FIRST SUNBURY PRESS EDITION: May 2017

Product of the United States of America
0 1 1 2 3 5 8 13 21 34 55

Set in Bookman Old Style
Designed by Crystal Devine
Cover by Terry Kennedy
Edited by Janice Rhayem

Continue the Enlightenment!

Contents

For DR

who set me on the road

Preface

ON October 12, 1492, Christopher Columbus set foot on the shore of a new island in a New World, the first part of America seen by any European since the time of the Vikings. Columbus named that island San Salvador, but the gentle Lucayan people who lived there called it Guanahani. Less than three days later, Columbus sailed away from Guanahani, never to return. The events of those days, on that island, forever altered the course of human history in ways that we are still feeling today. But as Columbus's three ships disappeared over the horizon, the island of Guanahani itself faded into the mists of time.

For five hundred years, the location and identity of Guanahani remained a mystery. For the last two hundred years, the actual site of Guanahani, Columbus's first landfall, has been the subject of controversy. Dozens of historians, geographers, and mariners have claimed to know the answer—or claimed that the answer was unknowable. And though all agree that it was somewhere in the Bahamas, ten different islands have been proposed as Guanahani at various times by various theorists.

The range of subjects bearing on this mystery is extraordinarily broad: anthropology, astronomy, botany, cartography, metrology, geomagnetism, oceanography, and seamanship are just some of the topics that a serious student of the problem must be prepared to grapple with. Most of the historical evidence rests on a foundation of documents in handwritten, sixteenth-century Spanish, plus a few place names in the lost language of the Lucayans.

This book is the story of that mystery and of those who tried to solve it. It is the story of how the scientific method can be successfully applied to historical problems. And in a small way it is also my story, because I am one of the detectives who cracked the case.

KAP

Watertown, Minnesota

1.

Technical Knockout

"GUESS what your old friend Joe Judge is up to?" The question was a little unfair, since Joe Judge wasn't really a friend of either of us; more of an adversary of my friend Dennis Rawlins, and known to me by reputation only. Judge had been senior editor of *National Geographic* during the 1980s, a controversial period in the magazine's history. And Judge had been involved in the most contentious issue of that period: the dispute over whether Robert E. Peary had actually reached the North Pole in 1909, as he claimed, or whether he faked the feat, as most historians now believe.

It was the Peary controversy and *National Geographic* that had first brought me in contact with Rawlins. In the January 1990 issue, *National Geographic* had run an article by retired Admiral Thomas D. Davies, USN, which defended Peary's claim. The article ran alongside a letter from society president Gilbert Grosvenor, stating flatly that Davies's new research had ended the controversy conclusively in Peary's favor.[1] Davies had relied heavily on an analysis of shadows seen on photos taken by Peary at his northernmost camp. From that he determined the Sun's angle above the horizon, and therefore his approximate position using celestial navigation. I had read the article, and later Davies's full report on the issue, which was published by the Navigation Foundation, a group of mariners and navigation

---

1. *National Geographic* 177:1 (January 1990), 44-61.

enthusiasts headed by Davies himself. As a systems analyst with strong interests in both photography and astronomy, I had found large gaps in Davies's computation of the errors in his photogrammetric process; I was certain that these errors were far larger than Davies admitted. So I did what I usually do in such situations: I wrote a letter to the editor of *National Geographic*, suggesting that the analysis be redone.

Although I frequently write letters to the editor of various publications, I had seldom received any response other than a boilerplate acknowledgement. So I was surprised when Barbara McConnell, a researcher at *National Geographic*, responded personally to my letter. She noted that I had not given many details of my objections and concluded that the society was standing behind Davies's article. And she was perfectly correct: I had been writing briefly, with the hope of publication, rather than in complete detail. But since McConnell had been kind enough to respond personally, I thought I owed her a more detailed analysis of the problems I had found. One week and four thousand words later, I replied to her with a detailed set of issues, along with suggestions for improvements in Davies's analysis. She sent a copy of my letter on to Davies.

At about the same time, *Scientific American* had run a brief article[2] reporting the *National Geographic*'s findings. They quoted astronomer Charles Kowal's opinion, quite similar to mine: the errors in Davies's analysis were too great to support the conclusion that Peary had reached the Pole. Kowal's name was well known to me; his work on solar system objects had made him world famous. (There is an entire class of objects today known as "Kowal bodies.") I wrote to Kowal at the Space Telescope Science Institute, and he promptly put me in touch with astronomer Dennis Rawlins, a leading critic of Peary's claim.

Rawlins phoned me in March 1990. He was intelligent, articulate, and full of interesting stories about the Peary controversy

---

2. *Scientific American* (March 1990), 99. The odd discrepancy I had initially noted in Davies's *Geographic* article stemmed from the photo layout (op.cit. p. 45) in which is shown an enlargement of one of the Peary photos with photogrammetric lines drawn on top. The photo shows not one, but two photogrammetric horizon lines, a few millimeters apart, apparently a highest- and lowest-possible horizon. That is not in itself a problem, since either horizon is defensible and since the computed error band should include the difference. But my back-of-the-envelope computation showed that the size of the published error band was barely large enough to allow for just this one source of error—not including any of the many other error sources.

and everyone involved. I liked him instantly. He was impressed that I had noticed a flaw in Davies's math that Rawlins had missed; I was impressed that he had noticed several flaws that I had missed. One tidbit I gleaned from Rawlins was that Joe Judge at the *Geographic* had hired Tom Davies to write the Peary article, and had even given Davies office space in the *National Geographic* headquarters building. Judge had chosen Davies because of a paper Davies had written some time earlier, dealing with Amerigo Vespucci's longitude measurement of 1499. The Vespucci paper had not been published, but both Rawlins and Kowal had read it, and they knew that Davies had made some colossal astronomical blunders,[3] which when corrected discredited the whole notion that Vespucci was a celestial navigator of any kind. Judge, with no background in astronomy, was apparently unaware of this when he hired Davies to defend Peary's navigation.

When no reanalysis of the photos seemed to be forthcoming from the *National Geographic*, I decided to do one myself, using Davies's published material, but with a more accurate accounting of the various possible sources of error. I sent copies of my analysis to Rawlins, Davies, and the *National Geographic*. Much later, I learned that either Davies or his Navigation Foundation had sent a copy of my analysis to a statistics professor at West Point for vetting; but apparently it came off clean, since I heard nothing further from them.

That round of the long-running Peary affair came to a head in April of 1991. The U.S. Naval Institute organized a debate over the Peary controversy as part of its annual meeting that year. Rawlins was on the panel as one of Peary's critics, and although Admiral Davies had died in the interim, his son Doug Davies represented the Navigation Foundation. I watched from the audience as an interested party. At that time I took the opportunity to join the Naval Institute, an academic society affiliated with the U.S. Naval Academy in Annapolis. Although most of its members are active or retired Navy and Marine officers, they are happy to accept anyone interested in naval affairs.

---

3. Davies had computed the Moon's position geocentrically, that is as seen from the center of Earth, rather than topocentrically, from a given position on Earth's surface. This is usually not a big difference, but in the specific case of the Moon, it is a huge difference because the Moon is so close to Earth. For further discussion of Vespucci's longitude, see Chapter 8.

At the Naval Institute debate, Peary's critics clearly won the day. When Boyce Rensberger, science editor for the *Washington Post*, wrote his article, he concluded that Peary's claim was "probably faked."[4] In addition to the principals of the debate, Rensberger interviewed both myself and Brad Schaefer, a NASA astronomer interested in historical matters, who had seen my analysis and said some complementary things about it. In the years since, doubts about Peary's claim have been voiced by an almost unbroken line of historians on both sides of the Atlantic.

Rensberger's article did not appear in the *Post* until June of 1991. Joe Judge was fired by *National Geographic* a few weeks later. He was the most visible victim of a major housecleaning by Grosvenor; a look at the masthead shows that Grosvenor himself took more direct control of the magazine and the society at this time. News accounts suggested that Judge had earned Grosvenor's ire by giving the magazine a less conservative slant; meaning that he had run some features with environmental and ethnic appeal. At our house, we wondered if the bruising the *Geographic* had taken on the Peary affair might also have been a factor.

So I was surprised to read, in the December 1991 issue of *Proceedings of the U.S. Naval Institute*, that Joe Judge was still alive and kicking, so to speak. The Naval Institute had again arranged a debate on another matter of historical and navigational interest for its upcoming 1992 annual meeting. The topic this time around was the Columbus landfall controversy: where, exactly, did Christopher Columbus step ashore in the New World on October 12, 1492? The five hundredth anniversary of the discovery was an appropriate time for the debate, and Judge was slated to defend his theory that the landfall was at Samana Cay, a small island in the Bahamas. Judge had published his theory in the November 1986 issue of *National Geographic*, and Samana Cay has been known as the *Geographic*'s theory ever since.

I called Dennis Rawlins with the latest. "Guess what your old friend Joe Judge is up to? He'll be debating the Columbus landfall problem at the Naval Institute next year." The Naval Institute had engaged advocates of three different landfall theories for its panel. In addition to Judge, Dr. Steven Mitchell was

4. *Washington Post* (1991 June 9), D3.

representing his theory that Columbus had landed at Conception Island; and Samuel Loring Morison was impaneled to represent the Watlings Island theory, which had been advocated by his late grandfather, Admiral Samuel Eliot Morison. Although Rawlins knew little of the Columbus landfall problem, he said that as far as he knew, Judge's theory was as good as any.

I knew even less about the Columbus landfall problem than Rawlins, but I shot off my mouth anyway. I told him that I had a copy of Columbus's log in my library; that I had read it, and that it was impossible to tell anything at all from the scanty evidence in it. Rawlins was interested; he suggested that I write up a paper on the landfall problem for *DIO*, the science history journal that he had recently founded. If my opinion was supported by the evidence, that was fine with him; but if my research supported Judge, he would be happy to publish that, too. This was typical of Rawlins: he could be ruthlessly critical of ideas and people he disagreed with; but he was also unstinting with praise for his opponents when their ideas had merit.

As it turned out, most of what I told Rawlins that day was dead wrong. First, I did not have a copy of Columbus's log in my library. What I had was a copy of Columbus's letter to the Spanish court announcing the discovery. Although I had been right about the letter—it was too short of details to be useful—I knew that Columbus's log did exist. And when I found a copy of the log and read it, the evidence I found there was far from scanty. In fact, the log was extremely detailed, containing a meticulous account of the voyage, especially in the area of the first landfall.

The landfall island was known to be somewhere in the Bahamas, an archipelago about which I was also mostly ignorant. I knew that there were a lot of them, that they were low lying, and that they ran roughly northwest to southeast. But I knew nothing of the geographical details of any of the islands. And except for the Columbus letter, I had never read an entire book devoted to Columbus.

But I also realized that I could use my own ignorance to my advantage. My plan was to read the log of Columbus's first voyage and see if I could make a map of the coastlines and islands visited by Columbus, using only the descriptions given in the log. Since I didn't know where the coastlines of any real islands actually ran, my map would be untainted by any subconscious bias for or against any landfall theory. I was in a position to be the perfect disinterested observer.

If, as I suspected, it was not possible to make such a map, or if it was not possible to do so in an unambiguous way, then I could say with some confidence that the landfall problem was impossible to solve definitively. But if such a map was possible, I could take the map I drew and compare it to a real map of the Bahamas, to see if my map matched any set of real islands. I frankly suspected that if such a map could be drawn, it would match more than one possible island as the landfall; otherwise, the problem would have been resolved long ago.

Visiting the University of Minnesota library, I discovered that the log of the first voyage, more properly known as the *Diario*, existed in a wide array of translations. I quickly settled on a recent edition by Oliver Dunn and James E. Kelley Jr.[5] The Dunn & Kelley translation was uniquely valuable, because it had a transcription of the original Spanish manuscript on the left-hand pages, while the English translation occupied the right. Even better, there was a concordance of the Spanish transcription in the back. I soon bought my own copy, and the *Diario* became my constant companion in the weeks and months that followed.

Within two weeks, I had read the *Diario* twice through. In common parlance, it is called the "log" of Columbus, but that is not strictly accurate, since it is an abstraction of the log, made in the sixteenth century by Bartolomé de Las Casas, a monk who was a friend of the Columbus family. The account breaks naturally into three sections. The westbound transatlantic portions are spare narrative, listing the ship's daily run (measured in leagues, a common maritime measurement of roughly three statute miles), courses sailed, plus brief accounts of any unusual occurrences or sightings, such as birds or seaweed. A day's entry typically runs a paragraph or two.

This pattern is abruptly broken on the night of October 11-12, when four pages are devoted to the night on which land

---

5. Oliver Dunn and James E. Kelley Jr., *The Diario of Columbus's First Voyage to America, 1492-1493* (University of Oklahoma Press, Norman and London, 1989). Unless otherwise noted, the English translations of *Diario* passages in this book are mine, based on the Spanish transcriptions of Dunn & Kelley.

was sighted and the events of the following day. Oddly, there is no separate entry for the day of October 12; the narrative just runs on from the previous night. This introduces the second major part of the *Diario*, the inter-island section, which is about two-thirds of the text. In this section, descriptions are generally longer and more detailed, with daily entries ranging from a couple of lines to several pages. The descriptions cover geography, animals, plants, native peoples, and the activities of the Spaniards. Navigational information is interspersed in the general narrative, which means that close reading is required. The last part of the *Diario* is the return voyage, which reverts to the original style: brief navigational descriptions of courses and distances, plus any unusual phenomena.

There is one obvious problem with the *Diario* from a navigational point of view: while Columbus is careful to specify courses and distances traveled every day in the transatlantic sections, that is not always true in the inter-island section. For that reason, it was clear to me that Columbus was using two different methods of navigation. In the deep-water portions, Columbus was using "dead reckoning" navigation. In dead reckoning, courses and distances are plotted on a chart from a known point, with each day's endpoint being the starting point for the next day's charting. But within sight of land, Columbus was using "pilotage": steering from one visible point of land to another. Columbus wrote that he was making a map of the lands he discovered, which would make up for any missing data in the log; but his map has not survived.

In spite of the occasional missing data, I hoped to construct a map of the coastlines and islands he visited by reading the descriptions carefully. There were a few places where Columbus's language was difficult or ambiguous, so I made reasonable assumptions in those cases. In some places where Columbus omitted the distances, he did give the time of travel, often an important clue to the missing distance.

In making my map, I encountered several surprises. First, I was surprised to find that the navigational data in the *Diario* were mostly free of internal inconsistencies. In fact, the data tended to be self-confirming in a number of important ways. Given the long history of the controversy, I had expected that the *Diario* would be frequently self-contradictory, or at least ambiguous in important and obvious ways; but this was seldom the case. Because of this internal consistency, I found that I actually could draw a map from Columbus's descriptions, and that there was, by and large, only one way that such a map could look and still be consistent with the *Diario*.

So I was satisfied that I had drawn a map of coastlines and islands consistent with the available data; and I was also fairly confident that any map conforming to the data must be quite similar to mine. In fact, drawing the map was so easy that I was increasingly pessimistic that the map I had drawn could be fit to any real set of islands in the Bahamas, or that it could fit only one set of islands. The fact that there was landfall controversy at all implied that the solution could not be so simple.

Finally, I took the plunge and examined a real map of the Bahamas and compared it to the map I had drawn. Would my map confirm Joe Judge's Samana Cay theory? Would Watlings Island, the official "San Salvador" on modern maps, be the solution? Or would the dark-horse Conception Island, which I had never even heard of two weeks before, claim the prize?

I knew the features I was looking for, and in my second big surprise, I found them immediately. The details of my map did indeed conform to one and (in another surprise) only one area of the Bahamas in every important respect. I could hardly believe my eyes, or my luck. But the biggest surprise was the identity of the first landfall island. The answer: none of the above!

Two small, closely spaced islands bore the words "Plana Cays," positioned right where my map indicated the first landfall island should be. The fact that there were two worried me. Maybe they were joined in Columbus's day? But then again, did the *Diario* specifically state that the landfall island was one and only one island, or that there was or was not another nearby? I couldn't be sure.

Suddenly, I caught myself. How foolish I was! Clearly, I had made a mistake somewhere. If, after decades of controversy, nobody was advocating the Plana Cays as the landfall, there must be an obvious reason for it, a reason I had missed. Determined to find the fatal flaw, I decided to read the *Diario* again, comparing each and every description in the *Diario* to the route starting from the Plana Cays. I also wanted to compare the descriptions to the routes from Samana, Watlings, and Conception. This required some additional research to find the routes proposed by Judge, Morison, and Mitchell. Judge's and Morison's routes were easy to find in the library; Mitchell's Conception Island route was not. However, Conception Island is quite close to Watlings, so I guessed that the routes were mostly the same. This guess eventually proved to be correct.

It turned out that the three islands represented on the Naval Institute panel were only a fraction of the possibilities. I found references to nine Bahamian islands that had been proposed as the Columbus landfall. I also discovered that the Plana Cays had in fact been suggested as the landfall by a previous researcher: Ramón J. Didiez Burgos, an admiral in the navy of the Dominican Republic, had published a book in 1974 proposing the theory.[6] But his book went unquoted and almost unmentioned by anyone else; nor were any other works by Didiez available.

By January 1992, I was frustrated and flummoxed. Having reread the *Diario* thoroughly, I had not found the fatal flaw in the Plana Cays route that I had expected to find. There was no explicit reference to the landfall being either a single island or multiple. There were many places where Columbus referred to "the island," singular; but if the landfall was multiple islands, those could simply be references to one specific island of the group. There were a few places where descriptions did not seem to fit the route from the Plana Cays perfectly, but in most cases those same descriptions fit the other islands' routes just as poorly or worse. With real maps in hand, I could trace Columbus's route through the Bahamas backward from Cuba, and the backward track inevitably ended at the Plana Cays.

By now it seemed to me that it was not the Plana Cays, but the other islands that had the fatal flaw, and that flaw was related to almost the first navigational clue in the inter-island section of the log: the only place in the *Diario* where Columbus describes the direction to the landfall island from anywhere else. After arriving at the second island on October 14, Columbus describes it like this: "I found that the face in the direction

---

6. Ramón J. Didiez Burgos, *Guanahaní y Mayaguaní* (Editoria Cultural Dominicana, Santo Domingo, 1974).

of San Salvador runs north-south." In my mind, it seemed clear
the coast of the second island running north-south was facing
towards San Salvador, the landfall island. The paradox is that
this critical description, which fits the Plana Cays perfectly, did
not fit either Samana Cay or Conception Island at all, and fit
Watlings Island quite poorly. But the Spanish at this point in
the log was obscure for me, so I consulted other translations.
With some variation, these all conveyed the same idea, a coast
that was facing San Salvador.

There was no escape. The Plana Cays, ignored and unloved,
seemed clearly to be the best solution to the riddle of the Columbus landfall. And since nobody else seemed willing or able
to carry the standard for the Plana Cays, I had two choices. I
could just let the whole thing drop, or I could carry the standard
myself. The first option was not my style, so there was really no
choice at all. I was on my own, at the end of a very long limb.

I had to call Dennis Rawlins with the bad news. "I've been
looking at the Columbus landfall problem," I said, "and I don't
think it's any of those islands. I think it's another island entirely. An island nobody else believes." Rawlins took it surprisingly well. "Well, if the evidence shows that, write it up, and we'll
run it." I was grateful for the support. Dennis had asked for an
overview of the landfall problem, which was one thing; but a
new historical theory, likely to be controversial, was a different
kettle of fish. To take Dennis off the hook, I told him I would
seek publication elsewhere first, if possible.

Next I wrote to James Barber, president of the U.S. Naval
Institute. I suspected that since the debate panel had already
been announced in *Proceedings*, it would be too late to add another participant; but I figured it was at least worth a try. Barber
did turn down my request, but was gracious about it. He passed
my letter on to his subordinate, Mac Greeley, a former Marine
fighter pilot working as an associate editor for *Proceedings*.

Mac was encouraging when he called. The panel discussion
was scheduled for the morning of April 24. Although the on-
stage panel was set, I would have an opportunity to air my views
in two ways. First, I could ask questions of the panelists from
the floor. Second, another landfall session was planned for the
afternoon. Since this conflicted with another major seminar for

the members, the audience for the afternoon session would be much smaller and composed only of Columbus aficionados, but Mac promised much of the afternoon session to me. These arrangements were similar to the Peary debate the previous year, and I was grateful for the time. Mac also mentioned that there would be yet another landfall theorist attending: Arne Molander, an advocate of the Egg Island theory.

Over the next three months I spent every spare hour researching Columbus's navigation and the various theories of the Columbus landfall and preparing my presentation for the afternoon session. The landfall debate had been going on for a surprisingly long time and had even developed its own special jargon. The modern Bahamian island of San Salvador was invariably referred to by its pre-1926 name, Watlings Island, to avoid confusion with Columbus's nomenclature. For the same reason, the Bahamian islands visited by Columbus were referred to by Roman numerals. "Island I" was the landfall island: called Guanahani by the natives, and named *San Salvador* by Columbus. "Island II" was the second island visited, named *Santa Maria de la Concepcion* by Columbus. Next visited was "Island III," named *Fernandina* by Columbus; like Island II, its native name was not recorded in the log. Finally, "Island IV," which was called Samoet by the natives, was named *Isabela* by Columbus. After leaving Island IV, Columbus came upon a string of islands running north-south, which he named the *Islas de Arena*, or Sand Islands, before arriving at Cuba. Given their geography and distance from Cuba, nearly everyone agrees that the Ragged Islands in the Bahamas are the only possible candidates for the *Islas de Arena*. Only the identities of the first four islands are in dispute.

I arrived at Annapolis the afternoon before the debate and found Mac Greeley sitting in the huge lecture theater in Mahan Hall on the Naval Academy campus. Mac was as pleasant in person as he was over the phone. By this time, my paper was well along, and Mac indicated that there was a chance it could be published in *Proceedings*. Over the previous century, *Proceedings of the U.S. Naval Institute* had published several papers dealing with the landfall problem, starting in the nineteenth century.[7] In the February 1992 issue, *Proceedings* published short articles by each of the debate panelists describing their theories. I had responded with a letter to the editor, advocating the Plana Cays theory; Mac Greeley told me it was due for publication in the May issue.

As the point man for the Naval Institute on the debate, Mac had been doing his own research on the landfall problem, so he and I had much to talk about. Mac gave his opinion that the landfall island could only be found by tracing Columbus's track backward from Cuba, a view I shared. But Mac also said that no one could trace the backward track satisfactorily. I told him that I could, and moreover that I would do so in the afternoon session. Mac seemed nonplussed by my confidence.

The Naval Institute had invited William F. Buckley to be moderator of the debate. As host of PBS's *Firing Line*, as well as a noted author and yachtsman, Buckley was a perfect choice. In addition to the three landfall theorists, the panel included two retired Rear Admirals as neutral participants: William Lemos was an acknowledged authority on Columbus's ships; and Bob McNitt was an ocean racing sailor and navigational expert.[8]

After opening remarks from Naval Institute president Jim Barber and from Buckley, Joe Judge was up first. Judge began by giving a biography of Gustavus V. Fox, who had been (among other things) undersecretary of the Navy during the Civil War, and in 1882 was also the first person to suggest that Samana Cay was the first landfall of Columbus. Judge next lambasted a diplomatic council of Spanish-speaking nations that had recently met in Puerto Rico, which had endorsed Watlings as the landfall. To honor the 500th anniversary, Spain had constructed replica ships to sail in Columbus's route. Judge was disappointed that as a result of the Puerto Rico decision, the replica ships would arrive at Watlings rather than Samana. In Judge's eyes, the debate had become political rather than scholarly. After this, he used the little time he had remaining to run through

---

7. J. B. Murdock, "The Cruise of Columbus in the Bahamas," 1492. *Proceedings of the U.S. Naval Institute* 10 (1884) 449-486. Murdock's inter-island track from Watlings Island was a significant improvement over the previous suggestion of A. B. Becher, and formed the basis of the track proposed by Morison in 1942.

8. U.S. Naval Institute, "Where Did Columbus Land? The evidence to date." 118th annual meeting & second Annapolis seminar, Tape 2 (VHS) (1992).

a quick but competent explanation of the Samana theory, using a map of the Bahamas projected on the large screen in the front of the hall.

Next, Dr. Steven Mitchell gave his presentation on Conception Island. Mitchell was a geologist from California State University at Bakersfield, and he had just returned from fieldwork on Conception. He began by outlining how his own opinion of the landfall problem had evolved over the years, from Watlings to Conception to Samana and finally back to Conception. Mitchell's approach was that of the scientist, and after describing his geological research and the Conception Island landfall, to his credit he spent time talking about an important weakness in his own theory: the use of Rum Cay as Island II. Columbus described Island II as having a coastline running north-south for five leagues, and another running east-west for ten leagues. These distances were about three times larger than the coastlines on Rum Cay. To explain the discrepancy, Mitchell employed an argument first suggested by Murdock in 1884. The idea was that Columbus had written his log originally in miles, not in leagues. The league distances in the existing manuscript of the log were unit conversion errors by Bartolomé de Las Casas, the transcriber and abstracter of the existing version. This hypothesis allowed Mitchell (as well as advocates of Watlings Island, which also uses Rum Cay as Island II) to suppose that Columbus had written five *miles* and ten *miles* as the original dimensions of Island II, and that the units of measure had been corrupted in the conversion process. We will see in chapter 6 that this idea is of crucial importance.

In contrast to the first two speakers, Samuel Loring Morison was excruciating. Morison was the grandson of the late Samuel Eliot Morison, a heavyweight figure in Columbus scholarship. The elder Morison had been rear admiral in the U.S. Navy, professor of history at Harvard, and 1943 Pulitzer Prize winner for his Columbus biography *Admiral of the Ocean Sea*, still considered essential reading for any Columbus scholar. Morison's legacy towered over the landfall debate like a colossus. Samuel Eliot Morison had stated that the landfall was at Watlings Island, and for two generations of schoolchildren, nothing more need be said. But the grandson, an analyst in the Defense Department, was decidedly out of place as a public speaker. Reading from a prepared script, he spoke slowly, often lost his place, sometimes repeated phrases, and threw in the occasional incomplete sentence. Morison's triumphant discovery, which took him two years to make, was that the *National Geographic* had made a 24-hour mistake in its transatlantic track reconstruction. Morison had looked at the reconstruction of Columbus's transatlantic track used by his grandfather, a reconstruction done by John McElroy in 1940. He compared it to the reconstruction done by Luis Marden in 1986 and published in the *Geographic*. On McElroy's map, the first day's position was labeled "September 8," while Marden's first day position was labeled "September 9, 6:00 am." To Morison, it seemed clear that Marden and the *Geographic* had made a major error. What Morison apparently didn't realize was that in the westbound portion of the *Diario*, a day's run was considered to end at dawn. McElroy's first daily position marked the end of the first day's run of September 8—an endpoint that actually occurred at 6:00 a.m. on the ninth. So McElroy and Marden were both right, they were just using different labeling conventions. I was surprised that no one, especially Judge, seemed to notice Morison's blunder. Or perhaps they were just taking it easy on him out of mercy.

After Morison, William Lemos addressed the problem of the length of the league used by Columbus. Although a league was four miles long in Columbus's day, many variants of "mile" were in use in the Middle Ages. Lemos came down in favor of Columbus using the Italian mile of 4,060 feet. The corresponding Italian league of 2.67 nautical miles was first suggested as Columbus's measure by James E. Kelley in 1983. Bob McNitt spoke on Columbus's navigational methods, concluding (as has every competent navigator who has examined the issue carefully) that Columbus navigated by dead reckoning, rather than by celestial means.

After this the agenda called for questions from the floor, but Buckley departed from the script to invite Arne Molander to the podium to speak on behalf of his Egg Island landfall theory. Much later I learned that Molander had been quite upset when he learned that he had been excluded from the panel, and that he personally importuned Buckley to intercede with the Naval

Institute on his behalf. I would soon discover that this was typical behavior for Molander. A retired civil engineer who had first published his Egg Island theory in 1981, in the intervening decade he had failed to convince anyone that the idea had merit. Since he just *knew* that his theory had to be correct, Molander concluded that this lack of support was due to bias that others felt against him. In Molander's view, he was being ignored and treated unfairly by the historical "establishment," and he was not shy about browbeating anyone over this perceived unfairness until he got his way.

Tall, lean, and gray-haired, with a nervous voice and a quick mind, Molander walked to the podium with the help of a cane. Egg Island was far to the north of all other landfall candidates, which presented the problem of explaining how Columbus had arrived way up there. Molander proposed that Columbus had sailed across the Atlantic using celestial navigation, rather than dead reckoning, to hold to a constant latitude. If he was right in this, all other landfall theories were falsified at a stroke. The obvious problem was that there are no celestial navigation data in the *Diario*, a strange state of affairs if Columbus had really been a celestial navigator. Molander got around the issue by proposing that Columbus navigated without instrumentation, by observing certain stars that brush the northern horizon in their nightly rotations.

But Bob McNitt saw a larger problem with the whole celestial navigation idea. Since the helmsmen aboard these ships were below decks and could not see the sky, they relied on their magnetic compass to steer. During this era, there was westerly magnetic declination in the North Atlantic; a compass needle would not point true north, but a few degrees west of true north. This westerly declination would have pulled Columbus leftward on any course, or a little to the south when sailing west. If Columbus had been navigating celestially, he would have seen from the stars that he was going too far south, and he would have corrected his course northward every few days to compensate. But the log does not show such course corrections. According to the log, Columbus stuck doggedly to his westerly course for weeks at a time, turning from west on only three brief occasions: twice to chase false signs of land and once because of contrary winds. McNitt's argument was cogent and irrefutable: since there were no course corrections, there could not have been celestial observations, which would have required them. Molander agreed with McNitt that there were no course corrections, but he did not seem to comprehend that this was in any way a problem for his theory.

As Molander moved back to his seat, Buckley threw it open to questions from the audience. I was first in line at the microphone, just beating out Brad Schaefer, the NASA astronomer I had met the previous year. I introduced myself as an advocate of the Plana Cays theory of the landfall and asked the panel a question that would prove embarrassing to all; it was the fatal flaw again:

> Gentlemen, there is only one place in the log where Columbus tells us the direction to San Salvador from any other point. For anyone who is searching for the location of San Salvador, this is arguably the single most important description in the log. After arriving at Island II on the 15th, Columbus writes, 'I found that the face in the direction of San Salvador runs north-south, and that in it there are five leagues.' Or in other words, San Salvador lies due east of a five-league long north-south coastline. This important description is not mentioned in Mr. Judge's *National Geographic* article, it is barely mentioned in Professor Morison's biography, and it is not mentioned in any of the three articles in the February *Proceedings*. It seems no coincidence that this description does not fit Conception Island, does not fit Watlings Island, does not fit Samana Cay, (and also does not fit Egg Island, Mr. Molander's theory); although it does fit the Plana Cays perfectly. Two questions, therefore, for each of the panelists. First, why have you omitted this important description from your writings? And second, how do you explain this description with respect to your individual theories?

A shocked silence fell on the panelists. No one seemed eager to speak. Buckley invited the befuddled Morison to answer, a prospect that drew soft chuckles from the audience. Morison was dumbfounded; he did not recall this description in the log. I assured him it was there. Morison suggested that it might not be in the Fuson translation he was using. I had read Fuson and again assured him that it was there. He finally stated that he could not answer the question, since he did not recall the description.

Buckley asked Dr. Mitchell if he recalled it, which of course he did. Mitchell tried to finesse the question, by pointing out that a north-south coast could face either east *or* west, a point I granted; but he went on to suggest that, if you looked at a map, the west coast of Rum Cay, his proposed Island II, did sort of face Conception Island, his proposed landfall. I instantly disputed the point, and Buckley asked that the map slide be projected on the screen again. It was then obvious to everyone, including Mitchell, that the coast of Rum Cay that faces Conception runs east-west, not north-south.

As the map was being projected, Joe Judge took his turn, pointing to the north-south coasts of both Rum Cay and Acklins Island (his own proposed Island II) and admitting that "Columbus's adjectival description does not fit either Watlings Island or Samana Cay."

Hearing this, Buckley asked, "Do we have a TKO?"

The audience roared with laughter. Judge tried to recoup by describing Gustavus Fox's tortured theory of Columbus's movements during the night of October 14, but finally admitted, "that's not a very good or convincing explanation." But the damage had been done. The score: Morison didn't know the log, Mitchell didn't know the geography, and Judge didn't know the answer. None of the panelists had even attempted to explain why the description had been omitted from their writings. In Buckley's apposite description, the Plana Cays theory had scored a TKO with its very first punch.

At the noon break, I managed to walk a little ways with Joe Judge on our way to the Preble Hall dining room. I tried to ask him why he had rejected the Plana Cays in his 1986 article, but he seemed about as happy to see me as a whale is to see a harpoon. After blowing me off with a quick excuse, he joined the group at the head table with Buckley and the other panelists. It was the first and only face-to-face conversation we ever had.

After lunch, about sixty Columbus enthusiasts reassembled in a smaller lecture hall on the academy campus for the afternoon session. Here at last was my chance to explain the Plana

Cays theory in full to an interested audience. Boyce Rensberger was there from the *Washington Post*, as were Steven Mitchell, Arne Molander, Brad Schaefer, and Mac Greeley. Judge, Morison, and Buckley did not attend. In about an hour I honored my promise to Mac Greeley and traced Columbus's route backward from Cuba to the landfall at the Plana Cays, using what seemed to me to be an obvious method, but one that had never been done before. (A summary of that backward track is given in chapter 2.)

I also fielded questions from the audience. Most of the questions I handled easily, but Molander raised a couple I could not. One of these was whether there was a safe anchorage at the place I proposed, off the southern point of the western of the two Plana Cays. The second had to do with the availability of fresh water on the Plana Cays. I noted both questions as topics for further research.

Leaving the lecture hall, I was walking on air. Mitchell told me privately that he thought Plana was clearly a better theory than Samana; Mac Greeley invited me to go sailing. Brad Schaefer, taking the skeptical attitude of the scientist, remained neutral.

My feelings at the time were that if there was a winner in Annapolis, it was the Plana Cays. The theory had never before had any public airing, at least in the English-speaking world, and it had come out strongly. By asking the TKO question, I had effectively won the debate from the floor. At this rate, I figured that the landfall controversy could be over in a few months, just as the Peary debate had fizzled out the year before, in the face of overwhelming evidence for one side.

Once again, I was dead wrong.

2.

The Backward Track

MANY things can change in five hundred years. Climate can change. Changing rainfall patterns can make deserts advance or retreat. Forests can be created and destroyed. Plants and animals can migrate and can go locally or even globally extinct. Violent storms can erode away coastal features, and can create new ones. People can migrate into or out of areas. Industries can rise and fall. Entire populations can be wiped out by disease or by war. Place names on maps can be created, move, or disappear.

All of these things have happened in the Bahamas in the past five hundred years, or may have. With so much that might have changed, how can we be sure that any of the descriptions that Columbus wrote in his log in 1492 are still true? Doesn't this immense cloud of uncertainty mean that finding the landfall is a hopeless task?

No, it does not, because there is a clearing in that cloud. There are some things that do not change in five hundred years: *islands cannot move.* And because islands cannot move, the distances and directions between islands are the same today as they were in Columbus's day. Which means that the distances and directions between islands are by far the most reliable indicators we have for determining the location of the landfall. It is possible, even likely, that these distances and directions may have been miscalculated by Columbus to a certain extent, and perhaps their transmission may have been imperfect. But the

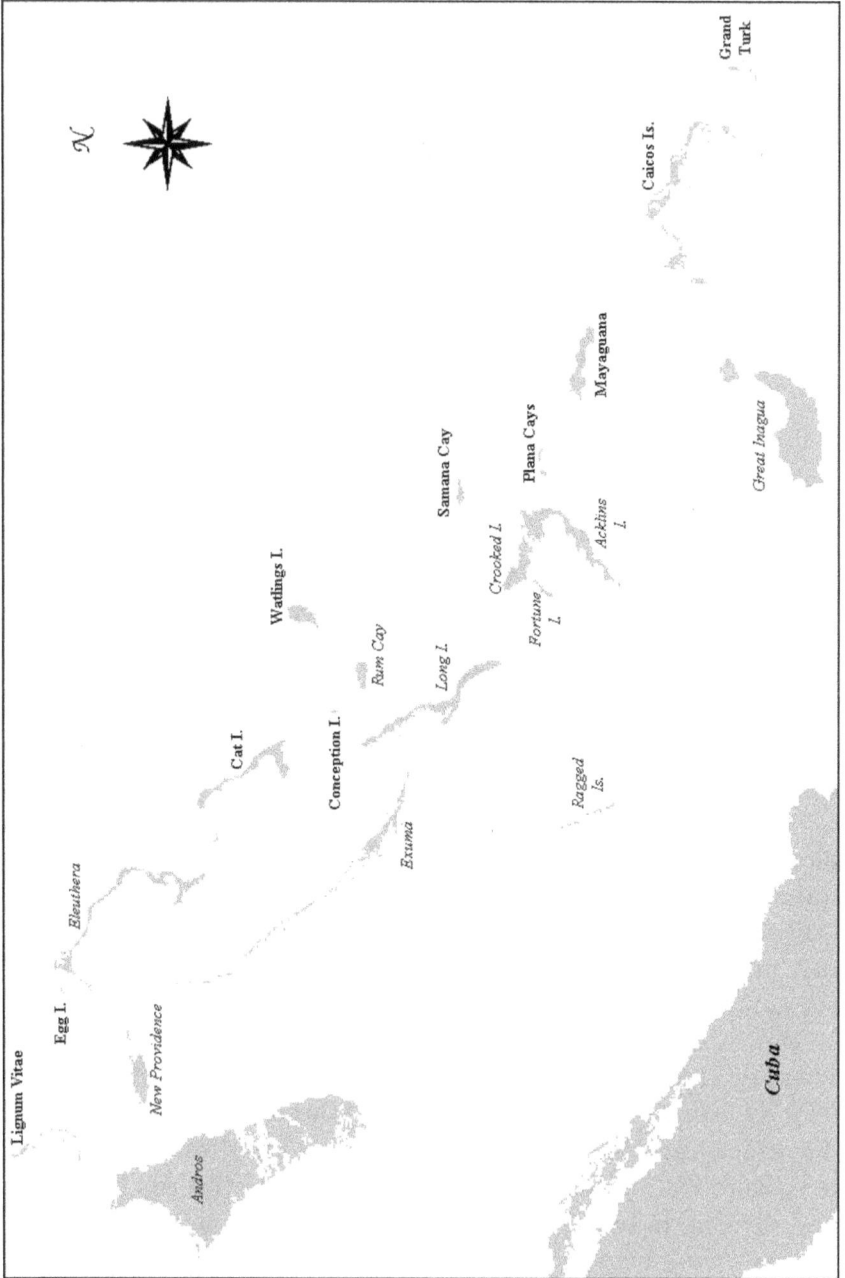

FIGURE 2.1. The Bahamas, with proposed landfalls in bold.

causes of such errors are generally known, and mostly can be accounted for. In addition to immobile islands, the directions of coastlines are also permanent, even if some coastal features may not be (especially features built up from sand).

By following the distances and directions in Columbus's log, there are two ways to arrive at Guanahani: we can follow the route of Columbus himself, westward across the Atlantic from the Canary Islands; or we can start at Cuba and backtrack through the Bahamas to find the landfall island. As we will see in chapter 8, the transatlantic track has major technical issues to deal with. But it turns out that the track backward from Cuba is fairly straightforward. At the afternoon session in Annapolis, I traced the track backward.

Distances in the *Diario* are given in leagues, so before we start we must know how long a league is. The Portuguese Maritime League was the standard[1] league used by Iberian sailors in the fifteenth and sixteenth centuries. Each Portuguese Maritime League is composed of four Roman miles of 1,000 paces each, or 4,860 feet, making the league 3.20 nautical miles long in modern terms. Prior to 1983, this was about the only league anyone had ever assumed that Columbus used.

Then James E. Kelley Jr. proposed[2] that Columbus used the Italian or Geometric League. Each Italian League is composed of four Italian miles of 5,000 palms, or 4,060 feet each, making the league 2.67 nautical miles long in modern terms. We will see that the Italian League solves many outstanding problems in Columbus's navigation. Nowadays, many students of his navigation, including William Lemos, Doug Peck, and Alejandro Pérez, accept it as the league used by Columbus. It has been so useful in my research that it is now the only league length I use.

But in 1992 I was much less sure about this. So I hedged my bets by tracing the backward track using both league lengths. The analysis here uses the Italian League only, so it's a little different from my afternoon presentation in Annapolis. Some of the specific arguments here also date from after Annapolis, but the basic ideas are still the same.

---

1. Morison, Samuel Eliot (1942). *Admiral of the Ocean Sea*. Little, Brown (Boston).
2. Kelley, James E. Jr. (1983). In the wake of Columbus on a portolan chart. *Terrae Incognitae*.

Columbus arrived at Cuba from the *Islas de Arena*, which he described as a group of seven or eight islands extending north and south.[3] Today it is almost universally acknowledged that these must be the Ragged Islands, but we will use this first easy step to demonstrate the technique we will use.

Columbus anchored five leagues off the southern end of the *Islas de Arena*. From there he sailed 17 leagues south-south-west, at which point he sighted Cuba. He doesn't say how far he was from land when he sighted Cuba, but since it was raining at the time, visibility would have been poor. So we can assume that he was pretty close, maybe a league or two.

We can make a little chart of these movements using graph paper (see Figure 2.2). We draw our chart at a scale of one graph paper square to one league. We start at any arbitrary

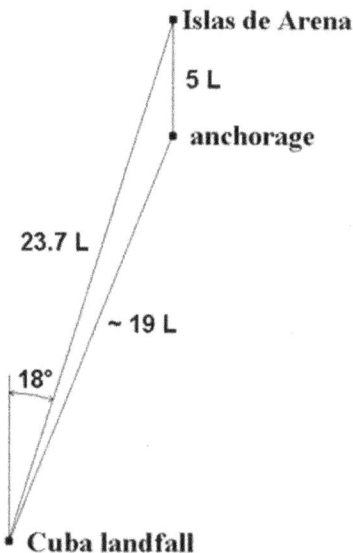

FIGURE 2.2. Vector addition, *Islas de Arena* to Cuba.

3. The extant *Diario* manuscript is written on 67 folio leaves front and back. When referencing the original text, I use the convention of Dunn & Kelley by putting the folio number first, followed by an *r* (for recto, or front of the page) or a *v* (for verso, back of the page) and the line number or numbers. So in this case, the description of the *Islas de Arena* is found at 17v23-24, i.e., folio 17 verso, lines 23 and 24. Dunn & Kelley 1989.

point that we label *Islas de Arena*, representing the southern point of these islands. From there, we draw a line five squares long southward, to Columbus's anchorage five leagues off the southern part of the islands. From the anchorage point, we use a protractor and a ruler to draw another line, 19 squares long to the south-southwest. This represents 17 leagues that Columbus sailed, plus another two leagues for the sighting distance. The end of this line represents a point on the coast of Cuba.

But since we're tracing the track backward, what we really want to know is the course and distance from Cuba directly back to the *Islas de Arena*. To find this, we use a technique called vector addition. The easiest way to do this is to simply use our ruler to measure the distance on our chart from the Cuba point to the *Islas de Arena* point and our protractor to measure the angle, as shown on Figure 2.2. If we're being fussy, we could use trigonometry instead (which gives the same answer). From Cuba to the *Islas de Arena*, the total distance is 23.7 leagues, and the combined direction is 18 degrees east of north.

If we knew exactly where on the coast of Cuba Columbus first sighted land, we could draw this course and distance from that point to find the *Islas de Arena*. Columbus's landfall in Cuba is now believed to be the modern Bahia Bariay, but for the time being we don't have to assume any particular landfall on Cuba. We just draw this course and distance from every single point on the north coast of eastern Cuba and see if any of these points hits any islands in the Bahamas. We have to allow for the possibility that Columbus may have erred somewhat in his distance measurements, and we also have to allow for the possibility that we may have erred in our assumption of the two-league sighting distance. So we'll include an arbitrary error band of plus or minus 15 percent in our drawing.

Now we draw all these points on a real map. Since a league is 2.67 nautical miles, 23.7 leagues is about 63 nautical miles, measured 18 degrees east of north from every point on Cuba's north coast. The endpoints of all these measurements join to form a line drawn through the sea north of Cuba, a line in the same shape as Cuba's coastline. Our 15 percent error amounts to a band nine nautical miles on either side of this line. If we have done everything correctly, the southern end of the *Islas*

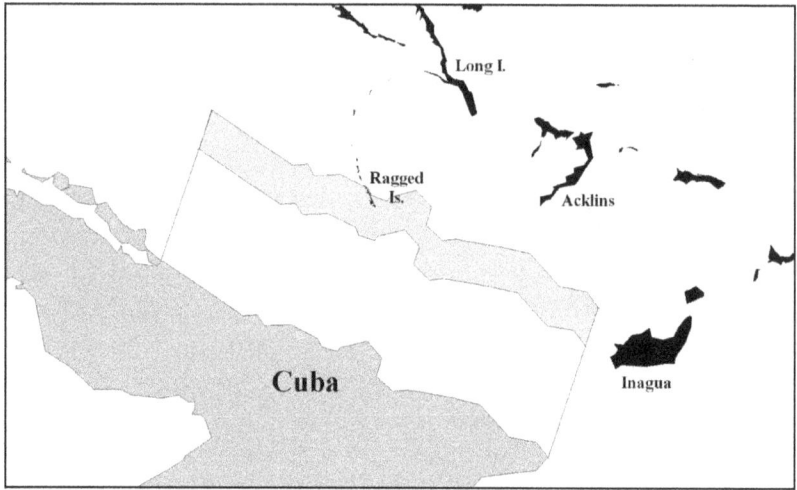

FIGURE 2.3. The light gray plot box shows all points 63 nmi. (plus or minus 15 percent) from eastern Cuba's north coast, on a bearing of 18 degrees.

de Arena should lie within the error band. As seen in Figure 2.3, there is indeed a group of islands in this band: they are the modern Ragged Island Range. Just as important, the Ragged Islands fit Columbus's description of the *Islas de Arena*: a string of seven or eight islands extended north and south.

The right *distance* from Cuba, the right *direction* from Cuba, and the right *description*: the Ragged Islands pass what I call the "3-D test." For this reason, there is no doubt that that Ragged Islands and Columbus's *Islas de Arena* are one and the same. In fact, with only a couple of minor exceptions, every landfall theory has identified the Ragged Islands as the *Islas de Arena.*

Columbus arrived at the Ragged Islands by sailing from Island IV, whose identity is in dispute. In trying to reconstruct the route from the *Islas de Arena* back to Island IV, we have a problem right away: Columbus has omitted one of the distances. Columbus left Island IV at midnight on October 24, and sailed west-southwest for an unknown distance. Beginning at noon that day, he was becalmed for the next six hours. At sunset the wind returned, and that night he continued for another seven leagues before changing his course to west. He then sailed another 11 leagues, at which point he sighted the Ragged Islands five leagues ahead.

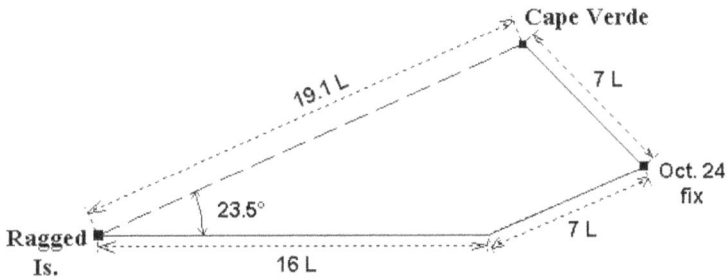

FIGURE 2.4. Adding the vectors from the *Islas de Arena* to Cape Verde on Island III.

Our problem is those first 18 hours from midnight to 6:00 p.m., for which we have a direction but no distance. Luckily, there is saving grace: at sunset on the 24th, Columbus writes that Cape Verde, in the southwestern part of Island III, is seven leagues to his northwest.[4] Joe Judge has named this point the "Cape Verde fix." This allows us to bypass Island IV for the time being, and to construct our vector addition from the Ragged Islands directly back to Island III. (We will return to Island IV later.)

So from Cape Verde on Island III, we go seven leagues southeast to the Cape Verde fix, Columbus's position at sunset on October 24. From there, seven leagues west-southwest and 11 leagues west brings us to the Ragged Islands landfall. The islands themselves are another five leagues west from that point. Adding up these vectors, as seen on Figure 2.4, we find that Cape Verde on Island III must be 19.1 leagues from the Ragged Islands, in a direction 66.5 degrees east of north.

We can draw this on a real map, again allowing for an arbitrary 15 percent error. The 19.1 leagues becomes 51 nautical miles. As shown in Figure 2.5, only Long Island[5] can possibly

---

4. More exactly, Cape Verde is in "the western part of the southern part" of Island III (17v1). The Cape Verde fix is given at 17v2-3.

5. Molander 1983 asserts that Andros is Island III, and that the seven leagues to Cape Verde is a transcription error for 70 leagues. But this only works if, in addition, Columbus raced madly at top speed across the treacherous Great Bahama Bank on October 18, a day when the *Diario* asserts he actually coasted along Island III. For Grand Turk, Power 1983 employs both Mayaguana and Acklins as Island III, even though they are separated by over 40 miles of open ocean; his Cape Verde fix simply does not work, and Power, too, must assert an ocean crossing on October 18. Here we employ the principle of Occam's Razor and eliminate any unnecessary (and conveniently bizarre) assumptions, along with their concomitant theories. As one who approaches the landfall dispute with the attitude of the scientist, I am often

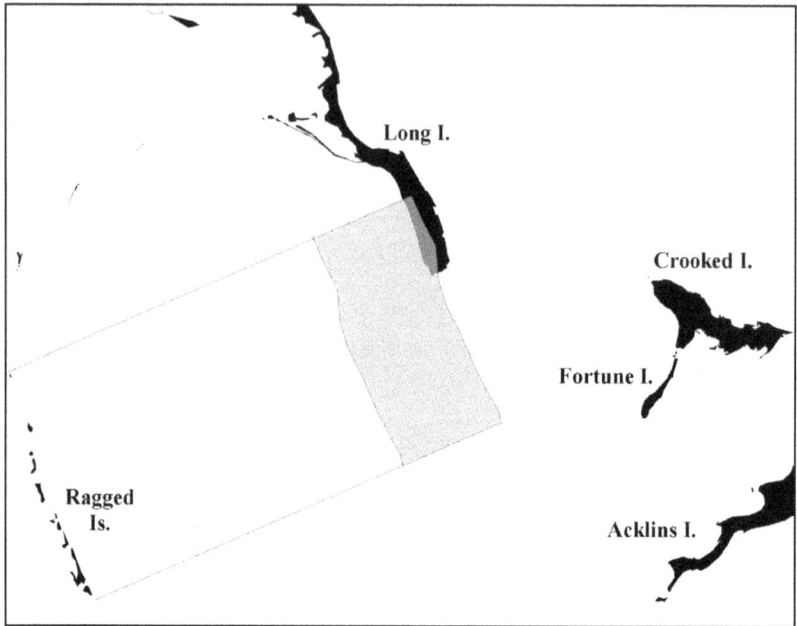

FIGURE 2.5. The gray plot box showing all points 51 nmi. (plus or minus 15 percent) from the Ragged Islands, on a bearing of 66.5 degrees.

be Island III. Cape Verde is described as being "in the western part of the southern part" of Island III, and the southwestern part of Long is just where our vector analysis takes us. Equally impressive, Long Island matches other descriptions given by Columbus: it is twenty leagues long, and it has a coastline running north-northwest.

Like the Ragged Islands, Long Island passes the 3-D test: right distance, right direction, and right description. For these reasons, few today doubt that Long Island is indeed Island III. Our next step backward is to Island II. Here, there is some ambiguity in the *Diario*, for Columbus repeats the description of his departure from the western end of Island II and passage to Island III. In the first account, the distance is nine leagues, and his course is west; in the second account, the distance is eight leagues, and the course is "almost east-west."

This makes our vector addition easy, since there is only one vector. To allow for both recorded distances, we draw our error

dismayed by the reluctance of historians to utilize this marvelous little blade.

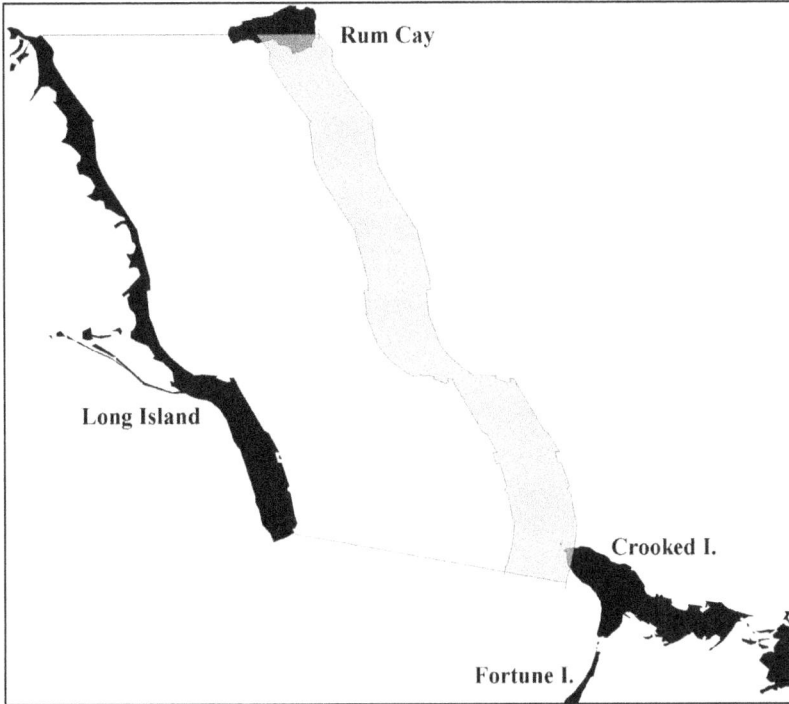

FIGURE 2.6. The gray plot box shows all points 8 to 9 leagues east or nearly east of Long Island, plus or minus 15 percent.

band two ways: first as 15 percent above nine leagues (or 28 nmi.), and also as 15 percent less than eight leagues (19 nmi.). But after drawing the vector, as shown on Figure 2.6, we find that there are two possible islands in the target area: Rum Cay to the north and Crooked Island to the south.

Determining which of these two possibilities is the real Island II is a critical point, so we will pay considerable attention to it. First, let's look closely at the distance and direction between Long Island and the two candidates. The western end of Crooked Island is really 10 leagues from Long Island, not nine. This falls within our error band, but we would still like an explanation for the difference. The direction between the two is almost directly west, as Columbus states.

We now know that one important source of error in Columbus's distance measurement is currents in the ocean. When his ships are sailing against the current, any dead-reckoning navigator will overestimate the distance traveled. If you imagine walking up a downward-moving escalator, you can see why: you will have to take many more steps to reach the top than if the escalator were standing still, so the distance seems longer. Likewise, if the ships were sailing with the current, Columbus would have underestimated distances.

Currents in the open ocean are variable, much like winds in the atmosphere; but like winds, there is a prevailing direction in which we should expect the current to move more often than any other. In this area of the world, the prevailing direction for currents is toward the northwest. Since Columbus was sailing west from Island II to Long Island, it is likely that he was traveling with the current, which would result in an underestimate of the distance. Currents in this region typically run less than one knot, but that would be enough to account for the difference. So if Crooked Island is Island II, Columbus's underestimate of the distance between the islands can be explained.

On the other hand, the distance from Rum Cay to Long Island also does not quite fit Columbus's description, but the fit is a little worse and in the opposite direction. When measured the shortest way, it is only six leagues from the western end of Rum Cay to Long Island. But this shortest route does not run west from Rum Cay to Long Island, it runs west-southwest. Even if we were to sail directly west from Rum Cay, it would be seven leagues before we came to the Long Island coast—still a league too short. Of course, it's possible that Columbus ran into a current running counter to the prevailing direction, which does occasionally happen.

But there is another problem here, other than just the distance. These islands are so close that from the western point of Rum Cay, the higher elevations of Long Island can be seen on a clear day, lying west-southwest. So if Columbus saw these hills to the WSW, why would he sail west, or "almost east-west" between these islands, as he reported? And even if visibility was bad, Columbus reports that he had learned about Long Island from the Native Americans he had captured as guides. These guides would surely have steered Columbus on the shortest route between the islands, west-southwest, just as they later steered him south-southwest on the shortest course from the Ragged Islands to Cuba.

So while neither Crooked Island nor Rum Cay is a perfect fit for the distance given by Columbus, Crooked is a better fit, and has a more likely explanation for the discrepancy. In comparing the direction between islands, Crooked fits perfectly, while Rum Cay fits somewhat, but has a nagging discrepancy.

But there is a third D in our 3-D test: description. And here things get very interesting. According to Columbus, Island II had a coast running north-south for five leagues, and another coast running east-west for more than 10 leagues. Neither Crooked Island nor Rum Cay is this big. But Crooked Island lies close by Acklins Island; only a narrow and shallow strait filled with shoals and islets separates them. Crooked and Acklins are so close that the north coast of Crooked and the north coast of Acklins can be considered to form a single coastline, and this combined coastline does fit Columbus's 10 league description. Further, Acklins has an adjoining coast running north-south for five leagues, a perfect fit to Columbus's description.

Of course, Columbus does not say explicitly[6] that two islands combine to form Island II. But Crooked and Acklins are close enough, and the strait between is narrow and clotted enough that he may not have noticed that the islands were separate. Or maybe he did notice after all. Here is his exact description of Island II, taken from the *Diario*:

> I found that the face towards the island of San Salvador runs north-south, and that in it there are five leagues; and the other, which I followed, runs east-west, and in it are more than ten leagues. And because from this island I saw another main one to the west, I filled the sails to travel all that day until the night; because [otherwise] I could not even have gotten to the western cape.[7]

---

6. Although at one point (12v22) the *Diario* refers to Island II as "las Isla," an erroneous construction of plural article *las* with singular noun *Isla*. So maybe Island II was multiple after all; or maybe not. Either way, the lengths of the coastlines of Island II as given in the *Diario* are not in dispute, and that is another good reason to concentrate on those data in our analysis.

7. *Diario*, 11r38-41. Most translators have rendered *mayor* as a "larger" island rather than a "main" island. As it turns out, Island III is in fact larger than Island II, but perhaps not by much. In any case, since the Spanish is ambiguous, I prefer an ambiguous word in English.

What is this other main island to the west? We are immediately tempted to say that it is Long Island, our Island III. Indeed, those who support Rum Cay as Island II invariably state this to be true. But if Crooked and Acklins are Island II, another explanation is possible: seen from Acklins, the other main island to the west is Crooked. But doesn't this conflict with Columbus's prior description that Island II is 10 leagues long east to west? Maybe not: notice that Columbus does not say that the *island* is 10 leagues long, he says that the *face*, the coastline, is 10 leagues long. Since on this route the coastline is comprised of two islands, perhaps Columbus is merely stating that the western of the two islands is also a main island yet still part of Island II.

Rum Cay is much smaller than Crooked, and does not have any nearby island to make up the difference. The size disparity is so great that both theories using Rum Cay as Island II (the Conception Island theory and the Watlings Island theory) will rise or fall depending on their ability to provide a convincing solution for this problem.

Samuel Eliot Morison was firmly convinced that Watlings Island was the landfall. To deal with the problem of the size of Rum Cay, Morison proposed a bold, new idea. Morison suggested that Columbus measured coastlines with a different league length than he measured distances across the sea. According to Morison, this "alongshore league"[8] was between 1 and 1.5 nautical miles long.

Morison used two lines of evidence for the existence of the alongshore league. First were the distances within the Bahamas themselves, according to his own Watlings landfall theory. Second were the exaggerated distances that Columbus reported along the north coast of Cuba as he explored that island in November of 1492.

In spite of Morison's reputation, the alongshore league did not gain much acceptance. There was no documentation that Columbus had ever used such a league; in fact, there was no documentation that anyone had ever used such a league at any time. The empirical evidence was fine, but alone it was not enough to convince. The alongshore league seemed all too *ad*

---

8. Morison (1942) I, 248. Morison adopted the "alongshore league" of J. Van der Gucht and S. M. Parajon, S. M. (1943). This league was 1.5 nautical miles.

hoc. And to some landfall theorists, the distances Morison used as evidence seemed to be a clear case of circular reasoning: the inter-island track from the Watlings landfall and the supposed route along Cuba was needed to prove the existence of the along-shore league, while the alongshore league was needed to prove the Watlings landfall and the inter-island track along Cuba.

The whole alongshore league idea fell apart in 1983, several years after Morison's death. When Jim Kelley published his paper proposing that Columbus used the Italian League of 2.67 nautical miles, he supported his thesis with an analysis of the distances that Columbus sailed, including the distances along the north coast of Cuba. Kelley noted that the Antilles current ran northwest along this coast. Since Columbus sailed mostly eastward along Cuba, the current was mostly against him. Kelley allowed for the effects of this current and found that the contrary current would have caused Columbus to overestimate his distances. These overestimates, combined with using the somewhat shorter Italian League instead of the Portuguese Maritime League, were enough to account for about 90 percent of the discrepancy[9] in the distances that Columbus reported in Cuba. After Kelley published his paper, there was no longer any credible evidence for the alongshore league.

That is why in Annapolis, Steven Mitchell relied on a completely different explanation for the problem of the size of Rum Cay, a much earlier proposal. In 1884, J. B. Murdock had proposed[10] that Columbus measured his distances in miles, not in leagues. In this scenario, Columbus recorded his distances (in miles) in the original log that he carried aboard ship. When Las Casas abstracted the log in the sixteenth century, he converted most of these mile distances into leagues. (These unit conversions would be needed to explain the current state of the *Diario*, in which most of the distances are league measurements.) According to this hypothesis, Las Casas made the occasional mistake in this conversion process. Sometimes, Las Casas slipped and wrote "leagues" when the distance was really meant to be miles. According to Murdock, the dimensions of Island II were two such places: Columbus, looking at tiny Rum

---

9. James E. Kelley Jr., "In the Wake of Columbus on a Portolan Chart." 77-111.
10. J. B. Murdock, "The Cruise of Columbus in the Bahamas, 1492," 449-486.

Cay, had written the dimensions of the coastlines originally as "five miles" and "ten miles," and Las Casas had mistranscribed them as "five leagues" and "ten leagues."

Murdock's idea was clever, and had the huge advantage that Las Casas's handwritten manuscript of the *Diario* contained many errors and crossed out words. In fact, there are a dozen places where Las Casas had written the word "leagues" (or part of the word) and then crossed it out and wrote "miles." This is solid evidence that Las Casas had actually done unit conversions in the *Diario* and was certainly enough to make Rum Cay a legitimate contender for Island II. The miles-to-leagues conversion hypothesis would eventually be disproved,[11] but in Annapolis in 1992, it was still alive and well.

So in our comparison of Rum Cay and Crooked Island, we can say that Crooked (combined with Acklins) fits the descriptions of Columbus pretty much as written, without serious error. Rum Cay does not fit at all, but there is a reasonable explanation for the two large errors: the miles-to-leagues conversion hypothesis. Once again, Crooked seems to be preferable, but once again the differences between the two are not impossibly great. Is there any other way to choose between the two?

There is one more line of evidence to consider. If Rum Cay is Island II, then Columbus arrived near the north end of Long Island, and explored the northern part of the island. But if Crooked-Acklins is Island II, Columbus arrived at the southern end of Long Island and explored the southern part. We can compare the two ends of Long Island and see which fits Columbus's descriptions of Island III better.

Columbus arrived at Long Island on the evening of October 16, too late in the day to anchor. But he did note that the coastline ran north-northwest and south-southeast[12] from a

---

11. See chapter 6.

12. The initial description of the coastline is: "this cape where I came and all this coast runs north-northwest and south-south*west*" (13r12-13). But that is (perhaps) corrected at 13v27-28 to, "it runs all north-northwest and south-south*east*." This may be a simple transcription error (since *este* and *ueste* are quite similar in Spanish), although these are not necessarily in contradiction. At the southern end of Long Island, for example, there is just such a cape where the coastline runs NNW one way and SSW the other way. But a little ways NNW from there, the coast runs NNW and SSE. The cape is the closest point of Long Island to Crooked, so this may be another point in favor of the route passing southern Long Island.

cape, and the coastline was a beach free of rocks. Natives came to the ship in canoes to trade that night, and in the morning Columbus found their village nearby and anchored. Columbus also wrote that the island was more than 20 leagues long, but since he had not actually explored the island at this point, his native guides must have given him this idea. After consulting with the captains of the other ships, Columbus decided to circumnavigate the island, and he learned from his native guides that going north-northwest was the easiest way to do that. (Since the wind had been from the south the previous day, this was the only logical choice in any case.) So he weighed anchor and sailed some distance north-northwest along the coast, until he came upon a "marvelous harbor" located two leagues from the end of the island. (But he does not say from which end these two leagues are measured.) The harbor had a small island in its mouth, which formed two narrow entrances. Columbus anchored outside of the harbor and sent boats inside to take soundings and to find fresh water. By the time Columbus left the harbor, it was around noon. He continued northwest along the island (note the change in direction here: from NNW to NW) and explored "all that coast as far as the coast that runs east-west." At this point the wind died, and when it picked up again at sunset, it began to blow up a storm. That night Columbus turned away from the island to ride out the storm.

There are quite a few geographical clues in this account:

1. A cape, at which Columbus arrives.
2. From the cape, coastlines run north-northwest and south-southwest.
3. The coastline is all beach without rocks.
4. Sailing NNW from the cape, Columbus sees harbor.
5. The harbor has a small island in its mouth, forming two narrow entrances.
6. The harbor is two leagues from one end of the island.
7. North of the harbor, the coastline runs northwest.
8. Following that coast northwest, Columbus sees a coast running east-west.

Of these clues, we should perhaps be most skeptical of the one about the beaches. As noted before, beaches can be created and destroyed in five hundred years. (Some beach rocks in the Bahamas today have Coke bottles imbedded in them.[13] In less than a century, these rocks have solidified from wet sand baking in the sun.)

But most of the other clues concern the direction of coastlines, which remain constant. The left hand part of Figure 2.7 is a rough sketch of the way these coastlines run on Island III, as reported by Columbus. The sketch is not to scale, though, since we don't know any of the distances, except that the harbor is two leagues from one end of the island.

Looking at the southern end of Long Island (Figure 2.7 center), we find that there is a cape, from which the coast does indeed run NNW-SSE. We also find a harbor just up the coast, Little Harbor. But this harbor has two small islands in its mouth, not one. (Joe Judge suggested that these two islands were joined at one time and have since been separated by the action of storms.) Little Harbor is very nearly two leagues from the southern end of Long Island, and the coast does take a bend at that point, to the northwest. And beyond the northwest-running coast, it turns again to run east-west; in fact, this is the only part of the east coast of Long Island that runs east-west. So it's a nearly perfect fit for southern Long Island with the descriptions of Columbus: only the island in the harbor's mouth does not fit perfectly, and a possible explanation has been suggested for that.

At the northern end of Long Island, the coast runs NNW-SSE, and there is also a little harbor, a small place with no official name, but called Newton's Cay Harbor by landfall theorists. Newton's Cay Harbor does have a small island in its mouth. But this harbor is not even remotely two leagues from the northern end of Long Island. However, it is about two *miles* from the northern end of the island; and we recall that this route has already used the miles-to-leagues conversion hypothesis twice to explain the too-short coastlines of Rum Cay. So we can press the hypothesis into duty once more, to explain the distance from

---

13. Neal Sealy, personal communication.

FIGURE 2.7. Left, Island III as described by Columbus. Coasts run NNW snd SSW from cape, then NW, and E-W. Center, the southern part of Long Island. Right, the northern part of Long Island.

the harbor to the end of the island. The coastline does change direction at Newton's Cay, but only very slightly, much less than the two compass points (22.5 degrees) that Columbus reported.

But significantly, north of Newton's Cay there is no coastline that runs east-west. The northern end of Long Island comes to a point, with the west coast running immediately to the southwest. As we will see, a variety of explanations have been employed by theorists to explain this, but none of them are very convincing. Finally, the coast of southern Long Island does have some beach, while the northern coast is completely rocky.

So southern Long Island fits Columbus's descriptions quite well, except for the small island in the mouth of the harbor, for which there is an explanation. Northern Long fits three descriptions well, one poorly, and two not at all.

Comparing Crooked-Acklins to Rum Cay as Island II, Crooked-Acklins is a better fit for the direction between the islands; it is a better fit for the distance between the islands; it is a better fit for the description of Island II itself; and the coast of southern Long Island is a better fit with Columbus's descriptions than the coast of northern Long Island. For these reasons, we should have no problem in choosing Crooked-Acklins as the correct Island II. Indeed, were it not for the miles-to-leagues conversion hypothesis, Rum Cay wouldn't have a prayer.

There is one more backward step to find Island I, the landfall island. Here are Columbus's words from the *Diario* as he leaves Island I, San Salvador, on October 14:

I set sail and saw so many islands that I did not know how to de-
cide which one to go to first. And the Indians began to name them,
and they named more than a hundred. Therefore I decided to go
to the largest, and I am doing so. It is about five leagues distant
from this island of San Salvador, and the others, from some more,
from some less.[14]

Night falls before he can reach this island—Island II. The
next morning, October 15, he continues: "And as the island was
farther than five leagues, rather it was seven, and the tide delayed me so it was about noon when I arrived at the said island.
And I found that the face towards the island of San Salvador
runs north-south. . ."[15]

Columbus's original eyeball estimate of the distance between
Island I and Island II is five leagues, but after actually sailing
the distance, he decided it was more like seven leagues. But he
also says that he was delayed by the tide. Tides cause currents
in restricted waters, but in this area of the Bahamas the sea is
too open for this to happen much. It seems likely that what Columbus experienced was a wind-driven oceanic current, which
he mistook for a tidal current. But regardless of the cause of the
current, we know that this would affect his distance measurements. In this case, since the current delayed him, it would
cause him to overestimate the distance; that is, the true distance is likely to be somewhat less than seven leagues.

The direction is clear: the north-south coast of Acklins Island faces San Salvador, so San Salvador, Island I, must lie
due east of that coastline. Returning to our vector plotting, we
draw both the five league and seven league distances each from
the east coast of Acklins, and after allowing for our usual 15
percent error band, we arrive at Figure 2.8. Only the Plana Cays
lie within the target area. Only the Plana Cays can be Island I,
Guanahani, the first landfall of Columbus in the New World.

---

14. The frequently mistranslated words from this passage (11r13-22) are "*y las
otras dellas mas dellas menos.*" It is beyond me why some translators render *dellas*
as "some" rather than the obvious "from some."

15. *Diario*, 11r31-35, Dunn & Kelly translation. See chapter 3 for a slightly vari-
ant translation.

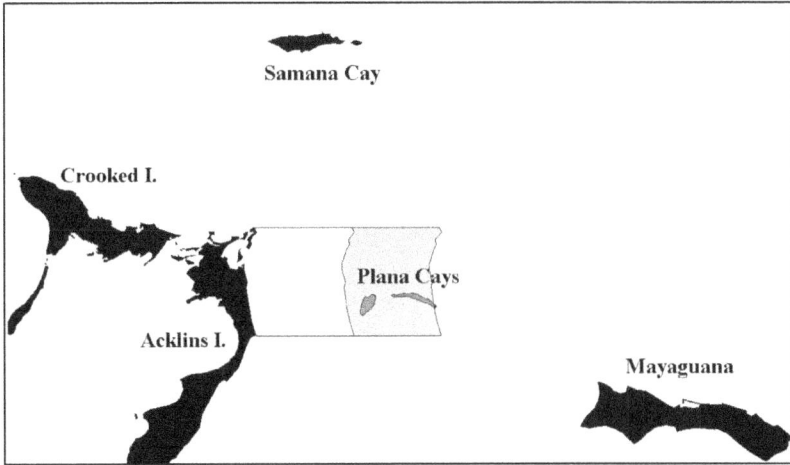

FIGURE 2.8. The gray plot box shows all points five to seven leagues east of the north-south coast of Acklins, plus or minus 15 percent.

Just to be sure, we must check the description of the is-land, the third D in our test. On October 14, Columbus explores Island I by boat, and he gives us only one description of the coastline of Island I: "I went north-northeast the length of the island, in order to see what was in the other part, the eastern part, which there is."

So Island I must have a coast running north-northeast. Plana does, at the western cay. (This western cay is the logical place for Columbus to anchor, since the west coast would be sheltered from the prevailing easterly winds.) Plana also has an eastern part, the eastern cay; and from Columbus's anchorage at the southern end of the western cay, the eastern part is in fact reached by going north-northeast the length of the island. So these descriptions fit Plana perfectly.

The only other possibilities in the region are Samana Cay, Joe Judge's choice for the landfall, and Mayaguana. But Sa-mana Cay does not lie in the correct direction from Island II (the famous TKO clue) although the distance is seven leagues. Samana doesn't fit Columbus's description either, since it has no coastline running north-northeast. It's just plain impossible to go north-northeast the length of the island at Samana Cay. Mayaguana, on the other hand, is in roughly the right direction, but the distance is at least twice too long.

But there is one important point that argues against the Plana Cays: they are two islands, and Columbus does not explicitly say that there were two islands at Guanahani. However, there is one subtle clue that this was indeed the case. Recall that on October 14, Columbus used the boats to explore "the other part, which is the eastern part" of Island I. But why didn't he just walk to the eastern part any time during the two previous days?

The question may sound absurd, but let's examine Columbus's use of boats. When Columbus explored Island II, he took a boat from ship to shore, and then explored by foot. At Island III, Columbus sent a boat into the harbor to take soundings, and his men then explored by foot. Columbus himself explored Island IV by foot. The same pattern of exploration by foot holds true at Cuba and at Hispaniola; some of the walking explorations there took days. In fact, except for Island I, there are only three other times on the first voyage where Columbus used the boats for an extended trip. The first was on November 15 through 17, when he used a boat to explore the many islands of Cuba's Bahía Tánamo. The next time was December 3, when the ships were becalmed in the harbor of Mata, Cuba, and foot exploration up the coast was blocked by the gorge of the river Yumuri. The last time was on New Year's Day, 1493. The *Santa Maria* had run aground and sunk the week before, just offshore from Hispaniola, and Columbus was building a fort from the wreckage. He sent some men by boat back to a place called Amiga, which he had seen several days before, to collect rhubarb. But Amiga is a small island separate from Hispaniola; his men could not have gotten there on foot.

So Columbus's use of the boats is consistent; he uses them when he cannot get to where he's going by foot. In fact, there is no point on the voyage when Columbus uses the ship's boat to get to a spot that he could have reached by foot. It is a simple rule of economy: use the boats when you need to, and don't use the boats when you don't need to. The same rule must also hold true for Island I, it seems to me. He wanted to explore the eastern part of Guanahani, and he needed to use the boats because he could not get there by foot. This can only mean that the eastern part of Island I was a separate island.

Finally, there is one other important clue that favors Plana over Samana. While still at sea in the Atlantic, at 10:00 p.m. on the night of October 11, four hours before the first sighting of land, Columbus saw a faint light in the darkness, "like a little candle of wax lifted and raised." Given the fast speed the ships were making that night, he must have been about 35 nautical miles east of Island I when the light was seen. This distance rules out any possibility that the light was on Island I itself. Morison proposed that the light was a figment of Columbus's imagination, but historical evidence indicates[16] that it was seen by as many as four people on two of the three ships. So the most reasonable explanation[17] is that Columbus bypassed another island in the night, an island we can call "Island Zero."

Going 35 nautical miles east from Samana Cay, there is nothing but empty sea; there is no Island Zero. But east of the Plana Cays lies Mayaguana, at just the right distance. In fact, at the time the light was seen, Columbus would have been at his closest approach to the highest hills on Mayaguana. A campfire on one of those hills would have been just bright enough to be the faint light seen that night.

Up to this point, this chapter has been a recap of the evidence I presented in the afternoon session in Annapolis, although with a few newer thoughts and expansions. There is a gap here, though: we bypassed Island IV on the way, and we

---

16. William D. Phillips Jr., (ed. & trans.) *The Columbian Lawsuits*, 245, 459. This records the testimony of one Hernan Peres Mateos, a cousin of Martín Alonso Pinzón (captain of the *Pinta*), who had met Pinzón at Bayone upon his return from the first voyage in March 1493. According to Mateos, Pinzón told him that a light was seen at night before the landfall, and although the identity of the observer is not stated, presumably it was someone aboard *Pinta*. The *Diario* records (8r39-8v9) that the faint light was seen aboard *Santa Maria* by Columbus personally that night, and he called to two others to verify it: Pero Gutiérrez and Rodrigo Sánchez de Segovia. Gutiérrez saw the light, while Sánchez did not. Oviedo records a story similar to that of the *Diario*, but adds that the light was also seen aboard the flagship a little while later by a ship's boy (the additional witness might also be implied by the *Diario* at 8v6-7, where "it was seen once or twice" more). For his part, Henige 1991 seems to doubt the story entirely, suggesting that it might have been a convenient fiction used to secure the Sovereign's annuity promised to the first to sight land. But Mateos's story indicates that Pinzón, at least, accepted it as true, and must have done so prior to the fleet's departure from Hispaniola.

17. Grand Turk advocate Josiah Marvel speculates (*The Islands' Sun*, March/April 1990, 6) that the light may have been caused by bioluminescent plankton in the rocks of the Mouchior Bank, just east of Grand Turk.

should now go back and pick it up. We will do this in two ways: first, by our usual backward track; and second, by tracking forward from Island III, Long Island.

You recall that earlier we said that the backward track from the Ragged Islands was not possible, because Columbus didn't give the distance sailed during the 18 hours on October 24 from midnight to sunset. But it may be possible for us to finesse the distance question. Columbus sailed west-southwest from the northern end of Island IV until he reached a point seven leagues southeast of Cape Verde on Island III. Cape Verde, Columbus tells us, is "in the western part of the southern part" of Island III. This is a perfect description of the modern South Point on Long Island, which is the most notable cape on the southern part of Long Island's west coast.

Let's start from South Point and draw a vector to the Cape Verde fix as before: seven leagues southeast. We then draw a line east-northeast to find the northern point of Island IV.

But as seen in Figure 2.9, we have a problem. The line does not intersect the northern point of any island; it runs aground along the western shore of Crooked Island, about midway between the northern point of Crooked Island and the northern point of Fortune Island, the only other possibility. For the Plana Cays theory, we have already used Crooked Island as Island II, so Island IV must be Fortune by default. But this point is in dispute for the Watlings Island theory: while most Watlings theorists use Crooked Island as Island IV, at least one, Bill Dunwoody, uses Fortune as Island IV. So it's worth exploring the differences.

Turning again to Figure 2.9, suppose that Crooked Island is Island IV. Columbus, departing from its northern end (Bird Rock) sails west-southwest as recorded in the log. But this course brings him closer than seven leagues to Cape Verde, the southwestern point of Long Island. On the other hand, if Fortune Island is Island IV, Columbus departs from the northern end sailing WSW, and comes out farther from Cape Verde than seven leagues.

The solution to this problem lies in Columbus's description of his sailing during the 18 hours between leaving Island IV and arriving at the Cape Verde fix. This a long time to go such a short distance, because he spent six hours adrift, making no headway at all. Since the current in this area usually sets to

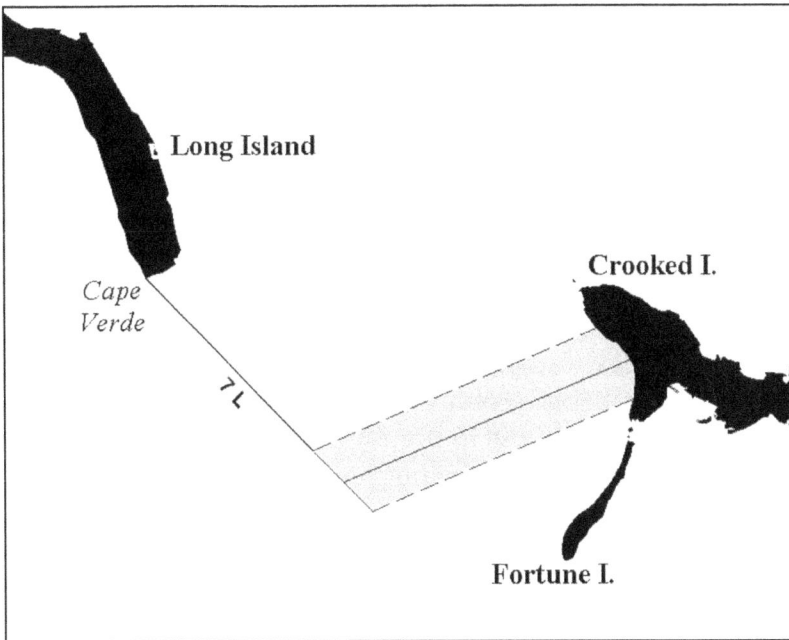

FIGURE 2.9. The north end of Island IV should lie roughly within the lines shown by the gray area.

the northwest, it is likely that Columbus drifted in that direction for several miles at least. A typical half-knot current would cause three nautical miles of drift during that time. When we consider this, we find that the track from Crooked Island gets much worse, while the track from Fortune Island gets much better. In fact, this drift can explain the entire discrepancy if Fortune Island is Island IV.

But all is not lost for the Watlings and Conception theories. We can explain the discrepancy by assuming that the correct distance is seven *miles* to the Cape Verde fix, not seven leagues as the *Diario* records. So for the fourth time, the miles-to-leagues conversion hypothesis comes to the rescue of these two theories.

And there is another way to trace the track to Island IV, directly from Island III on the forward track. While Columbus was at Island III, his captured native guides told him of an island called Samoet[18] where, they said, lived a king who had much

18. Also variously spelled as "Saometo" (twice) and "Saomete" (once).

gold. Columbus decided to search for this island of Samoet. He left Long Island at dawn on October 19, and split the fleet to increase the area he could search. *Niña* sailed to the south-southeast, while *Santa Maria* sailed southeast. *Pinta's* course is described as "east and southeast."[19] After three hours, Columbus, sailing aboard the *Santa Maria*, sighted Island IV to the east. He signaled the other ships, and they rejoined at the island's northern end at about noon.

But where was Columbus anchored when he left Long Island to look for Samoet? Since *Pinta* sailed initially east from Long Island, that rules out the entire west coast of the island as the starting point. (*Pinta* would have instantly run aground otherwise.) *Niña's* course to the south-southeast similarly rules out the east coast; *Niña* may not have run aground if the starting point was on the east coast south of Little Harbor, but it seems odd that Columbus would send *Niña* running along the coast of a known island in order to search for a new island. The most reasonable possibility is that Columbus's starting point for his search for Samoet was somewhere on the narrow southern coast of Long Island.

No distances are given in the log for this day's sail, but the times here are important: Columbus sailed three hours on a southeast course, followed by another three hours sailed to reach the northern end of Island IV. Since he sighted the island in the east, we can assume that he changed course to the east at the time the island was sighted. Further, since these two legs sailed by *Santa Maria* (to the southeast, and to the east) were both three hours long, we can also assume that the distances sailed on the two legs were about the same.

---

19. *Diario* 14v23. The course of the *Pinta* ("east and southeast") is so odd that Morison mistranslates the direction as east-southeast rather than try to explain the reasoning behind this maneuver. But on the Plana track, the reason is obvious. From Island III, Columbus knew that Island II was almost directly east; he recorded that course in his log. So *Pinta* sails east until Island II is firmly within her horizon, then turns southeast, paralleling the *Santa Maria*'s course, keeping both Island II and the flagship in simultaneous view at all times. Meanwhile, *Santa Maria* keeps *Pinta* in view to the north while *Niña* keeps the flagship in view. In this manner the fleet sweeps the sea south of Island II, secured by always keeping a known island in sight while searching for a new island—a typically cautious procedure for Columbus. On the track from most other landfalls, there is no known island to anchor the sweep, and no clear reason for *Pinta*'s stated maneuver.

Let's do vector addition again. From any arbitrary point, we draw a line for some distance southeast, and then another line of the same distance east. Adding the vectors, we find that the total direction must be east-southeast. The distance cannot be determined, but for right now all we need is the direction. Returning to our real map of Long Island, we plot a vector east-southeast from Columbus's departure point. Starting from the south coast of Long Island, we draw a plot box east-southeast until we run aground, as seen in Figure 2.10. These lines run to the northern end of Fortune Island. Since Columbus did indeed arrive at the northern end of Island IV, Fortune Island fits, but Crooked Island does not.

What about the third D, the description of Fortune Island? Alas, the description of Island IV is one of the few places that the log seems to be corrupt and self-contradictory. The *Diario* states that from the northern point of Island IV, the coast runs west for 12 leagues. But this clearly cannot be true. First, when Columbus departed from Island IV, he sailed WSW from the northern point. If the coast really ran west from there, this course

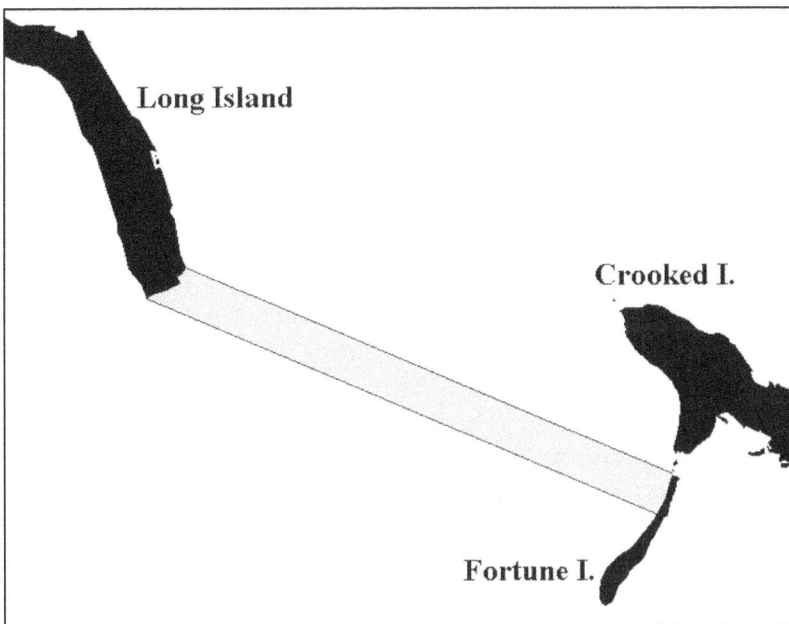

FIGURE 2.10. The northern end of Island IV should lie within the gray plot box, running east-southeast from the south coast of Long Island.

would put him aground. Second, Columbus arrived at Island IV sailing east, and the northern point was the first point he came to. If the coast ran west from the northern point, he would have come to the western point of the island first. Therefore, the coast cannot really run west from the northern point of Island IV. This turns out to be another saving grace, however, because neither Fortune nor Crooked has a coastline running west from the northern point. (And neither of them has a coastline 12 leagues long either; we will explain this discrepancy later.) Columbus also says that at the northern end of Island IV there is a small island nearby, called an *isleo* in Spanish; but this fits both Fortune and Crooked perfectly well. Finally, Columbus states that Island IV is the largest island he has visited thus far in the Bahamas; but this, too, cannot be the case, since he had earlier described Island III as being more than 20 leagues long, while the longest coast of Island IV is given as only 12 leagues.

In our 3-D test, the vector addition has been done two ways: the forward track from Long Island favors Fortune Island over Crooked; and the backward track from the Cape Verde fix favors Fortune, too, although the miles-to-leagues conversion hypothesis may again just save Crooked as a possibility. The description of Island IV is corrupt and seems to fit neither island better than the other. And the log does not mention any distances to or from Island IV to any other point.

Or does it? Buried deep in the *Diario*, there is a crucial description written on November 20, 1492. By this time, Columbus has been coasting along Cuba for three weeks, but now he turns back north, away from the Cuban coast, chasing another "island of gold" story told by his native guides captured from Guanahani. Columbus sails so far north that he computes that he is only 12 leagues from Isabela, his name for Island IV. And, he writes, he does not want to go to Isabela, fearful that his kidnapped Indian guides will try to escape and return to their home on San Salvador, Island I—because *Isabela is only eight leagues from San Salvador*.[20]

Fortune Island is about 12 leagues from both the Plana Cays and Samana Cay, the two theories that use Fortune as

---

20. *Diario* 25v36-37.

Island IV. This is a poor fit, but other theories are much worse: Crooked Island is more than 20 leagues from Watlings and about the same from Conception.[21] In other words, although the discrepancy is significant, Fortune Island is much closer to Plana and Samana than Crooked is to Watlings and Conception. The discrepancy is about 50 percent for Fortune-to-Plana, but 150 percent for Crooked-to-Watlings.

Almost unbelievably, not only has this major discrepancy never been explained by any advocate of any landfall, it has seldom even been mentioned by any theorist either. Like the coast of Island II that faces Island I, landfall advocates have been happy to sweep inconvenient evidence under the rug.

However, this distance can be explained quite easily when we recall that Columbus didn't actually sight this distance by eye; he must have been measuring the (now lost) map he was making of the islands. And from the *Diario* we can reconstruct this result—provided we can compute the distance from Island III to Island IV, a distance not given in the log.

We use two clues to do this: first, according to the log, Island IV was on a direct east-west line from Island III. (This is not quite true on the Plana route, but Columbus apparently thought it was.) And second, the Cape Verde fix was seven leagues SE of Island III, and some unknown distance WSW of the northern end of Island IV. This gives us just enough data to solve the charted distance using trigonometry, and it comes out as 17 leagues.

From Island I, the westerly distance to Island II was five or seven leagues; then more than 10 leagues west along Island II; then another eight or nine leagues west to Island III. The total westerly distance from Island I to Island III, therefore, would have been 23+ to 26+ leagues on Columbus's map. Then working back eastward, it was 17 leagues from Island III to Island IV, which means the remaining east-west distance on Columbus's map, from Island IV to Island I, would have been in the range of 6+ to 9+ leagues—a nice fit to the given distance of eight leagues.

---

21. But that's still better than Grand Turk, where the distance is almost forty leagues, or Egg Island, where it's over fifty. Occam's Razor cuts these theories to ribbons.

We have now identified all of the islands on Columbus's route through the Bahamas: Island Zero, the source of the light in the dark, is Mayaguana; Island I, the first landfall, is the Plana Cays; Island II is Crooked-Acklins; Island III is Long Island; Island IV is Fortune Island; and the *Islas de Arena* are the Ragged Islands.

This is a somewhat more detailed version of the analysis I presented at the afternoon session in Annapolis in 1992. But if these arguments haven't convinced you, don't worry: as we shall see, you're in very good company.

3.

Too Many Clues

ARNE Molander had given me some interesting news in Annapolis: there was a group of Columbus scholars who had been exchanging letters about the landfall problem over the past several years. Molander was an active member of the group, and he invited me to participate. I wrote to him when I returned home, and he sent me a copy of his mailing list. This group, known as the Columbus Round Robin, contained some familiar names: besides Molander, Mitchell, and Judge, whom I had already met, I found authors whose works I had been reading, such as James E. Kelley Jr., translator of the *Diario* and author of a seminal paper on Columbus's navigation; Dr. David Henige, an erudite historian at the University of Wisconsin; and Alejandro Pérez, who had written a recent book advocating Samana Cay. There were also names that were new to me, but that I would come to know well. Bill Dunwoody, a yachtsman and Watlings Island advocate, was also a skilled cartographer who created beautiful hand-drawn maps to illustrate his letters. Doug Peck, a retired Air Force officer and solo ocean sailor, turned out to be a friend of my uncle, both of whom were past Commodores of the Bradenton Yacht Club in Florida. Peck was noted for his personal retracing of Columbus's transatlantic route. In all, Arne's list contained over twenty names.

The Round Robin had its roots in 1981 as occasional correspondence between Henige and Kelley, a systems analyst interested in historical matters. By 1984, half a dozen others had joined the group. The members hoped that a final consensus on the location of the landfall could be reached before the upcoming quincentennial of Columbus's discovery in 1992. To understand why a consensus was needed at all, we need to look at the history of the landfall controversy and the important evidence surrounding it. This evidence is vast, detailed, and occasionally contradictory. For that reason, the remainder of this chapter should be viewed as more of a reference than a narrative; readers with more literary tastes can safely skip to chapter 4 and return here when needed.

Maps

The first person to suggest in print a location for Columbus's first landfall was Mark Catesby, an English naturalist, who in 1731 stated that Cat Island was Guanahani, or San Salvador. A similar assertion was made in 1767 by historian John Knox, while in 1797 the Spanish historian Juan Bautista Muñoz proposed Watlings Island.[1]

Since this was long before the log of the first voyage was published, we have no idea on what evidence Catesby, Knox, and Muñoz made their assertions; indeed, they gave no arguments to support their statements. But many maps drawn from the sixteenth to eighteenth centuries do show an island labeled "Guanahani" lying in the central Bahamas, and the island labeled "Guanahani" can usually be identified as either Cat Island or Watlings Island, if it can be identified at all (early cartography of the Bahamas is notoriously confusing). So it seems likely that Catesby, Knox, and Muñoz were simply going by the testimony of these old maps.

Some people place a great deal of faith in old maps, especially the place names found on them. I am not one of those. If you trusted the old maps, the landfall would most likely be Cat Island, which is a terrible theory (as we will see in the next chapter). It's simply impossible to say how any particular Indian toponym may have gotten to any particular place on European maps drawn decades or centuries after the first voyage—and

---

1. Robert H. Fuson, *The Log of Christopher Columbus*.

long after the last Lucayan Indian was dead. Further, when Columbus returned to Europe, he published a letter to the Spanish
court announcing the discovery. That letter was translated into
many languages and quickly became an international bestseller. In his letter, the only Indian name mentioned for any island
was Guanahani, and that name also became internationally
famous. Some old maps call the entire Bahamas archipelago
"Las Islas Guanahani."

When you consider that the Spanish had wiped out the entire native population of the Bahamas by 1513, any map drawn
after that time (which means almost every map in existence)
cannot be a trustworthy source for placing Indian toponyms in
the Bahamas. Where did these cartographers get their information? Who provided it? How accurate is it? Is the information
secondhand, third-hand, fifth-hand? One useful exercise is to
try and find on old maps the other two Lucayan toponyms Columbus mentioned in his log: *Samoet* and *Baneque*. It turns out
that you can't; only the famous and widely publicized Guanahani survived on maps of the seventeenth century and later,
even though Guanahani was in all likelihood smaller and less
important than the other two as
far as the Lucayans themselves
were concerned.

There is one exception to
all of this, and that is the map
of Juan de la Cosa. The owner
and master of the *Santa Maria*
was also a cartographer, and
his beautiful full-color world
map of 1500 is not only the
first European map to show
any part of the Western Hemi-
sphere, it is also the only extant
map known to be drawn by
any member of the first voyage.
This map shows us Guanahani,
Samoet, and Baneque (spelled
"Banacoa" by La Cosa). The Bahamian portion of the map (as

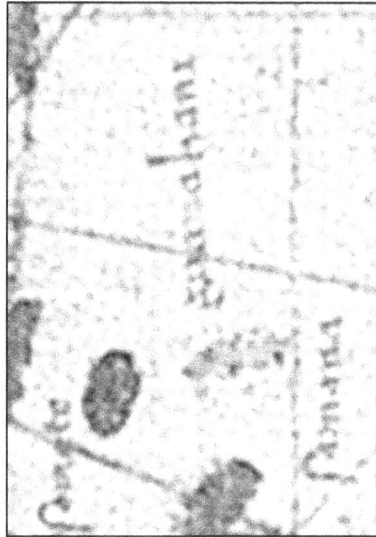

FIGURE 3.1. A fragment from the Juan
de la Cosa map, showing the island of
Guanhani. Islands labeled "Samote"
and "Samana" are also visible.

is typical for maps of that era) is hopelessly confused, with only a few islands firmly identifiable with their known counterparts. It was apparently drawn not only from his own experience, but also from information he must have gotten from other expeditions, most of them now lost to history. The map does show Guanahani, the landfall island, apparently as a small group of (possibly four) islets, lying roughly east-west. Watlings advocate Jim Kelley has suggested that the island was originally drawn as one, but that some of the paint has flecked off the parchment in the intervening years. Whether this is true or not, it is also clear that the shape of Guanahani is longest in the east-west direction, which favors Plana and Samana, but almost no other proposed landfalls. Guanahani is also shown as lying at the longitude of the Windward Passage, between Cuba and Hispaniola, and east of "Samote," (which may be Samoet, Island IV) and north of an island called "Samana" (which may or may not be the modern Samana Cay.)

But the overall depiction of the Bahamas archipelago is so poor that there is no strong context for identifying Guanahani, and the map becomes little more than a Rorschach test. I see good support for the Plana Cays on the La Cosa map, while Molander sees perfect congruence with Egg Island and Pérez notes similarities with Samana Cay.

The Log and Its Derivatives

Spanish King Charles IV upset the applecart in 1789. Wanting an authoritative history of the Spanish colonization of the world, he commissioned a naval officer named Martín Fernández Navarrete to comb various official and unofficial archives in search of any significant documents. In 1795, in the library of the Duke del Infantado, Navarrete found a manuscript in the hand of Bartolemé de las Casas containing an abstraction of Columbus's logs of the first and third voyages. This document is now known as the *Diario* (which simply means journal) among landfall historians. Navarrette transcribed and published this document in 1825, along with his assertion that the true landfall was at Grand Turk, the easternmost of the Bahamas. This was the first time that anyone had used the remains of Columbus's own log to try to determine the landfall.

The *Diario* is without question the single most important document for determining the location of the first landfall of Columbus. We have other historical documents that refer to it, and from these we can make a decent guess as to the history of the document itself.

The first copy of this document was the actual log that Columbus kept aboard ship and updated nearly every day between August 3, 1492, when he left his home port of Palos, Spain, and his return to Palos on March 15, 1493. This original document, called the *diario de abordo* (the on-board log) he gave to Queen Isabela when he reported to the royal court upon his return. The queen ordered the original log copied, with the copy being given to Columbus. This would have been necessary, since it contained navigational information that would have been vital to the safety of the second voyage. Since the court was meeting in Barcelona at the time, this copy is called the Barcelona Copy.

The original *diario de abordo* has not been seen since that time, but the Barcelona Copy remained with Columbus until his death, when it passed into the hands of his heirs. His younger son Fernando was a noted scholar with a large library, and that is the most likely place it would have gone. Fernando used (and quoted) parts of the Barcelona Copy when he wrote his biography of Columbus in 1538. But the biography languished for decades without being published, until it finally made print in an Italian edition published in Venice in 1571. The original Spanish manuscript of Fernando's biography has also been lost.

Somewhere along the line—and it's uncertain when—Bartolome de las Casas got ahold of the Barcelona Copy and wrote up the *Diario* as we know it today. About 80 percent of the text is not an exact copy, but rather an abstraction written in third person. The remaining 20 percent is written in first person, and las Casas claims that this is directly quoted from his source. Fortunately, the Bahamian portion of the log, the most important for the landfall question, is entirely in first person, and is by far the largest directly quoted part of the *Diario*. It contains a huge amount of information on the events of the first voyage, which we will examine in detail.

Approaching the New World

At two hours before midnight on October 11, Columbus saw a dim light "like a little wax candle, rising and falling." He mentioned this to at least two others aboard the *Santa Maria*, Pero Guiterrez and Rodrigo Sanchez de Segovia. Guiterrez also saw the light, but Sanchez did not. The light was seen once or twice more, but then was not seen again. According to later testimony in a lawsuit, the light was also seen aboard the *Pinta* at about the same time.[2]

The actual landfall island was seen four hours later (at 2:00 a.m. on the 12th) at a distance of two leagues. The fleet was traveling 12 miles per hour that night (eight knots in modern terms), so they must have been between 32 and 37 nautical miles east of the landfall island when the light was seen.

The problem here is that you can't see a low-lying Bahamian island from these distances. Morison suggested that Columbus's eyes were playing tricks on him, which sounds reasonable until we realize that according to various sources, the light was seen by perhaps as many as four people on two different ships.

In 1959 Ruth Wolper organized an experiment in which she set a giant bonfire at High Cay (an islet off the coast of Watlings) and sailed east from the island until the bonfire's light was no longer visible. The last glimmer was lost at a distance of 29 nautical miles, significantly short of the requirement (although that did not deter Wolper from claiming success in her experiment). Wolper was able to see as far as she did only because of the phenomenon known as "looming." When a very bright light illuminates the air above, the air itself becomes visible even when the light source is below the horizon. It is unlikely in the first place that the Indians would have made a bonfire this large; and even if they had, it would have become more visible as the fleet approached, while Columbus lost sight of the light almost immediately.

---

2. The testimony of Hernan Perez Mateos can be found in William D. Phillips Jr., ed. and trans., *Testimonies from the Columbian lawsuits.*

More recently, Josiah Marvel, an advocate of the Grand Turk theory, proposed that the light was caused by bioluminescent protozoa on the rocks of Mouchior Bank (located east of Grand Turk). But the light Columbus described—like a little wax candle—strongly suggests a point source. This would rule out both bioluminescence and looming effects.

However, from some proposed landfall islands there are other islands to the east, which would have been bypassed in the night, but which could provide a source for the light in the form of an Indian campfire or other habitation. From other proposed landfalls, notably Watlings and Grand Turk, there is no such easterly island. So it is no surprise that advocates of Watlings and Grand Turk have been at the forefront of the effort to find alternative explanations for the light seen that night, while advocates of other landfalls face no such difficulties.

Island I. Native name: Guanahani.
Columbus's name: San Salvador.

Columbus anchored at Island I on the morning of October 12, 1492, and reported that it was "green" and "flat," descriptions that fit almost every island in the Bahamas. He also said that the island was "*bien grande*," a phrase that could be translated as "fairly large," or alternately "good sized." It's anyone's guess as to what this really means. Elsewhere in the *Diario*, Las Casas refers to Guanahani as an "islet." Both Fernando and Las Casas (in his much later work, *Historia de las Indias*) describe San Salvador as being fifteen leagues long, but since Columbus apparently saw most or all of the island on a single-day boat trip, this seems quite exaggerated.

Columbus said that there was a very large *laguna* in the middle of the island. The English translation of *laguna* has been a bone of contention in the landfall dispute. The word in normal Spanish usage is a small lake or pool, usually (but not necessarily) fresh, but smaller than a *lago*, or lake. Watlings advocates often translate this phrase as "lake" (which fits Watlings nicely). Some others prefer "lagoon," but this seems weak. First, just because the English "lagoon" has its root in the Spanish *laguna*, that does not mean the words are identical. The English word "lacuna" is also derived from *laguna*, yet nobody would claim that Island I had a very large gap in a manuscript. In point of fact, this was a period in history before any European had seen a coral atoll, so nobody would have used any single word for a coral lagoon and expect his reader to understand what he meant without an explicit description. As it happens, Columbus did describe the water between the reef and the island, and after he did so, he used the word *puerto* (harbor) as his term, not *laguna*. So it stands to reason that when Columbus used *laguna* he did so with its common meaning in mind: a body of water smaller than a lake. In other words, Island I had a very large pond in the middle.

Having been anchored at Guanhani for two days, Columbus explored by boat on October 14 with a specific purpose in mind. "I went the length[3] of the island on a north-northeast course," he wrote, "in order to see the other part, which is the eastern part, which there is."

On the boat trip, he reported seeing the following things in this order:

1. Two or three Indian villages.
2. People who came to the beach, offering gifts and asking the Spaniards to go ashore.
3. A big stone reef that encircled that island all around.
4. A harbor between the reef and the island, with enough depth for ships, some shallow spots, and enough room "for all the ships in Christendom."[4] The harbor entrance was "very narrow."

---

3. This *Diario* passage, at 10v8-9, has been controversial at times. In Spanish it reads "*fue al luego dla isla en camino del nornoreste.*" The translation of *al luego* as "the length of" was proposed by linguist Consuelo Varela, in a letter to Arne Molander frequently quoted by him in the Round Robin. There is one other possible translation of this phrase in English: "along" the island, rather than "the length of." But Varela's opinion seems fully justified by other passages in the *Diario*, where Las Casas uses *de luego* to clearly mean "along" at 32r28, and *al luego* to mean "the length of" at 27r12, as here.

4. Columbus uses similar hyperbole elsewhere in the *Diario*, at times calling harbors large enough for all the ships in the world. Some analysts, notably Jim Kelley, have tried to quantify this, as though Columbus had done some actual measurements; but it seems clear to me that he was just using figures of speech that we should not take too literally. He also rhapsodized that the 4,000-foot mountains of Cuba were higher than the 13,000-foot volcano of Tenerife.

5. A good place for a fort, formed like an island, although it was not an island. But it could be cut through to make an island in two or three days.

The boat trip started at dawn, and Columbus does not say how long it took; however, they must have returned to the ships before sunset. The speed made by the boats can be inferred from another boat trip taken on the north coast of Hispaniola, when a boat sailed from their settlement Navidad to the island of Amiga (modern Rat Island) and back, a distance of 30 miles. The boat left at midnight and returned at vespers, so the distance was made in about 17 hours, for a speed of 1.8 knots; although, some time was spent ashore, so the actual speed would have been a little higher. It is an open question as to whether the boats were rowed, sailed, or some of both, on either October 14 or January 1. In each case, the trip was there-and-back, so it is likely that one leg would have been against the wind. To my mind, sailing seems more likely. For the 12 hour (or less) trip, then, the greatest distance they could have made would have been about 24 nautical miles.

Some of Columbus's remarks make it seem as though he had seen all or substantially all of Island I, either on the boat trip, or that combined with the approach to Island I on the morning of October 12. First, Columbus mentions the reef that circles the island "all around"; second, Columbus says that the entire population of the island could be subdued by fifty Spaniards. Both of these statements, taken together with the maximum length of the boat trip, imply that Guanahani could not have been very large.

The last important description of Island I comes much later, while exploring the north coast of Hispaniola. Columbus comes across an island with multi-colored stones of a kind "like those seen on" Island I. The stones, he says, could be used for paving or for building a church.

Island II. Native name: unknown.
Columbus's name: Santa Maria de la Concepcion.

While anchored at Island I, Columbus learned of other islands in the vicinity from the natives. One of these, to the south or southwest, Columbus understood to be the source of the natives' gold. Columbus wrote of his intention to sail southwest when he left Island I. But after returning from the boat trip, he weighs anchor on the afternoon of October 14, and he has a surprise:

> I set sail and saw so many islands that I did not know how to decide which one to go to first. And those men whom I had taken told me by signs that there were so very many that they were without number, and they named by their names more than a hundred. Therefore I looked for the largest and decided to go there, and so I am. It is about five leagues from this island of San Salvador, and the others, some more and some less.

Columbus was unable to make this modest distance in the time remaining before nightfall, and he spent the night jogging off and on. The following morning, he started again for his target island:

> The breeze[5] detained me, and it was farther than five leagues, closer to seven. So it was already around noon when I reached the island, and I found that the face in the direction of San Salvador runs north-south and in it there are five leagues, and the other, which I followed, runs east-west, and in it there are more than ten leagues.

In Annapolis I called this paragraph the single most important landfall clue in the *Diario*, because this is the only place where Columbus tells us the direction to Island I from any other point. If the north-south coast faces San Salvador (Island I), then Island I must lie due east of that north-south coast. Watlings

---

5. The Spanish word here, *marea*, is most often translated as "tide," which delayed Columbus. Tides cause noticeable currents in restricted waters such as harbors, but not in the open sea, so it might seem that the detaining current was wind-driven rather than tidal as Columbus believed. Bill Dunwoody has recently pointed out that *marea* has an alternate meaning: a light breeze. At first I was skeptical of this idea, since the same word is used one other place in the *Diario* (in the Las Casas abstracted portion) to mean tide. But in another document, a letter to the Spanish Sovereigns of February 6, 1502, Columbus again uses the word *marea*, and it is clear from the context that he definitely uses the word to mean breeze. [See Cristóbal Colón, *Textos y documentos completos*, 307.] So now I am inclined to agree with Bill on that point; but it is still unclear whether it was the strength of the breeze that caused the delay, or the direction. I would opt for the latter, while Watlings theorists like Dunwoody would prefer the former.

advocate Mauricio Obregón has used this clue as a bludgeon against the Samana Cay theory, since the north-south coast of Samana's Island II (Acklins) most definitely does not face Samana Cay. Unfortunately, the north-south coast of Rum Cay does not face Watlings either.

Here is the rest of the description of Island II as given by Columbus: "And since from this island I saw another large one to the west, I spread sail to go forward all that day until night, for otherwise I could not have reached the western cape."

The important thing about this passage is that it is entirely unclear whether Columbus was adjacent to one island this day or two. As you read the passage, consider the western cape, which Columbus reached at the end of the day: is it part of the island with the five- and ten-league coastlines? Or is it part of the other large island to the west? Both positions have been advocated by various theories. Perhaps even both interpretations are correct in different contexts. Those who interpret this passage to mean that Columbus was adjacent to two islands refer to them as Island IIa and Island IIb. For those who interpret the passage to mean one island, the large island to the west is Island III.

Columbus anchored at or near this western cape that night, and went ashore the next morning, October 16. He found that the natives were similar to those on Island I, and did not stay long. However, one of the natives from Island I escaped at this point, and at least one of the Island II natives was captured by the *Pinta* and taken to Island III as a replacement.

Island III. Native name: unknown. Columbus's name: Fernandina.

Upon leaving Island II, Columbus repeats himself in the log. He gives two different descriptions of his departure from Island II, his sail to Island III, and his initial activities there on October 16, and they have slight but significant differences.

In the first description, Columbus says he left Island II at 10 o'clock to sail to the large island that he "saw" in the west. The distance sailed was nine leagues and the course between the islands was east-west.

In the second description, Columbus says he left Island II at noon to sail to the large island that was "indicated" in the west. The distance sailed was eight leagues, and the course between the islands was "almost" east-west. Some have interpreted the adjective "almost" to refer to the distance ("eight leagues almost") rather than the course.

During this passage between islands, Columbus overtook an Indian in a canoe who was also heading for Island III. Columbus gave the Indian a lift and noticed that the native was carrying a Spanish coin—indicating that he had come from Island I, where the Spaniards had done a lot of trading with the natives.[6]

Columbus arrived at Island III at sunset on October 16, and hove to for the night. The following morning, Indians came out to trade in canoes, and Columbus anchored at their village nearby for a while, then continued his exploration of the island.

Before arriving at Island III, Columbus wrote that the island "may be" 28 leagues in length. Then after arriving at the island (but oddly, before actually exploring any of it) Columbus wrote that "I have seen quite 20 leagues of it and it does not end there." He also said that the coast was all beach without rock, although like all sandy coastal features, these might be considered impermanent.

In the first description, Columbus says that he came to a cape that ran north-northwest and south-southwest. This may (or may not) be an error, though. For the second time around, the coastline runs north-northwest and south-south*east*. He sailed north-northwest along this coast until he came to a "marvelous harbor." He wrote that the harbor was two leagues from the end of the island, but he did not say from which end. This harbor had "one entrance, or you might say two, because there is an *isleo* (small island) in its mouth. And both entrances are very narrow." Columbus at first thought the harbor was a river mouth, and sent boats into the harbor to look for fresh water.

---

6. It is interesting that twice later in the *Diario* Columbus mentions that the Indians can make seven leagues per day by canoe. This incident may have been the source for Columbus's belief: if the distance from Island I to Island II is seven leagues as stated in the *Diario*, and if it is 10 leagues west along the coast of Island II as stated in the *Diario*, and if the Indian was halfway between Island II and Island III when he was picked up, he would have paddled 7 + 10 + 4, or 21 leagues from Island I in three days, which is indeed seven leagues per day.

The harbor was not a river, and turned out to be too shallow to be very useful as a port.

When he left the harbor, his course along the island changed to northwest. At some point thereafter, Columbus came to a coast that ran east-west. This is as far northward as he explored; at sunset on the night of October 17, Columbus turned east-southeast under bad weather. The following morning, he continued trying to circumnavigate the island southward. He anchored that night at an unspecified place, but did not go ashore.

Island IV. Native name: Samoet.
Columbus's name: Isabella.

At dawn on October 19, Columbus left Island III in search of an island called Samoet. He had heard of this island from his native guides, and they had told him that it was very large and was the home of a king who had gold. But the exact direction to the island was apparently not well understood by Columbus, because he split his fleet: *Niña* sailed south-southeast, *Santa Maria* sailed southeast, and *Pinta* sailed east at first, then turned southeast.

The fleet weighed anchor at dawn, and after three hours sighted land to the east. All three ships arrived at the northern end of this new island at noon. Columbus named this island (Island IV) "Isabela" after the Spanish queen.

Columbus arrived at the north end of Island IV at noon on October 19. The *Diario* reports that from that northern end, the coast ran west for 12 leagues, as far as a cape that Columbus named "Cabo Hermoso" (beautiful cape).

We should pause here to point out that this direction for the coastline (west) is inconsistent with other descriptions in the *Diario*: (a) Columbus arrived at the northern end of Island IV sailing east (and yet somehow did not arrive at Cabo Hermoso first); (b) Columbus departed from the northern end of Island IV on October 24, sailing WSW, and yet did not run aground on this coast. For these reasons, the actual direction taken by this coast is almost always taken to be an error of some kind.

From Cabo Hermoso, Columbus described a "great bight" to the northeast. Twice in the next few days, Columbus tried to enter the bight, but found it too shallow for navigation. On the first attempt, Columbus mentioned that he could see Cabo Hermoso from his position in the bight. On the second attempt, Columbus returned to Cabo Hermoso because "the way south-west was very roundabout." Columbus described the coast of Island IV as "almost all beach," and had much water and large ponds. He also said that it had many large trees and a small height not large enough to be called a mountain.

The sail to Cuba

Columbus departed from Island IV at midnight on October 24, sailing west-southwest. His point of departure was Cabo del Isleo, at the northern end of the island. He sailed for six hours under very light winds, with all sails set, even the sail on the ship's boat. At dawn, the wind died completely, and he was adrift until noon, when the wind rose again. The distance made good that night was not recorded, probably because the ship's speed was too slow for a complete record to be made.

At sunset on the 24th, Columbus reported that he was seven leagues southeast of Cabo Verde on Island III. (He had not mentioned this cape previously, but he says now that Cabo Verde is in "the western part of the southern part" of Island III.) From this point, he sailed seven leagues (continuing WSW), then turned west and sailed another 11 leagues. At this point, he sighted six or seven islands in a north-south line, at a distance of five leagues. He named these islands *Las Islas de Arena* (the islands of sand). These islands are now generally acknowledged as the Ragged Islands in the Bahamas.

On the night of October 25, Columbus anchored five leagues off the southern part of the *Islas de Arena*, where the water was still shallow enough for an anchor cable. (This is one of the reasons that we know that the *Islas de Arena* must have been the modern Ragged Islands: there is a bank of shallow water extending south from there for 20 miles or so. This feature is today called the Columbus Bank.)

The final important navigational clue in the log occurs on November 20, when Columbus has sailed north from the Cuban coast. He is apprehensive of sailing further, he says, because he is approaching the island of Isabela (Island IV), which he says is only eight leagues from San Salvador (Island I).

Fernando's Biography

In 1571 a biography of Christopher Columbus, written in Italian, was published in Venice. The book was a translation of a Spanish manuscript written by Columbus's second son, Fernando Colon, between 1537 and 1539. The Spanish manuscript was eventually translated into Italian and published by Alfonso Ulloa, a Spaniard making his living in Venice as a professional translator.

Although the Spanish manuscript has not survived, it may have been in the hands of Las Casas as he wrote his *Historia*, since Las Casas cites Fernando as a source several times there. There are also large passages in the *Historia* that are closely similar to the biography, indicating that the two documents have a common source (although which is the original has been hotly debated). An analysis by Cioranescu supports the idea that the biography is actually the work of Las Casas, and was later published under Fernando's name. But regardless of who the author is, there are many details in the biography absent from the *Diario*, showing that Fernando (or whomever) had access to Columbus's log, and was not simply copying the *Diario*.

So are there any new clues for the landfall in Fernando's biography? Not many. Fernando reports that Island I was fifteen leagues long, a statement repeated in the *Historia*. If true, this would rule out all landfalls except Cat Island. Fernando also reports that the coastlines of Island II are five leagues north-south, and 10 leagues east-west (agreeing with the *Diario*.) If true, this would rule out all landfalls except Samana, Plana, Mayaguana, and Grand Turk.

The *Historia de las Indias*

You may recall that the transcription of Columbus's log was done by Bartolome de Las Casas. Las Casas was a Spanish monk and historian, who also wrote a massive history of the Spanish conquest of America, the *Historia de las Indias* (History of the Indies), or *Historia* for short. This work covers Columbus in detail, but there isn't much there that isn't also in the *Diario*, so it has been mostly overlooked by landfall historians.

One of the important arguments made against the Samana Cay theory had been that Columbus could not have returned to the vicinity of Island II (as the theory required) without mention-ing it in the log. But in 1992, Alejandro Pérez noticed a key pas-sage in the *Historia*. Here is Las Casas describing Columbus's decision to leave Fernandina, Island III, in search of Samoet (emphasis added):

> Because the Indians he had taken in the first island of Guanahani or San Salvador told him and indicated through signs that the island of Saometo, **which had been left behind**, was larger than Fernandina, and that they should **return** to it (and they must have done this in order **to get closer to their land**, from where he had taken them), the Admiral decided to **turn around** toward the east . . .

Since the emphasized passages make geographical state-ments not completely obvious from the *Diario*, Pérez has specu-lated that Las Casas had Columbus's map in front of him when he wrote this. (We know Columbus made a map of his discover-ies on the first voyage, but it has been lost for centuries.) And since there is another place in the *Historia* where Las Casas explicitly claims to have Columbus's map, Pérez's idea makes a lot of sense. The key information here: (1) That in sailing from Island III (Fernandina) to Island IV (Saometo), Columbus re-turned in the way from which he had come; and (2) in so doing, he came closer to Island I (Guanahani).

Soon after Henige and Kelley began the Round Robin, Joe Judge joined in the correspondence. After a lot of research, Judge eventually became convinced that Gustavus Fox had the right idea after all, way back in 1882: the landfall was Samana Cay. With the considerable weight of *National Geographic* maga-zine at his command, Judge published his views in the Novem-ber 1986 issue, supplemented computer analysis, color paint-ings, and a typically gorgeous National Geographic map. After a century of dominance, the Watlings Island route proposed by Murdock seemed to be in trouble. Although it was nowhere near dead, it was beginning to resemble a wildebeest being harassed by a pack of hyenas.

4.

The Wheat and the Chaff

WHEN researching the various theories of the Columbus land-fall, one is soon struck by the fact that maybe half of the pro-posed theories are truly dreadful, at times relying on excuses so unbelievable that one is astonished that the authors can actually suggest them with a straight face. For example, in sup-port of his Grand Turk theory, Robert H. Power suggested that Island III was composed of both Mayaguana and Acklins Island, even though these two islands are separated by over 40 miles of open sea. Power's excuse for this was that Columbus (and apparently his entire crew of experienced mariners) mistook a cloud bank for a 40-mile-long coastline.

At other times, theorists have proposed that Columbus float-ed his ships down three-foot-deep creeks, discovered islands and coastlines that don't actually exist, sailed at motorboat speeds on courses that run him aground, or have moved islands in hundred-mile leaps from one day to another. Sometimes a theorist takes us only so far, then leaves us hanging well short of getting Columbus to Cuba. Most authors are more subtle (and less forthright) than Power, disguising or simply omitting the worst absurdities of their theories—which is perhaps the only reason they make it into print in the first place.

I have heard some people who are not closely acquainted with the Columbus landfall problem speculate that the debate has continued for so long because Columbus's log, the *Diario*, does not contain enough detailed evidence to solve the problem.

Actually, the reverse is true: as we saw in chapter 3, the log contains so much detail that it is a relatively easy job to pick up a scrap here and a description there, and piece together the outlines of a hypothesis. In fact, the *Diario* is so expansive that any reasonably competent scholar could pick a Bahamian island *at random* and patch up a theory that would consume 10 or 20 pages in a handsome journal of navigation or history—provided he follows the all-too-standard procedure and carefully omits any mention of those places where he is contradicted by the evidence. Such theories can be made to sound so reasonable at first blush that only a person intimately familiar with the *Diario* would recognize the patchwork-quilt nature of the enterprise.

This stratagem is called "cherry-picking," and it is considered anathema among scientists. Any child set loose in a cherry orchard at harvest time will proudly return home with a basket full of cherries. Someone who had not seen the orchard might believe, on the evidence in the basket, that the child was a world-class cherry picker. But the truth is that we cannot determine the skill of the cherry picker by merely examining the cherries in the basket: we must also examine how many cherries are left on the tree.

This is also the essence of the scientific method. Any competent scientist can come up with a hypothesis to explain some as-yet-unexplained phenomenon. But to be accepted, the hypothesis must not only explain the phenomenon, it must also agree with everything else we already know about the universe. A hypothesis that explains the flight of birds by invoking a suspension of the law of gravity will win no support, regardless of how well it explains the phenomenon.

For this reason, the most important factor in determining the usefulness of any hypothesis is not what it explains, but rather what it leaves unexplained. Failure to explain the evidence in the *Diario* is simply fatal for any hypothesis, and this should always be foremost in our minds with regard to the many hypotheses of the Columbus landfall. So when we evaluate the various landfall hypotheses below, we won't waste much space evaluating the good points of any theory; the advocates of the various theories are only too happy to do that for you. Instead, we will concentrate on the bad points. If we want to separate the wheat from the chaff, we must look at the lapses, gaffes, embarrassments, and failures to explain. Our goal is to lay the worst theories permanently to rest, so that we may concentrate on the few remaining good ones. In the exegesis below, I will take the theories in roughly reverse order, from worst to best, on the basis of the improbability of their worst explanations.

The Virgin Islands, or Maybe Not.

This idea, proposed[1] by Dr. Luis M. Coin Cuenca in 1991, is actually not so much a theory of the first landfall as it is a theory of the transatlantic track of the first voyage; I include it here for the sake of completeness. Belief in this theory requires a mindset that sees vast conspiracies behind every important historical event, plus an inexplicable lack of knowledge of the known properties of ocean currents.

Dr. Coin bases his theory on Columbus's logged observation that the Atlantic currents were against him on September 13, 1492. Coin correctly notes that this is unusual in the area that Columbus was supposedly traversing at the time, and uses this unlikelihood to suppose that Columbus actually sailed southwest (instead of the logged west) from Hierro. The reason that the log says west, according to Coin, is that the log was altered to avoid the appearance of Spanish incursion into the Portuguese sphere of influence.

The first problem that Coin misses is that northeast-setting currents are even *less* likely in the area that Coin has Columbus sailing through, than in the area that everyone else assumes. In other words, Coin fails to adequately address the very problem he himself raised. Currents in the open ocean, like winds in the atmosphere, often move in directions different from, or even contrary to, the prevailing direction (we will discuss this further in chapter 8), so an unusual current is a very thin thread upon which to hang a theory.

Coin also makes a great deal of the various bird sightings recorded in the log, in areas of the Atlantic that (according to Dr.

---

1. John Dyson, (with nautical research by Luis Miguel Coin Cuenca) *Columbus: for gold, God, and glory.*

Coin) no birds are found. But recent research by John Parker[2] has identified nearly all of these sightings with their correct species, and in areas that they have been documented to exist.

Coin uses the alleged log-fixing to pull Columbus far enough south to be in sight of the Virgin Islands on September 25, which the fleet bypasses in the night. From there, Coin has the fleet making west-northwest for another two weeks (missing Puerto Rico, Hispaniola, and all other islands along the way) until the "real" landfall of October 12, at some unspecified point in the Bahamas. This northward movement is attributed to a northward setting current of *five knots*, about twice the speed of the massive Gulf Stream, and at least 10 times greater than the typical current speed in that area of the ocean. It is true that in restricted waters, such as in the straits between large islands, tidal currents can be fairly swift; but that's not where Columbus was on this day (nor on any other day in the subsequent two weeks), even according to Coin. He might as well have given Columbus a diesel engine instead.

Lignum Vitae Cay

This little-known theory was first proposed by John H. Winslow in a 1989 lecture[3] in Lancaster, Pennsylvania. Winslow identified Lignum Vitae Cay (and nearby Great Harbour Cay) in the Berry Islands as Island I. For Island II, he used a combined Bond Cay and Chub Cay, also in the Berry Islands, and more distant New Providence, the island on which Nassau now sits. The northern part of Andros Island is his Island III, while the southern part of Andros is Island IV. Unlike most theorists, Winslow does not use the Ragged Islands as Columbus's *Islas de Arena*, but instead hypothesizes a string of nonexistent islands on the Great Bahama Bank, west of Andros.

---

2. John Parker, *A Great Sign of Land. Columbus and the Sea-Birds: Ornithology and Navigation in 1492.*

3. Lancaster *Intelligencer Journal*, October 16, 1989. In 1990 and 1991, Winslow published an expanded version of the theory in (apparently the only editions of) the now-defunct journal *HRD News*, but a proposed third installment of the series, needed to cover Columbus's track from Island IV to the *Islas de Arena* and Cuba, never appeared.

The first problem with Lignum Vitae is that it is way up in the northern Bahamas. In order to reach Lignum Vitae, Columbus would have had to have been a celestial navigator. But as we saw in chapter 1, Bob McNitt has proposed an unrefuted argument that Columbus's navigation could not have been celestial, and must have been by dead reckoning instead.

Arriving at Island I, the theory runs into more problems. Winslow suggests that the *Pinta* left Island I and reconnoitered ahead of the fleet between October 12 and 14, even though it is not mentioned in the log. But that is not possible, since Columbus used the boats from all three ships in the exploration of Island I on October 14. On this boat trip, Columbus went north-northeast the length of the island. At Lignum Vitae, the boat trip starts north-northeast, but does not go the length of the island on this course, nor even along the coast. And oddly, Columbus wrote of his intention to sail southwest when he departed from his Guanahani anchorage, at the suggestion of the Indians. But this makes no sense at Lignum Vitae, since a southwest course from there runs right across unnavigable shallows, as Columbus would have easily seen.

These problems may be minor, but it gets worse as we go to Island II. The *Diario* records that Island II had a five-league-long coast facing Island I; while there is a coast running north-south at Bond Cay, it does not face Island I at all. Although Columbus's language is difficult here, Winslow's tortured translation of it is unconvincing. Columbus clearly implies that he saw, but did not follow, this five-league coast; the theory has Columbus following it anyway. Island II also had a coast running east-west for 10 leagues, while the east-west coast at Chub Cay isn't even remotely close to this size.

Like many others, this theory has a split Island II, relying on the ambiguity of Columbus's language in the *Diario* on this day. By itself, this is not necessarily a weakness. But in splitting Island II, Winslow has Columbus sailing from Chub Cay to New Providence while in search of ever-larger islands, apparently on the advice of his captured Indian guides. This is bizarre, since Andros Island is not only 10 times larger than New Providence, it is half as far from Chub Cay. Worse, in order to make this large distance, the theory requires a speed of nine knots for the fleet on the afternoon of October 15. It is generally regarded that the top speed for these ships was no more than eight knots,[4] based on the transatlantic portions of the *Diario*. Once again, this may not necessarily be fatal on its own, but even if there were such perfect wind conditions on the afternoon of the 15th, why did the fleet poke along at less than half that speed in the morning?

Yet it is at Island III that things get truly strange. First, Columbus describes the harbor at Island III as having a small island in the mouth forming two narrow entrances. There is only one entrance to Conch Harbor on Andros Island, and it's gigantic. Then after leaving the harbor at Island III, Columbus sailed northwest, according to the log. But that course from Conch Harbor puts Columbus aground on Andros.

Unbelievably, the theory requires the fleet to sail through the Middle Bight of Andros on October 18. This Middle Bight is actually a shallow tidal creek of the type seen in many places throughout the Bahamas; a similar strait separates Crooked from Acklins, for example. But none of these waters, including Middle Bight, are navigable for any except small craft. Indeed, such waters are obviously unnavigable, since one can clearly see the sandy bottom along with its starfish and other denizens. It is simply beyond belief that Columbus would put his fleet into such a shoal in the first place, and certain that they would have run aground if he had.

Having blithely sailed Columbus through this strait, things get no easier. Winslow then requires the fleet to sail onto the Great Bahama Bank on October 18. These waters are charted with depths of only one meter in this region, again far too shallow for ships this size.

But the worst is yet to come, for this theory has no credible candidate for Island IV. Leaving his Island III anchorage,

---

4. On the westbound passage, the highest speed recorded by the fleet was on October 4, when they made 63 leagues in 24 hours, for a speed of seven knots exactly. The sluggish *Santa Maria* sank in the islands, freeing the swifter caravels to sail faster on the eastbound passage; the fastest run on the way back was on February 6 when the caravels made 38.5 leagues during the 11 hours of daylight, or 9.2 knots. (Other than that one day, they twice recorded speeds of 6.7 knots on the return.) But in the Bahamian portion of the voyage that we are concerned with, a maximum of eight knots for the slow *Santa Maria* is, if anything, overly generous. To be conservative, I view anything over seven knots with suspicion, and over eight knots with disbelief.

it took three hours sailing for Columbus to sight Island IV. But from Winslow's proposed anchorage on the west side of Andros, his Island IV—which is simply the southern part of Andros—is already visible. The *Historia de Las Indias* reports that upon leaving Island III, Columbus "returned" to Island IV, "which had been left behind." The Indians wanted to do this, reports Las Casas, in order to get closer to their home on Island I. These descriptions do not fit the Lignum Vitae theory. In getting to Island IV, Winslow now has the fleet to sailing through the South Bight of Andros on October 19. By now it's no surprise to learn that, like Middle Bight, this, too, is a tidal creek, unnavigable for ships of this size.

From Island IV, Columbus noted a large bight (*angla*) to the northeast, which (the *Diario* says) was not navigable. There is no such feature at south Andros, except for South Bight, which the theory has already (and incorrectly) claimed *is* navigable. Finally leaving Island IV, Winslow's theory has Columbus sailing (again) across the Great Bahama Bank, which is (still) not navigable for ships this size. If you're keeping track, we are now on our fourth day of sailing through unnavigable waters.

On October 24 Columbus saw the *Islas de Arena*, a line of seven or eight islands running north-south, commonly identified with the Ragged Islands. But on the Lignum Vitae route, our Island IV, Andros, is so far north of the Ragged Islands that no amount of speculation can allow the fleet to get there. Even considered separately, the times, distances, and courses in the *Diario* each disallow it, and considering all three together, the Ragged Islands are out of the question. So Winslow simply conjures the *Islas de Arena* out of thin air, speculating that these islands were actually sandbars on the Great Bahama Bank that storms temporarily pushed above sea level at the time of Columbus, and that have since been swept away. Of course, if the sea was so shallow on the bank (as it is), one wonders again how the ships managed to remain afloat. But as it happens, even these magician's act *Islas* don't get Winslow off the hook, because his Cuba landfall is so far west that the coastlines and harbors don't even remotely match Columbus's descriptions, as they do at the conventional Cuban landfall of Bahía Bariay.

Grand Turk Island

This is an old theory, going back to Navarrete in 1825, and regularly revived since then. Grand Turk is the easternmost island in the Lucayan archipelago (although it is not part of the Bahamas politically). In recent years, Grand Turk has been advocated by H. E. Sadler,[5] Robert H. Power,[6] and others, and enthusiastically supported by the British colonial government of the Turks and Caicos, which has taken to the habit of re-naming[7] various land and sea features for Columbus and his crew. These theorists agree that Grand Turk is Island I, and some combination of the Caicos Islands is Island II; but there is disagreement beyond that.

Problems for this theory start (like some others) before Co-lumbus even reaches landfall. Columbus saw a light on the night of October 11, indicating that there was an island east of the landfall island that was bypassed in the night. Grand Turk is the easternmost island in the archipelago, so there is no more easterly island for the light to be.

Grand Turk has at least one minor problem with Island I itself. According to the *Diario*, there was a peninsula with a very narrow neck at Island I. The peninsula proposed at Grand Turk has a very wide neck, certainly too wide to be cut through in two days, as Columbus described. After that, Caicos as Island II looks good and is the theory's strongest point: the distances and directions from Island I are perfect, and the coastlines also match quite well. But after a slow morning sail, Power's theory requires Columbus to sail 58 nautical miles in six hours on the afternoon of October 15, at an impossible speed of 10 knots, in order to reach the northern point of the Caicos chain. The problems continue as Power must then sail Columbus from Caicos (his Island II) to Mayaguana (Island III) at a distance of

---

5. H. E. Sadler, *Turks Island Landfall: A history of the Turks and Caicos Islands.* Marjorie E. Sadler, Grand Turk. This is a reprint of Sadler's 1967 work in *Turks Island Review.* Sadler died in 1992.

6. Robert H. Power, "The Discovery of Columbus's Island Passage to Cuba," 165-167.

7. Although this practice is not necessarily untenable. Even if Columbus landed elsewhere, the *Pinta* under Martín Alonso Pinzón probably sailed through the Turks and Caicos later on the first voyage, during the time when Pinzón had abandoned Columbus to strike out on his own.

14 leagues northwest, while Columbus states that his course between these islands was actually east-west, or "almost east-west," and the distance no more than nine leagues. Upon arriving at Island III, Columbus reports the coast running north-northwest; but Mayaguana has no such coastline, and following Columbus's stated north-northwest course at Mayaguana would put him aground. The harbor at Abrahams Bay on Mayaguana has no little island in the mouth, as Columbus described, and Columbus's northwest course upon leaving the harbor again puts us aground.

And then there is the little matter of the split Island III, as Power asserts that a cloud bank led Columbus to believe that Mayaguana and Acklins were connected by a phantom coastline, instead of being separated by 40 miles of open sea as they really are. To his credit, Power readily admits the problem, but that does not make his explanation any easier to swallow. Finally, Power has Columbus leaving Island III entirely on October 18 for an unlogged anchorage at the tiny atoll of Hogsty Reef. The log has Columbus continuing his circumnavigation of Island III on this day.

While Power tells us that Columbus looks at the ocean and sees land, his fellow Grand Turk theorist Sadler tells us the opposite: that Columbus looks at land and sees the ocean. Sadler gets around Power's manifest problems by arbitrarily stopping Island II halfway up the Caicos chain. He splits up Middle Caicos and North Caicos to form Island II on one side and Island III on the other. The problem is that Columbus twice describes the distance from Island II to Island III as first nine leagues, then eight leagues, while recording a reasonable six hours to cross between them. But only a tiny meandering tidal creek separates Middle and North Caicos, perhaps 200 yards wide at its narrowest point. Given the view Columbus would have had from north of the outlying reef, it is impossible that anyone could even have seen that these were separate islands, much less imagined that they were divided by eight or nine leagues of ocean, which took six hours to cross. It is equally impossible that Columbus would have stated his intention to circumnavigate Island III (which he did) when the tiny creek between Island II and Island III was clearly unnavigable—if indeed it was visible at all.

This problem is an absolute killer for Sadler's whole Grand Turk theory, and he deals with it in a fashion all too typical of landfall theorists: he fails to inform his readers that the problem even exists. Does he imagine that we will not notice the elephant in the parlor? Either he is being unpardonably careless, or he distrusts his own reasoning.

It would be hard to argue with the view that these problems alone are enough to eliminate Grand Turk as a viable landfall. But the wheels continue to come off both theories as Power and Sadler each lamely attempt to get Columbus into and out of Island IV, which both claim is Inagua Island. While the *Santa Maria* sailed southeast and then (presumably) east from Island III to Island IV, Sadler must sail southwest instead. Power does get the direction about right, but on both routes Island IV shows up to the south, while Columbus says he first saw Island IV to the east. Columbus departed Island IV to the west-southwest for the *Islas de Arena*, yet both Grand Turk routes require an unlogged detour to the northwest. Columbus describes the Cape Verde fix being to the northwest at a distance of seven leagues; but the distance is far longer on Power's route, while Sadler's theory doesn't match either distance or direction. Finally, the distance from the Cape Verde fix to the *Islas de Arena* is 16 leagues in the log, but for Grand Turk, it's over 30 leagues on the route from Inagua. Indeed, after leaving Island II, there is hardly a single distance or course in Columbus's log that match either of the proposed routes from Grand Turk.

Once again, most of these major problems go unremarked by either Power or Sadler; we are left to discover them on our own, *Diario* in hand. So if Power and Sadler cannot come up with anything to cover their own theories' nakedness, should we expend any effort to do so? We will instead mark down Grand Turk as one more emperor embarrassed by his new clothes.

Cat Island

One of the few blessings we have in studying the landfall dispute is the fact that nobody believes this outmoded theory any more. Cat Island was in fact the first recorded landfall suggested in literature, and its identification as "Guanahani" or as "San Salvador" on old maps goes back to the seventeenth century.

The theory gained traction in 1828 with the help of Washington Irving, the American fiction writer and historian (who sometimes did not distinguish between the two). In preparation for a biography of Columbus, he asked Commander Alexander Slidell MacKenzie, USN, to examine the evidence and determine the location of the landfall. MacKenzie evaluated the then-traditional idea of a Cat Island landfall against Navarette's new theory of Grand Turk (similar to Sadler's) and he came away favoring Cat—which is perhaps no surprise. MacKenzie was hampered by a lack of accurate charts of the Bahamas, which led him to propose a route passing by islands that we now know do not exist.

Irving published MacKenzie's analysis in 1828 as an appendix to his biography of Columbus. Irving's book also contained numerous fictionalized[8] incidents in Columbus's life that gripped the imagination and made the book a bestseller. As a result, the Cat Island theory enjoyed a flurry of support in the next decade from the likes of Alexander von Humboldt.

MacKenzie's proposal has Cat Island as Island I, a split Island II composed of Conception Island and northern Long Island, Exuma as Island III, and back to Long Island as Island IV. For the *Islas de Arena*, MacKenzie proposed not the usual Ragged Islands, but rather the Mucaras, a group that was charted on the Great Bahama Bank in the eighteenth century.

The problems with Cat are pronounced even at Island I, which is a poor fit to the descriptions in the *Diario*. Columbus wrote that Island I (or its eastern part, at least) was "completely surrounded" by a reef. Cat Island, almost uniquely in the Bahamas, has no such reef. Columbus says that the reef enclosed a large harbor, but again there is no such feature at Cat Island. From his anchorage, Columbus went north-northeast along the coast of Island I. But there is no coastline running this direction on Cat Island for any appreciable length at all. Columbus described a peninsula with a narrow neck at Island I; and there is no such peninsula at Cat.

Upon arriving at Island II, Columbus reported that it had a coast running north-south. There is no such coast at Conception

---

8. Sadly, even at the beginning of the twenty-first century, some of Irving's inventions (such as, everyone except Columbus thought the world was flat; and Queen Isabella hocked her jewels to pay for the voyage) are still being taught as fact in some American schools.

Island, this theory's Island II; and even if there were such a coast, it would not face Island I, as reported by Columbus. Worse, this coast must be at least five leagues long, which is far larger than the entire tiny island of Conception. Then there is the 10-league-long east-west coast of Island II, which is again far larger than the entire island of Conception, and also does not fit northern Long Island (the other half of Island II, according to MacKenzie). Northern Long Island has no east-west coast at all, much less one of 10 leagues. In fact, aside from the usual generic adjectives like "flat" and "green," there is not a single part of Columbus's explicit descriptions of either Island I or Island II that fits the Cat Island theory well.

Columbus reported the distance from his anchorage at Island II to Island III as eight or nine leagues. The distance from Long Island to Exuma, this theory's Island III, is only five leagues. (And Conception to Exuma is 15 leagues, so there is no way to finesse the issue.) Columbus reported the coastline of Island III runs north-northwest and south-southeast, but the coast of Exuma runs west-northwest and east-southeast, a significant difference to a sailor. Columbus reported a harbor two leagues from the end of Island III. Although there is a fine harbor at Exuma, it is farther than two leagues from either end of the island. The two harbor entrances at Island III were both "very narrow" and separated by a small island, according to the log. This does not fit Exuma, where the harbor has many entrances both narrow and wide, separated by many islands large and small. After leaving the harbor to the northwest, Columbus reported a coast running east-west. There are no such coastlines at Exuma.

Columbus did not sight Island IV until three hours after leaving Island III. But the west coast of Long Island, MacKenzie's Island IV, is already in view from his departure point at Exuma. Columbus reported that the coast of Island IV runs west[9] from the northern point. At Long Island, the coast runs south-southeast from the northern point.

Columbus reported many ponds near the northern end of Island IV. There are no such ponds at the northern end of Long Island.

---

9. This clue is probably corrupt, based on other evidence in the *Diario*, but we should still consider it for the sake of completeness.

Columbus's initial course when departing from the northern end of Island IV was west-southwest. This course from Long Island would put Columbus aground on Exuma. Further, his stated departure time of midnight seems most unlikely given the extremely shallow water west of Long Island; if Columbus had really wanted to traverse this region, he surely would have waited for daylight to avoid the numerous shoals. In fact, the entire proposed leg after leaving Long Island crosses the very shallow and dangerous Great Bahama Bank, an unlikely if not impossible course for these ships.

And finally, the *Islas de Arena* are proposed to be the Mucara Islands—which do not actually exist. MacKenzie was apparently swayed by inaccurate eighteenth-century charts, some of which show these islands. In fact, only a single tiny islet called Cay Lobo is in this region, not the seven or eight islands reported by Columbus.

Caicos Islands

The Caicos theory was proposed in 1947 by Pieter Verhoog,[10] a Dutch sea captain, and gained support from Robert Fuson and Edwin Link, inventor of the Link trainer for airplane pilots. But since the 1950s the theory has gained no further adherents, and there appears to be no one alive today bearing its standard. This is perhaps all for the best, since the theory's many shortcomings are clear. Verhoog's theory has Caicos as Island I, Mayaguana as Island II, Acklins as Island III, and Inagua as Island IV.

Caicos comprises five islands, but Columbus does not specifically say that there are five islands in the log. Further, the *Diario* (which may mean Las Casas in this case rather than Columbus) describes Guanahani as an "islet,"[11] which hardly fits the expansive Caicos group in any sense. Verhoog points out that Fernando Colon's biography of Columbus, as well as Las Casas's *Historia de las Indias*, describe Island I as 15 leagues long; but he does not tell us that there is nothing in the *Diario* that says this, and much in the *Diario* that seems to contradict it.

---

10. Pieter H. G. Verhoog, "Columbus Landed on Caicos," *Proceedings of the U.S. Naval Institute* 80, 1101-1111.

11. *Diario*, 8v25.

The major problems with the Caicos theory start at Island II. The distance from Island I to Island II is reported as first five, then seven leagues. The distance from Caicos to Mayaguana is 40 nautical miles, or 15 leagues—two or three times the distance Columbus reported. Island II has a coast running north-south for five leagues, according to Columbus; but there is no such coast at Mayaguana. The distance from Island II to Island III is eight or nine leagues according to the *Diario*, while the distance from Mayaguana to Acklins is nearly twice that.

And things get no better at Island III, which is Acklins Island according to Verhoog. The coast of Island III runs north-northwest and south-southeast according to the *Diario*, while there is no such coast on Acklins. The harbor at Acklins is not two leagues from the end of the island, as Columbus reported; and the harbor at Acklins has a narrow entrance and one very wide entrance, not two very narrow entrances. After leaving the harbor at Island III Columbus sailed northwest along the coast; but this course makes no sense at Acklins, since the harbor is at the northeast corner of the island. Having seen the east-west coast of Island III, Columbus steered east-southeast on the evening of October 17. At Acklins, this course puts him aground on the Plana Cays.

From this point forward, Verhoog's theory is similar to Power's route from Grand Turk, and shares the same weaknesses. While the *Diario* tells us that Columbus continued his attempt to circumnavigate Island III on October 18, Verhoog has Columbus sailing away from Island III to an unlogged anchorage at Hogsty Reef. This unlogged Hogsty anchorage is needed to make landfall at Island IV plausible in the timeframe given in the *Diario*. Sailing from Island III (or from Hogsty Reef, if you believe Verhoog and Power), Columbus sighted Island IV to the east after sailing on a southeast course. But sailing from Hogsty Reef on this course, Inagua comes into view in the south, not the east.

Columbus's initial course departing from Island IV was west-southwest. Verhoog ignores this and requires Columbus to sail west and west-northwest to make the Ragged Islands landfall. After leaving Island IV, Verhoog also requires a course change from west-southwest to northwest that is not recorded in the *Diario*. After passing seven leagues southeast of Cabo Verde on

Island III, the Ragged Islands were then 16 leagues farther west, according to the log. But on the Caicos route, the Ragged Islands are about 30 leagues from this point, on a course west by north.

In defense of his theory, Verhoog wrote, "I have never found a single serious objection against Caicos as the landfall of Columbus in 1492." If this is true, it can only mean that he wasn't looking for objections very diligently—or more likely, he was not looking at all.

Egg Island

Arne Molander, a retired civil engineer, first proposed[12] this theory in a 1981 lecture and 1983 in print. He has been a tireless advocate of it ever since, both in the Columbus Round Robin and in various magazine and Internet articles. Like Lignum Vitae cay, Egg Island is also in the northern Bahamas, and therefore must also rely on the idea that Columbus held his latitude by celestial means. We saw in chapter 1 how Bob McNitt put the refutation of this idea directly to Molander at the 1992 Annapolis debate. Molander has yet to counter McNitt's argument.

Molander proposes that Egg Island and its nearby companion Royal Island together form Island I; New Providence is Island II; Andros is Island III; and Long Island is Island IV. Like most other theorists, Molander uses the Ragged Islands as the *Islas de Arena.*

Egg Island is quite tiny, perhaps a hundred acres or so, and Royal is only a little larger. However, Columbus's description of the size of Island I is vague enough that this may be no major issue. Like Grand Turk, Egg has no other island to the east that could have been the source of the light bypassed on the night of October 11. Other than that, there is only one serious problem with the description of Island I, that being the reef, which Columbus described as encircling the entire island. At Egg and Royal, the reef is on the west coast only, with the east coast fronting on the broad shallows of the Great Bahama Bank.

At Island II things begin to go more seriously astray. Columbus's descriptions here are explicit: Island II has a coast

---

12. Arne B. Molander, "A New Approach to the Columbus Landfall," 15, 113-149.

running north-south for five leagues, a coast that faces Island I; and another coast running east-west for more than 10 leagues. But New Providence is a lozenge-shaped island with points at the east and west ends, and so has no coastline running north-south at all. Also, New Providence is only about six or seven leagues long east to west, well short of the more than ten leagues reported in the *Diario*. Molander tries to make up for the difference by suggesting that Columbus also counted the east-west distance of nearby Rose Cay, but a wide and obvious channel that Columbus could not have failed to notice separates the two islands.

To alibi the missing north-south coast of Island II, Molander has come up with a clever argument. Columbus had kidnapped several Indians from Island I for use as guides, and he took them through the islands with him (and eventually back to Europe). Molander proposed that these Indians drew a map for the Spaniards, that Columbus relied on this map, and that the map was inaccurate. So the north-south coast was charted on the Indian map, from whence the idea made its way into Columbus's head (bypassing the evidence of his own eyes) and from there into his log. The missing north-south coast of Island II is the first place that Molander relies on this hypothesis, but it is not the last, so we should take a critical look at this idea.

Certainly the Indians understood the concept of physical representations of geographical features. For example, the Indians taken on the first voyage reportedly created a sort of map out of beans for King John II of Portugal. But did they actually create a *map*—drawn to scale, as the distance of the north-south "coast" of Island II implies—that Columbus actually possessed and used?

There is good evidence in the historical record that Columbus did not receive cartographic information from the natives via maps. For example, in Columbus's 1493 letter to the Spanish Sovereigns, he wrote:

> After I arrived at Juana [Cuba] . . . I thought it was probably not an island, but rather a mainland . . . but I could not verify this because everywhere I arrived people fled and I could not speak with them. . . . In the meantime I already understood something of

the speech and signs of certain Indians I had taken on the island of San Salvador, and I understood [from them] that this was still an island.[13]

So Columbus needed cartographic information from the Indians, and he was unable to get it until he had learned their language. Of course, if the natives had been drawing maps, language would have been no barrier. Therefore, the inaccurate Indian map hypothesis is quite unlikely, and the missing north-south coastline of Island II has no convincing explanation on the Egg Island route.

From New Providence, Molander has Columbus next reaching Andros Island as Island III. While the direction, distance, size of the island, and coastline directions are all pretty good, there are some inconsistent details. Columbus describes the harbor at Island III as having two entrances, both very narrow, separated by an islet. The harbor at Andros, Conch Harbor, has one huge entrance that nobody would call very narrow. After leaving this harbor, Columbus sailed northwest, a course that would put him aground north of Conch Harbor at Andros.

But it is Island IV that throws the Egg Island theory into reverse. In order to arrive at the Ragged Islands, Molander must start from an Island IV somewhere near there—which in this case means Long Island. But Long Island is a long, long way from Andros. As it turns out, Columbus does not give us an explicit distance from Island III to Island IV (which is good for the theory); but he does state that it took him only three hours of sailing from Island III before Island IV came into view. And that's very, very bad for the theory, since the closest distance from Andros to Long is 120 nautical miles, and on that route the large Exuma Island is directly in the way. Therefore, Molander must instead aim for the even more distant southern part of Long Island, and he must do so on a course that keeps Columbus out of sight of Exuma.

Recall that Columbus was searching for an island when leaving Island III, so it's no use bypassing or ignoring any large, visible island. But the only course that keeps Columbus from

13. Margarita Zamora, Christopher Columbus's Letter: "Announcing the Discovery."

seeing the unreported Exuma Island takes him directly across the treacherous Great Bahama Bank. And so that is exactly where Molander takes him.

The bank is not as shallow southeast of Andros as it is on the west side, so unlike Winslow, Molander does not run Columbus aground immediately. But although the water here may average about five meters (while the ships draw two meters or so), many places are shallower than that, and a glance at the charts does not give much confidence—the nautical chart here is strewn with constellations of + marks denoting underwater rocks. This area of the bank is marked with notations such as "Numerous rocky heads and reef navigable only for small craft," and "Numerous unsurveyed rocky heads," and "Numerous rocky heads with 5 to 7.5 meters between them." You get the idea. The Great Bahama Bank is a sailor's worst nightmare: a wide shallow sea studded with a maze of rocky coral heads, ready to rip the hull out of any passing ship. Not deep enough for safe passage, not shallow enough to keep you from drowning or being smashed against the coral by the sea. Today, even ships with engines avoid it; in Columbus's day, without an engine, without a chart, and without any hope of rescue, it would have been suicidal.

Further, the time problem here is stark: From the northern end of Andros, which Columbus must have seen on the afternoon of October 17, Molander must sail the fleet nearly 300 miles in less than 48 hours, to arrive at Long Island at noon on the 19th. And 12 of those hours, the night of the 18th, Columbus spent anchored, meaning that the entire distance must be sailed at eight knots, faster than any single day on the transatlantic voyage. To make things even worse, according to the *Diario*, Columbus spent the entire day of the 18th continuing his circumnavigation of Island III.

The only solution for Molander is to abandon the *Diario*, in both greater and lesser ways. Upon leaving the east-west coast of Island III (which in this theory is the northern end of Andros), Columbus sailed east-southeast, turning downwind away from an approaching storm. But this course (if followed at high speed, which the theory requires) would put Columbus aground on the Exuma Cays on the night of the 17th. So Molander simply sails the fleet south-southeast instead, in spite of Columbus's logged course.

Then on the 18th, instead of continuing his circumnavigation of Island III as the *Diario* reports, Molander has Columbus sailing directly away from the coast of Andros and across the treacherous Great Bahama Bank, with the excuse that Columbus somehow considered the bank to be part of the island. According to Molander, Columbus anchored that night in the Jumentos Cays, west of Long Island and on the opposite side of the bank from Andros.

Here the distance and speed problem shows its greatest difficulty. A sailing ship reaches top speed[14] when the wind reaches force seven or eight on the Beaufort Scale. Winds that strong leave the waves streaked with foam and whitecaps. Now recall that this is supposed to be happening in a region of the sea strewn with rocks, where the sailors are keeping a sharp eye out for breakers on the numerous coral heads separated by as little as five meters, about the same as the widths of the ships themselves. In a rough sea covered with whitecaps, is it even remotely possible that anyone could have discerned a wave breaking on a barely submerged rock? And that all three ships could have avoided such breakers for 12 hours? And even if the rocks were actually seen, could a ship plowing ahead at eight knots take evasive action through this maze of reefs without losing speed? And, having allegedly survived such a harrowing ordeal, would it then go completely unremarked in the detail-packed *Diario*? Hardly. Molander's timeline turns the suicidal into the impossible, and not even an inaccurate Indian map can rescue the fleet.

The problems do not end there, however, since Columbus describes his arrival at Island IV as being at the north end of the island. But the theory has Columbus arriving near Sandy Cay at the western end of Long Island, more than 30 miles south of the northern end. Indeed, the northern end of Island IV jumps around quite a bit for this theory, since Columbus departs from Island IV at the northern end, too, yet Molander has Columbus departing from the southern end instead (which is needed in

14. John Harland, *Seamanship in the Age of Sail.* See the graphs of ship speed vs. wind speed on p. 46, and the effects of the Beaufort Scale on p. 53.

order to reach the Ragged Islands). And to explain the much-later *Diario* entry that Island IV is only eight leagues from Island I, Molander moves the northern end of Island IV *again*, to somewhere around Highbourne Cay on Columbus's inaccurate Indian map—about 150 miles north of Sandy Cay!

San Salvador, or Watlings Island

From this point forward, all remaining theories use Long Island as Island III, which avoids some major issues of previous theories: the thorny problem of getting Columbus to the *Islas de Arena* is easily solved by having Long Island as Island III.

Watlings Island has been the favored landfall theory for much of the nineteenth and twentieth centuries. It was first suggested as the landfall as early as 1793 by Juan Muñoz (apparently on the basis of old maps alone, as the *Diario* had not then been published). The idea was turned into a real theory by British admiral A. B. Becher, who gave it a book-length treatment in 1856. And indeed, compared to the then-popular ideas of Grand Turk and Cat Island, Watlings must have seemed like a beacon of sanity in a sea of nonsense. Yet Becher's explanations for the problems of his own theory were hardly convincing; for example, he invoked the possibility of volcanic action (in the completely non-volcanic Bahamas) to alter the coastlines since Columbus's day. Becher's route was also in some ways oddly similar to MacKenzie's unpalatable route from Cat Island. But James B. Murdock markedly improved the route from Watlings in 1884, and his route has since become standard for Watlings advocates.

In 1926, Father Chrysostom Schreiner convinced the Bahamian parliament to officially rename Watlings Island as "San Salvador, or Watlings Island," and the island is usually just called "San Salvador" on maps (and airline schedules) today. Among landfall theorists, however, Watlings is still the preferred toponym, to avoid confusion with the more generic San Salvador that was Columbus's name for Island I.

Murdock's route gained the support of Samuel Eliot Morison in his 1942 Pulitzer-winning biography *Admiral of the Ocean Sea*, an endorsement that brought the landfall debate to a standstill in the mid-twentieth century. Since then, the Watlings bandwagon has included many members of the Landfall Round Robin, including *Diario* translator James E. Kelley Jr., anthropologist Bill Keegan, and single-handed sailor Doug Peck. A few of these (notably Mauricio Obregon and Bill Dunwoody) have tinkered with the route in order to try and resolve some of its problems. The Murdock-Morison identifications: Island I is Watlings; Island II is Rum Cay; Island III is Long Island; Island IV is Crooked Island. (Dunwoody substitutes Fortune Island as Island IV, a notable improvement.) Because Watlings has been one of the most widely supported and studied theories over the years, it will be worthwhile to spend some time here and look closely.

Like some other proposed landfalls, there is no other island east of Watlings that could have been the source of the light on the night of October 11. The description of Island I itself is pretty good: flat, with a reef and large pond in the middle—although the reef does not entirely surround the island as the *Diario* says it should, and Columbus would have seen that. And although Columbus's descriptions of the size of the island are vague, there are some nagging doubts about Watlings in this regard: the island might just be too large, and the wrong shape. This stems from a close analysis of the boat trip that Columbus took on October 14, during which he explored Island I. In the first place, Columbus's trip took him "the length of the island on a north-northeast course." Some of the things that Columbus saw on the boat trip were a reef surrounding the island, a harbor between the reef and the island, and a peninsula with the narrow neck, formed almost like an island. Morison proposed that Graham's Harbor, along the north coast of Watlings, was the harbor described by Columbus, and a small cay at the eastern end of the harbor was this island-like peninsula.

But this scenario is beset with a series of small but nagging problems. Columbus's proposed anchorage is at Fernandez Bay, actually a wide bight on the west coast[15] of the island. But leaving from there, the initial course along the coast takes you north, not north-northeast. Further, you don't go the whole

---

15. In this region of prevailing easterly and northeasterly trades, the west coast of Watlings provides much better anchorage than the more exposed east coast.

length of the island, but rather less than half the length, before arriving at the northern coast. Columbus reported entrance through the reef and into the harbor was "very narrow." At Graham's Harbor, the reef gap is a huge 1,400 meters wide.

But the biggest issues here are time and speed. It's a long way north from Fernandez Bay to the north end of the island, where coral reefs form Graham's Harbor and the little cay at the eastern end. Although the description of the peninsula fits the *Diario* well enough, this would mean that the boats were rowed (or sailed) about 11 nautical miles to get there, and another 11 back to the ship's anchorage. That distance is just within the boats' range; but then after getting back, the boats were hoisted aboard the ships, the ships weighed anchor, and the fleet sailed far enough away from Island I to see Island II—and apparently other islands—before nightfall. And all this occurred on a day when the wind was weak enough that the water in the harbor was, according to Columbus, "no more disturbed than the bottom of a well."

Further, you only see one island when sailing southwest from Watlings, and that is Rum Cay. Since Columbus reported seeing many islands, Morison proposed that the hills of Rum Cay would have appeared to be separate islands to Columbus. Although the idea is not inherently unreasonable, there are a couple of problems here. First, Columbus also said these many islands were at varying distances from Island I, some more than five leagues away and some less. But the visible hills of Rum Cay would have all been at about the same distance. Also, as Joe Judge pointed out, all the hills of Rum Cay lie in nearly the same direction, so it is doubtful an experienced mariner like Columbus would have been fooled into believing that they were separate islands in the first place. Finally, in order to see many hills on Rum Cay (rather than just the highest), the ships must have been off Southwest Point of Watlings, perhaps six or seven nautical miles from the anchorage. Given the light winds that day, it would have taken about three hours for the boats to be hauled in, anchor weighed, and the distance sailed. That would leave perhaps nine hours of daylight for the boats to make the required 22 nautical miles, a speed of about two and a half knots. And that's quite fast for these boats on an all-day trip.

The only other time the boats spent all day away from the ships, on January 1, they made less than two knots on the journey.

If only we could move the anchorage from Fernandez Bay down to Southwest Point, we could solve a couple of problems: the boat trip would then start on north-northeast course, as Columbus said, and it would go the length of the island, as he said. But that would mean that the boats would have to travel not 22 miles, but 32—and that's just not possible, not even with the whole 12 hours of daylight. Another idea is to move the anchorage from Fernandez Bay northward to Cockburn Town. This nearly resolves the boat speed issue (at 18 nautical miles, the speed drops to two knots from two and a half), but it means that the initial course is now shifted to north-northwest, a rather startling departure from the logged north-northeast. Yet regardless of which anchorage one chooses, there is another problem with the boat trip at Watlings: Columbus went on this trip, he tells us, to see "the other part of the island, which is the eastern part." But at Watlings, Columbus is actually exploring the northern part of the island, and spends the entire trip in the northern quadrant from his anchorage. As I said, each of these problems, considered alone, might be considered minor, especially compared to the absurdities of some previous theories we have seen. But put them all together and the events of October 14 seem to leave the theory in a state of some confusion, like a witness who can't get his story straight.

But it is at Island II, Rum Cay, that the Watlings theory faces its biggest test. Columbus wrote "I found that the face in the direction of San Salvador runs north-south and in it were 5 leagues; and the other, which I followed, runs east-west; and in it were more than ten leagues." Rum Cay's proportions are about right, but as we saw in chapter 2, its size is about a third of Columbus's descriptions. We also saw that Watlings theorists have a longstanding explanation for the discrepancy, the miles-to-leagues conversion hypothesis. This supposes that Columbus wrote "five miles" and "ten miles" as the original dimensions, but that these figures were miscopied as "five leagues" and "ten leagues." We will discuss this in greater detail in chapter 6.

Columbus also said the north-south coast of Island II was facing Island I, while Rum Cay's north-south coast, even though convex, does not face Watlings. And the exact language used by Columbus is once again difficult for Watlings, because the clear implication is that Columbus saw the north-south coast but did not follow it. Since the north-south coast of Rum Cay bows outward, the only way Columbus could have known the length of this coast with any confidence is if he had followed it anyway. Some theorists have speculated that it is the north coast of Rum Cay that Columbus followed, rather than the south coast as Morison postulates. This fixes the coast-not-followed problem, but then it is unclear how Columbus would have known the length of Rum Cay's east coast.

Once again the timeline is a problem at Island II. After spending the night marking time, it took Columbus from dawn until "around noon" to arrive at Island II, a distance of less than seven leagues. From then until nightfall he sailed the more than ten leagues along the east-west coast to the western end of Island II. So it would seem that the fleet accelerated from morning to afternoon, which makes perfect sense, as Columbus wrote that the tide (or a current) detained him in the morning, while in the afternoon he crowded on more sail. At Rum Cay, the distance sailed in the morning was about 18 nautical miles (any less, and the timeline on the 14th goes from bad to worse) and in the afternoon amounts to no more than 10 nautical miles (if the north coast was followed) or 12 (if the east and south coasts were followed). In other words, the theory must suppose that Columbus slowed down significantly between morning and afternoon on October 15, in spite of both implicit and explicit statements to the contrary in the *Diario*.

Upon leaving Island II, Columbus reported sailing on an east-west course from there to Island III. And in fact, if you sail west from the western end of Rum Cay, you get to the northern tip of Long Island, this theory's Island III. But the problem is that from the west end of Rum Cay, the highest hills of Long Island are already visible to the west-southwest—which is also the course giving the shortest distance to Long Island. Therefore, Murdock and Morison simply slide by Columbus's logged course and sail him west-southwest anyway, to a landing about 10 miles south of the northern end. (This is mandatory, since from his Island III landfall, Columbus sailed north-northwest along the island; hence, landing at the northern tip of Long Island is a total non-starter.) And while Columbus wrote that the distance from Island II to Island III was eight or nine leagues, the actual distance from Rum Cay to Long Island is only six leagues.

Columbus found a harbor two leagues from the end of Island III, with a small island in its mouth forming two narrow entrances. Newton Cay harbor (at the northern end of Long Island) is the only candidate on this route, but it is less than half that distance from the end of the island. So once again, the miles-to-leagues conversion hypothesis comes to the rescue of the theory. Columbus's initial impression of the harbor was "marvelous." But at Newton Cay, a maze of reefs covering the entrance makes approach from seaward hazardous if not impossible for large vessels. Leaving the harbor, Columbus wrote, "I sailed to the northwest far enough that I discovered all that part of the island until the coast that runs east-west." At Newton Cay, the distance he would have needed to sail to discover this coastline would have been zero, since the harbor is already at the northern end of the island, with the northern cape in plain view. Worse, there is no such east-west coastline north of Newton Cay harbor at all, since that northern cape of Long Island comes to a point.

Upon leaving Island III in search of Island IV, which had been described by his kidnapped Indian guides, Columbus split his fleet to widen the search area. The *Santa Maria* sailed southeast for three hours and then was the first to sight Island IV, which showed up to the east. In the Watlings theory, Island IV is Crooked Island. The problem is that, sailing southwest from the southern end of Long Island (his required starting point: see chapter 2), Crooked Island comes into view much sooner than three hours, and shows up to the northeast on a southeasterly course from Long Island. The geometry is just wrong. And although Columbus describes the coast of Island IV as trending 12 leagues west from his arrival point at the northern end, the coast of Crooked Island is not that long.

Finally, and perhaps most tellingly, the *Diario* tells us that Island IV was eight leagues from Island I. Crooked Island is about 20 leagues from Watlings, two and a half times farther away. This is a huge problem for the Watlings theory, and its biggest single distance discrepancy with the *Diario.* Yet you would hardly know it from reading either the popular or the academic literature on the landfall. As is so depressingly common in landfall literature, most writers have simply declined to inform their readers that the problem even exists.

Conception Island

Conception Island is a small (two square km) island lying in the Long Island Passage, between Cat Island, Long Island, and Rum Cay. It was first proposed[16] as the landfall by Lieutenant R. T. Gould (RN) in 1927, chiefly as a means of resolving some of the problems with the Watlings theory (particularly the problem of the light of October 11). The theory attracted little attention at the time, but was recently revived by Dr. Steven Mitchell, a geologist at California State University at Bakersfield, who did some archaeological field work on the island in the 1980s.

Mitchell's route, similar to Murdock's route from Watlings, proposes that Island I is Conception, Island II is Rum Cay, Island III is Long Island, and Island IV is Crooked/Acklins. Although Conception is small, we have seen that Columbus's descriptions of Island I are generic enough that few Bahamian islands have problems here, and that includes Conception. But its size does have the advantage of avoiding all the speed and distance problems with the boat trip as we saw at Watlings; and there is also a coastline running north-northeast from the southern end of the island. According to Mitchell, the "eastern part" of Island I explored on this trip was Booby Cay, a small islet just off Conception's east coast. So the descriptions of Island I fit the *Diario* somewhat better here than at Watlings.

The coast of Island II is somewhat worse, though, since the coast of Rum Cay that faces Conception does not run north-south at all, but is rather the north coast of Rum Cay, which runs nearly east-west. The problems that Conception has from Rum Cay and beyond are identical to the problems for Watlings, since the two routes merge from this point forward. Rather than

---

16. R. T. Gould, "The landfall of Columbus: An old problem restated," *Geographical Journal* 49 (1927), 403-429.

repeat these same issues, I refer the reader to the latter parts of the Watlings theory above.

Samana Cay

Samana Cay is a small island lying north of Acklins Island in the central Bahamas. The Samana Cay theory was first proposed[17] in 1882 by Gustavus V. Fox, a former undersecretary of the Navy. Fox identified Island I as Samana Cay, Island II as Crooked-Acklins, Island III as Long Island, and Island IV as Fortune Island.

The theory fell into disrepute when it was severely criticized by Watlings advocate James B. Murdock in 1884. Sadly, Fox had died in 1883 and was unable to rebut Murdock's criticism. Murdock's major gripe was that in Fox's track to Fortune Island (the theory's Island IV), Columbus returned to a point within sight of Crooked Island (Island II). Murdock argued that Columbus couldn't have backtracked without specifically mentioning it in the log. This was a convincing line of reasoning that held sway for a century.

The Samana theory was revived in 1986 by Joseph Judge,[18] senior editor of *National Geographic,* and has since enjoyed a resurgence in popularity. Ironically, Judge did not deal with Murdock's "Columbus couldn't have returned" argument at all. But in 1992, another Samana advocate, Alejandro Pérez, noticed a key passage in Las Casas's masterwork *Historia de las Indias* and made a convincing case to the Columbus Landfall Round Robin. Here is Las Casas describing Columbus's decision to leave Fernandina, Island III, in search of Saometo (emphasis added):

> Because the Indians he had taken in the first island of Guanahani or San Salvador told him and indicated through signs that the island of Saometo, **which had been left behind**, was larger than Fernandina, and that they should **return** to it (and they must

17. Gustavus V. Fox, "An Attempt to Solve the Problem of the First Landing Place of Columbus in the New World." *Report of the Superintendent of the U. S. Coast and Geodetic Survey* (Appendix no. 18, June 1880). Washington: Government Printing Office.

18. Joseph Judge, "Where Columbus found the New World," *National Geographic,* 170 (November 1986), 566-599.

have done this in order **to get closer to their land**, from where
he had taken them), the Admiral decided to **turn around** toward
the east . . .

Since the emphasized passages make geographical statements not obvious from the *Diario* alone, Pérez argued that Las
Casas must have had Columbus's map in front of him when he
wrote this passage. (We know Columbus made a map of his discoveries on the first voyage, but it has been lost for centuries.)
And since there is another place in the *Historia* where Las Casas
explicitly claims to have Columbus's map, Pérez's idea makes
sense.

The problems with Samana are relatively few compared to
some other theories. First, as with Egg, Watlings, and Grand
Turk, Columbus saw a light on the night of October 11, indicating an island bypassed in the night. From Samana, there is
no island to the east and nowhere for the light to be. But the
description of Island I itself is the major headache for Samana
advocates. First, Columbus reported a very large pond (*"una
laguna muy grande"*) in the middle of Island I, while the only
ponds at Samana are quite small. After being criticized on this
point, Judge sought a way out by convenient translation, ren-
dering the Spanish *laguna* into the English "lagoon," whereupon
he claimed that the area of the sea between the offshore reef
and the island forms the required lagoon. We saw in chapter 3
that this argument is weak on a number of grounds.

The problems with Island I do not stop there, however. Columbus reported a peninsula with a narrow neck, formed like
an island. There currently is a peninsula at Samana that fits
the bill, a low-lying sandpit at the eastern end of the island's
southern bight. Unfortunately, after further geological research,
it is now apparent that this peninsula is a recent feature that
did not exist at the time of Columbus, as Judge admitted in the
1992 debate. The coastlines of the island are even more problematical, since Columbus went north-northeast the length of
Island I, and Samana has no coastline running in this direction
at all, much less for its entire length.

From there, Island II is a blessing, especially compared to
other theories. The closely spaced Crooked and Acklins Islands

form a single coastline on the north, a coast that runs east-west for more than 10 leagues, just as described by Columbus; and Acklins has an east coast that runs north-south for about five leagues, again matching the *Diario*. But the coast of Island II that faces Island I runs north-south, while the coast of Acklins-Crooked that faces Samana is the one that runs east-west. Further, in order to see the north-south running coast of Island II at all, and to correctly judge its length, the theory requires that Columbus made an unmotivated jog eastward, going many miles out of his way for no clear reason. This seems very odd, especially considering he spent the entire afternoon crowding on sail to arrive at the western end of Island II. If he was heading for the western end of Island II, why not just go there directly instead of jogging east?

From this point, the Samana and Plana tracks merge and share the same few problems (and the same many virtues). Island III is virtually a perfect match with the *Diario* when coming from Crooked. But, as with most other theories, the coast of Island IV does not run west from the northern point, and it is not 12 leagues long.

All in all, though, one must admit that the Samana route is pretty good. If only Island I were not such a poor match to the *Diario*, it would be hard to beat.

Plana Cays

The Plana Cays theory was first proposed by Ramon Julio Didiez Burgos, an admiral in the Navy of the Dominican Republic. His book *Guanahani y Mayaguain* has been almost completely neglected since its publication in 1974, perhaps due to its unwelcome thesis, or perhaps due to Didiez's difficult prose.

Didiez theorized that Mayaguana was the source of the light of October 11, and that the first landfall was at the western of the two Plana Cays. From that point, Didiez has Columbus following the north coast of Crooked Island (Island II), then circumnavigating Long Island (Island III), and arriving at Fortune Island as Island IV.

The theory had no further activity until I stumbled across the idea independently in late 1991. I improved things a little by substituting a route similar to Fox's Samana Cay theory, up and down the east coast of Long Island in place of Didiez's complete circumnavigation. Like Fox and Judge, I also put Columbus's anchorage at Island II at Landrail Point, the western end of the island, rather than within the reef on the northern coast as Didiez prefers.

The Plana Cays is the most likely landfall, not because it's a perfect theory (there is no such thing in this debate) but simply because it has fewer and less serious problems than any of the others—in some cases, a lot fewer. But since I've subjected everyone else to the wringer, it would be unfair to let the problems with my own ideas go unmentioned, so here they are.

First, there are no clear references on old maps to Plana as Guanahani. Some people make a great deal of this, but I don't; if you trusted the old maps, the landfall would most likely be Cat Island, which is a terrible theory. As mentioned in the previous chapter, it's simply impossible to say how the Indian toponyms may have gotten to any particular place on European maps drawn decades or centuries after the fact.

The next obvious problem with the Plana Cays is that they are two islands, while Columbus does not specifically say that there are two islands. Although the map of Juan de la Cosa may be helpful in this regard, I prefer to rely on the implicit statement made by Columbus by taking boats to explore "the other part, which is the eastern part" of Guanahani on October 14. As we saw in chapter 2, Columbus never uses a boat to go somewhere he can walk instead; and this strongly implies that the eastern part of Guanahani was indeed a separate island.

There are a couple of minor problems here with the description of Island I. Columbus described a large pond in the middle of Island I. Unlike Samana Cay, there are large ponds at Plana that fit the bill, but they are not centrally located on the island. They are, however, near the southwestern end of the island where Columbus would have anchored, so they would have been easy for him to find. Also, there is no peninsula with the narrow neck that Columbus described on his boat trip, on either the eastern or western cay. Here, I must throw up my hands and punt; I must assume that there was such a feature there in 1492, perhaps a temporary sandpit like the one now at

Samana, which has been washed away by storms in the mean-time. Another alternative is that the large pond at the eastern end of the eastern cay was, in 1492, joined to the sea, making a hooked peninsula. The separation of the pond from the sea is very narrow these days around most of its circumference. But this is obviously a weak point for the theory.

Next, Acklins Island is marginally visible from the Plana an-chorage, yet Columbus does not mention other visible islands until after leaving Island I. Personally, I think this is a small point; he mentions seeing other islands immediately after weigh-ing anchor, even in the same sentence, so it is clear that they could not have been too far away. Further, the distance from these islands to Guanahani was, according to Columbus, less than five leagues in some cases, and there is no way an island that close would not have been visible, given good weather—al-though it's always possible that the first two days at Island I were hazy.

Also in the visibility department, from Island II Columbus mentions that he can see Island III. Using the standard equa-tion to determine distance to the horizon, it is just a bit too far to see Long Island from Crooked. But the standard equa-tion is based on the standard atmosphere, which is a daytime atmosphere. Just before sunset, the energy balance of Earth's surface changes as it begins radiating away more energy than it gets from the Sun; this causes a temperature inversion (called the nocturnal boundary layer) that starts at the surface and gets thicker as the night proceeds. One effect of a temperature inversion is to increase atmospheric refraction, and hence sight-ing distance. Even a very modest temperature inversion in the lowest 50 meters of the atmosphere would be enough to make Long Island visible to Columbus. On the Plana route, Colum-bus rounded Bird Rock (at the western tip of Crooked Island) at around sunset, when the nocturnal temperature inversion would have just formed; and he would have had the highest hills of Long Island silhouetted darkly against a bright sky in the west. These are ideal sighting conditions.

Finally, as with so many other theories, the description of Island IV is problematical. The coast of Fortune Island does not run west from the northern point, and it is not 12 leagues long. But we saw in chapter 2 that the westerly direction of the coastline must be a flat-out error, from other descriptions in the *Diario*. And as for the 12-league distance, there is one possible transcription error that would resolve it. This was a period in history when both Roman and Arabic numerals were in wide use, and both appear frequently in the *Diario*. It is possible that Columbus wrote the size of the island as the Roman numeral IV leagues, and that a later copyist misread it as the Arabic numeral 12 leagues.

But all in all, it is gratifying how many difficult problems melt away when starting from the Plana Cays as Island I. There is an island to the east (Mayaguana) that would have been the source of the light seen on the night of October 11. There is a coast that runs north-northwest at Plana, and it runs the whole length of the island, and you must follow that coast to reach "the other part, which is the eastern part" that Columbus explored by boat. The island is small enough that the boat trip does not have the speed problems seen at Watlings. Island II does have a coast that runs north-south for five leagues, and that coast does face Island I. Island II also has a coastline running east-west for more than 10 leagues. We saw in chapter 2 how the coastlines of southern Long Island are a dead-on match for the descriptions of Columbus's Island III. We also saw how only Fortune Island fits the track both from Island III and backward from the Ragged Islands. The eight-league distance reported by Columbus between Island IV and Island I isn't quite right, but we saw in chapter 2 that it can be easily resolved.

Mayaguana

Finally, there is one theory we have not discussed: Mayaguana Island. This was proposed as the landfall by Francisco de Varnhagen in 1864, in an obscure Chilean journal that is impossible to find anymore; even the Library of Congress does not have it. Certainly, lying so close to the Plana Cays, it would be possible for someone today to make a very good case for Mayaguana, if motivated to do so, by tacking most of the Plana Cays route onto a new Island I. But since nobody is beating the band for this theory, I prefer to let it rest in peace.

5.

Coming of Age in Samoa

ON January 14, 1995, Jim Kelley wrote a challenging letter to the Round Robin, and the contents were addressed partly to me:

"Keith, I really enjoyed your letter of 25 Nov. Delighted you are tackling the difficult technical problems associated with reconstructing CC's voyage tracks. More thinking by technically capable people is just what the doctor ordered. I'd like to help as a resource person if I can. I have some comments on your letter—challenges to your thinking, to stir the pot."

Jim proceeded to stir vigorously.

"It is readily established that the landfall island must have been in the central Bahamas. Then, by a process of elimination, one can readily discount Cat I, Rum Cay, Conception, Samana, Long, Crooked, and, yes, even the Plana Cays. Just on the basis of population and harbor size alone, the smaller islands like Conception, Samana, and the Planas can be eliminated."

Jim supported his statement by citing two papers of his own, relating to harbor size in one case and population in the other. I had not seen the harbor size paper, but I had read the population argument.[1]

---

1. James E. Kelley Jr., "Epistemology 101 for Landfall Students: An Appreciation of an Important New Book," 101-110. The upper limit of population reported here (1,115) differs slightly from the upper limit of this same paper in offprint, given as 945; but the difference is not important for our purposes.

While at Guanahani on October 13, Columbus wrote of the natives approaching the Spanish ships in canoes. "They came to the ship with dugouts that are made from the trunk of one tree . . . and so big that in some of them 40 and 45 men came. And others smaller, down to some in which came one man alone." Working from this description, Kelley had started with the fair assumption that there were more small canoes than large ones. Then he made a reasonable extrapolation as to how many canoes of each size came to the ships that day, and arrived at a total number of men in canoes. From this, a minimum population of Guanahani could be determined. According to Kelley's analysis, the population of Guanahani must have been at least 634 to 945 persons.

Anthropologists Allen W. Johnson and Timothy Earle had made a study[2] of the likely population densities of societies at various stages of technological development. From their work, Kelley postulated that the population density of the Bahamas at the time of Columbus was between four and eight people per square kilometer. This implied that Guanahani could be no smaller than 79 square kilometers. Watlings Island is 101 square kilometers; Samana Cay is 39, the Plana Cays are 16, and Conception is only four.

This was a credible analysis that demanded a credible response. While I could not fault Kelley's analysis of the number of canoes, I knew little of population densities in a subsistence economy, so reading Johnson and Earle's book was enlightening. They had studied populations in a continental setting, and I wondered if things might be different on small islands. If small islands were capable of supporting higher population densities than continental areas, then I should be able to find evidence of it.

But the population of Caribbean islands at the time of European contact turned out to be another highly controversial topic among historians and demographers. Pre-Columbian population estimates for Hispaniola alone range from 60,000[3] to 8 million.[4] So the native population for small islands such

2. Allen W. Johnson and Timothy Earle, *The Evolution of Human Societies: From Foraging Group to Agrarian State.*
3. Angel Rosenblat, *La Poblacion de America en 1492: Viejos y Nuevos Calculos.*
4. Cook & Borah (1971).

TABLE 5.1. Early Populations of Caribbean Islands.

Island/group	Size (km²)	Population	Date	Density
Bermuda	52	10,000	1750	192
U.S. Virgins	373	10,000 30,000	1700 1750	27 80
Barbados	430	40,000 80,000	1700 1750	93 186
Br. Leewards	624	30,000 70,000	1700 1750	48 112
Neth. Antilles	873	10,000 30,000	1700 1750	11 34
Br. Windwards	1,316	10,000 30,000	1700 1750	8 23
Guadeloupe	1,378	20,000 50,000	1700 1750	15 36
Martinique	1,394	20,000 80,000	1700 1750	14 57
Trinidad & Tobago	4,962	20,000	1800	4

as the Bahamas are open to wide differences in interpretation. I initially thought that perhaps I could get some ideas by studying the populations of small islands prior to the industrial revolution. Table 5.1 contains some early examples from the Caribbean region I found, arranged by island size.

It was clear that small islands are capable of supporting very high population densities; and I also noted the uneven trend for the smaller islands to support higher population densities. But it was also clear that the Caribbean was undergoing a population explosion in the eighteenth century, driven by immigration from Europe and the African slave trade. And it seemed wholly inappropriate to apply population densities supported by the European urban economy to the small island subsistence economy of the pre-contact Lucayans.

Undoubtedly a better model could be found in the Pacific, where European influence was far less intense, and where the indigenous peoples had a technology, lifestyle, climate, and geography similar to that of the early Lucayans. I began by collecting early population reports from the Pacific Islands from various sources, looking for the earliest reliable estimates or counts in all cases. Unfortunately, many of these islands were ravaged by epidemics before reliable counts could be taken. On the other hand, many of the islands were discovered late enough in history that the discoverers were aware of the importance of accurate population counts or estimates.

I made an effort, as far as possible, to count individual islands instead of doing group averages. This is because group averaging can be deceiving when the group contains islands of widely differing sizes. For example, western Samoa has four inhabited islands, two very large ones (Savai'i and Upolu) and two very small ones (Apolima and Manono). Averaging creates four medium-sized islands that retain the lower population densities of the larger pair.

But population estimates for individual islands are not available in many cases (notably in Micronesia, the Tuamotus, and many atolls) so I reluctantly let these group averages stand. There were also some tough calls in determining whether an atoll island counts as one island or more than one. My rule of thumb was that if the water between two pieces of land can be easily waded, it counts as one island, otherwise it's two. I also excluded any islet smaller than 20 hectares from the atoll counts, on the grounds that it would be uninhabitable; and (in the case of Mangareva) excluded islets known to be uninhabited. For atoll groups for which I had no large-scale maps, I assumed an average of 3 islands per atoll, which was consistent with the mapped atolls.

In the Hawaiian Islands, pre-discovery population estimates range from 200,000 to 300,000[5] for the group as a whole, but there are no estimates for individual islands. By the time of the first island-by-island count in 1831-32, the population had dwindled to about 130,000. In order to get the individual island estimates given in the table, I adopted the same ratios of island populations found in 1831, and estimated the likely 1778 population by multiplying the 1831 counts by a factor of 1.9.

Finding the areas of many of the smaller islands turned out to be more difficult than finding early population estimates. In some cases (such as the smaller Marquesas), I found large-scale

5. See Robert C. Schmitt, *Demographic Statistics of Hawaii, 1778-1965.* And Eleanor C. Nordyke, *The Peopling of Hawaii.*

maps, which I measured. The island count for Micronesia was derived from an atlas[6] of the region, by counting named islands and atolls in the gazetteer. I also found two island population counts I excluded from my study: Kahoolawe in Hawaii (1778 population estimate:152, size:174 km^2) and Manuae in the Cooks (1829 population:10; size: 6.2 km^2). In these cases, the island is clearly able to support a larger population than these early estimates. Therefore, these populations could not have been at stable levels; they must have been growing or (more likely) shrinking rapidly. And in fact, both of these islands were uninhabited within a few years of their counts. Sizes and populations of the various Pacific Islands are listed on Table 5.2 (see pp. 100-101).

Note again the wide variation in population densities. But also notice something odd: even more clearly than in the Caribbean, small islands tend to be more densely populated than large islands. This can be most clearly seen in Samoa, where in 1839 tiny Manono supported a density of over 300 per square kilometer. Remarkably, this density is 14 times greater than that of its much larger neighbor Upolu—even though the two islands are enclosed by a single reef and separated by only a mile of water.

Further, this population estimate was not a mere fluke or error, since the first real count (in 1900) showed that, while the populations of both islands had declined, the smaller island still supported 15 times greater population density than the larger.[7] The same trend is apparent throughout Samoa and broadly throughout the Pacific.

What accounts for this unexpected observation? In the first place, the population of an island tends to grow rapidly until some critical resource is no longer easily available; at that time, growth slows until the population and the critical resource achieves a static balance. At this point, the island has reached its "carrying capacity." This is the logistical model of population growth, first proposed by demographer Raymond Pearl,[8] and later extended to human populations.[9] I hypothesized that if the

---

6. Bruce Karolle, *Atlas of Micronesia.*

7. Norma McArthur, *Island Peoples of the Pacific.*

8. Raymond Pearl, *The Biology of Population Growth.*

9. William F. Keegan, Allen Johnson, and Timothy Earle, "Carrying Capacity and Population Regulation: A Comment on Dewar," 659-663. Also, William F. Keegan, *The People Who Discovered Columbus: A Prehistory of the Bahamas.*

TABLE 5.2. Early populations of Pacific Islands, and relevant data.

Group	Island(s)	Size (km²)	#	Mean Size	Population	Date	Density	Mean Pop	Log Mean Pop	Log Mean Size
Tuvalu		26	27	1	2,700	1900	104	100	2.00	-0.02
Tokelau		12	10	1	1,000	1850	83	100	2.00	0.08
Micronesia		2,707	317	9	100,000	1500	37	315	2.50	0.93
Fr. Poly.	Mangareva	15	4	4	2,141	1838	143	535	2.73	0.57
Fr. Poly.	Tahiti	1,041	1	1,041	20,000	1769	19	20,000	4.30	3.02
Fr. Poly.	Mai'ao	8.9	1	9	210	1825	24	210	2.32	0.95
Fr. Poly.	Tuamotos	712	240	3	20,000	1866	28	83	1.92	0.47
Tonga	Tongatapu	256	1	256	12,000	1777	47	12,000	4.08	2.41
Tonga	Lifuka	30	1	30	5,000	1777	167	5,000	3.70	1.48
Marquesas	Nuku Hiva	329	1	329	8,000	1842	24	8,000	3.90	2.52
Marquesas	Hiva Oa	399	1	399	6,000	1842	15	6,000	3.78	2.60
Marquesas	Ua Pou	80	1	80	2,000	1842	25	2,000	3.30	1.90
Marquesas	Ua Huka	89	1	89	2,000	1842	22	2,000	3.30	1.95
Marquesas	Tahuata	49	1	49	700	1842	14	700	2.85	1.69
Marquesas	Fatuhiva	84	1	84	1,500	1842	18	1,500	3.18	1.92
Samoa	Upolu	1,118	1	1,118	25,000	1839	22	25,000	4.40	3.05
Samoa	Savai'i	1,810	1	1,810	20,000	1839	11	20,000	4.30	3.26
Samoa	Apolima	1.3	1	1	500	1839	385	500	2.70	0.11
Samoa	Manono	4	1	4	1,100	1839	306	1,100	3.04	0.56
Samoa	Tutuila	104	1	104	4,000	1839	38	4,000	3.60	2.02
Samoa	Manu'a	36	3	12	2,000	1839	56	667	2.82	1.08

Group	Island(s)	Size (km²)	#	Mean Size	Population	Date	Density	Mean Pop	Log Mean Pop	Log Mean Size
Fiji	Vanua Levu	5,535	1	5,535	29,000	1874	5	29,000	4.46	3.74
Fiji	Viti Levu	10,386	1	10,386	91,000	1874	9	91,000	4.96	4.02
Cook Is.	Rarotonga	67	1	67	3,000	1845	45	3,000	3.48	1.83
Cook Is.	Mangaia	52	1	52	3,500	1845	67	3,500	3.54	1.72
Cook Is.	Atiu	27	1	27	900	1845	33	900	2.95	1.43
Cook Is.	Mauke	18	1	18	250	1845	14	250	2.40	1.26
Cook Is.	Mitiaro	22	1	22	100	1845	5	100	2.00	1.34
Cook Is.	Aitutaki	18	1	18	2,000	1845	111	2,000	3.30	1.26
Cook Is.	Tongareva	9.8	4	2	300	1871	31	75	1.88	0.39
Cook Is.	Manihiki	5.4	2	3	407	1871	75	204	2.31	0.43
Cook Is.	Rakahanga	4.1	2	2	400	1871	98	200	2.30	0.31
Cook Is.	Pukapuka	5.5	3	2	340	1871	62	113	2.05	0.27
Hawaii	Oahu	1,549	1	1,549	56,535	1778	36	56,535	4.75	3.19
Hawaii	Kaui	1,417	1	1,417	20,856	1778	15	20,856	4.32	3.15
Hawaii	Maui	1,886	1	1,886	66,618	1778	35	66,618	4.82	3.28
Hawaii	Lanai	360	1	360	3,040	1778	8	3,040	3.48	2.56
Hawaii	Molokai	676	1	676	11,400	1778	17	11,400	4.06	2.83
Hawaii	Hawaii	10,399	1	10,399	87,005	1778	8	87,005	4.94	4.02
Hawaii	Niihau	251	1	251	1,989	1778	8	1,989	3.30	2.40
Trobriand Is.	Kiriwina	182	1	182	7,000	1900	38	7,000	3.85	2.26
	Niue	259	1	259	1,600	1900	6	1,600	3.20	2.41
	Rapa Nui	163	1	163	3,000	1770	18	3,000	3.48	2.21
	New Caledonia	16,912	1	16,912	70,000	1850	4	70,000	4.85	4.23

critical resource is land-based, then the population of an island should be proportional to its area. But if the critical resource is ocean-based, the size of an island's population should be roughly proportional to the length of its coastline rather than its area. Then, too, there was the possibility that early population counts by Western mariners were biased in a coastwise fashion: populations may have been estimated by looking only at the people visible along the coast, while skipping the difficulties of expeditions to the interior. If this were true, reported populations would also be proportional to coastline length.

To test these hypotheses, I plotted the logarithm of the islands' sizes against the logarithm of the islands' populations (Figure 5.1). In this plot, it is clear that the points lie roughly along a line. There is a standard statistical procedure that we can use (called regression) to determine the best-fit line for these points, called the regression line. The closer the actual points are to the regression line, the stronger the correlation between the two variables. (In this case, the variables are the log of the area and the log of the population.)

The length of an island's coastline varies roughly according to the square root of its area. If population density did not change as island size increased, we would expect that the data points on such a log-log plot of population and area would be linear, highly correlated, and have a slope of one. But if the population varied according to the length of the coastline, we would expect that the data points would be linear, highly correlated, and have a slope of 0.5 (since the logarithm of 0.5 corresponds to the square root of the area). When I actually plotted the data, I found that the data points were linear, highly correlated, and had a slope of 0.726. This showed clearly that the increase in population density with decreasing island area was a real phenomenon, but it did not support the idea that island populations vary according to coastline length.

It is not immediately obvious why island populations should vary in such a manner. Nor is it clear why this relationship should hold for such a broad range of island sizes, from 1 to over 10,000 km^2. It is logical to suppose that there is an interplay among fishing, cultivation, and the capacity of the island's aquifer; and that this interplay, along with socio-economic

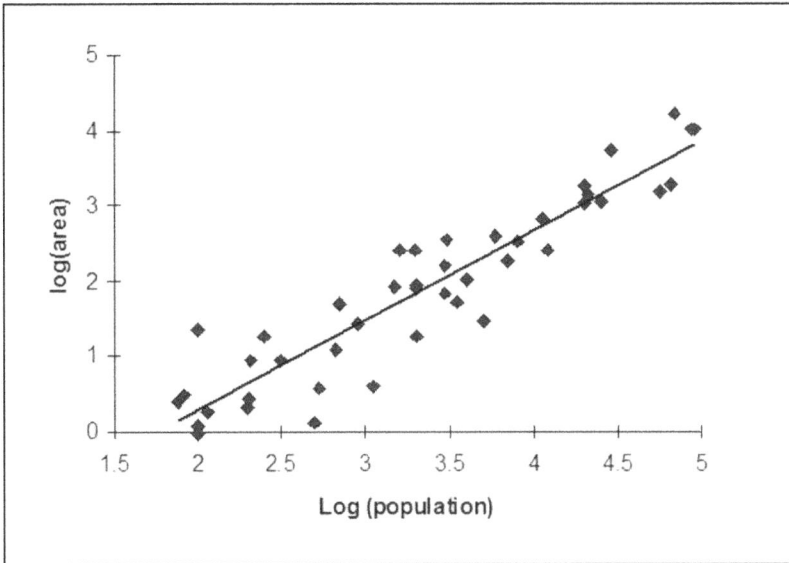

FIGURE 5.1. Scatter plot of the Pacific Islands' size and population, with the regression line.

factors, determines an island's carrying capacity. This in turn implies that the underlying population-vs.-area function may be polynomial rather than logarithmic. For example, if the interior portion of a Pacific island supported nine persons per km² (from cultivation and forage) and if the coastal region supported 26 persons per linear km. of coastline (from fishing), the resulting population vs. area function would be close to the regression line seen in Figure 5.1, provided the function is applied over the same range of island sizes.

One quite useful result that can be gained from the Pacific data is a formula for determining the likely pre-contact or early post-contact population ranges for any inhabited Pacific Island (or the carrying capacity of an uninhabited island) provided we know its size. From the regression line in Figure 5.1 we can find the relation:

$$P = k \, a^{0.726} \qquad\qquad (1)$$

When the island area a is measured in square kilometers, we can use equation (1) to find the mean expected population

P and one-sigma (i.e., one standard deviation) limits, by taking the following values for k: for the mean population, $k = 96$; for the upper limit, $k = 202$; and for the lower limit, $k = 45$. We can use a similar formula for determining the population density range for an island:

$$D = k \, a^{-0.274} \qquad (2)$$

Expected population density D per square kilometer and one-sigma limits can be found from equation (2), using the same values for k as in equation 1.

Naturally, we want to know: does this relationship between island size and population hold for the pre-discovery Caribbean islands? Given the wide uncertainty in population estimates for the area, it is difficult to say for sure. But there are some tantalizing clues.

The Pigeon Creek region on the southeast coast of Watlings Island has been the subject of a number of archeological investigations in this century.[10] Michael Craton and Gail Saunders[11] reported that the main settlement and its nearby satellite sites could plausibly hold a population in the range of 500 to 1,000. But what fraction of the island's population does this represent? It is reasonable to assume that the forage and cultivation range for these sites covered roughly the southeastern quarter of the island: south of Granny Lake and east of Great Lake. This region is defined by three natural choke points, which would make convenient boundaries with other population centers on the island. The land area within these choke points is about 23 square km. Since the total land area of Watlings is 101 square km (excluding the large inland lakes), this implies a total island population of about 4.4 times the Pigeon Creek population, or 2,200 to 4,400. On the other hand, Craton and Saunders speculated that the Pigeon Creek population could represent as much as half of the island's total population,[12] which implies a total of 1,000 to 2,000.

---

10. Richard Rose, "Pigeon Creek," 35:129-145; and Richard Rose, "Lucayan Lifeways."
11. Michael Craton and Gail Saunders, *Islanders in the Stream: A History of the Bahamian People.*
12. Craton & Saunders (1992).

If we take an intermediate value for the population of Pigeon Creek (750) and an intermediate value for the multiplier (3), this would give us a total population for Watlings Island of 2,250, within a range of 1,000 to 4,400. The density range would be 10 to 44 per square km, with 22 as an intermediate figure.[13] The Pacific model predicts that an island the size of Watlings should have a population of 2,700, with a range of 1,300 to 5,700. In general this suggests that the Pacific model is an acceptable population predictor for a Bahamian island the size of Watlings, and specifically that it is more useful than the four per square km minimum of Johnson and Earle.

As mentioned above, the population of Hispaniola has been the subject of wide debate. One of the best recent estimates has been made by Samuel Wilson,[14] who extrapolated from the Spanish censuses of 1508 and 1514 to estimate a total pre-contact population of 381,000 for the island. Bill Keegan, an occasional Round-Robin contributor, had suggested[15] a population of 302,000 by applying the four per square km minimum density of Johnson and Earle to the island. The Pacific model predicts that an island the size of Hispaniola would have a population of 330,000 within a range of 160,000 to 700,000. Extrapolating the Pacific model to islands so far outside its verifiable limits of island size should be viewed with some caution, yet this does again suggest that the model is an acceptable predictor in the Caribbean, even outside those limits. It also suggests a useful maximum size for which the model is valid: when the predicted density falls below four, the island has reached essentially continental size for a subsistence economy under the regional polity economic structure of Johnson and Earle. This occurs when the island is about 100,000 square km, or roughly the size of Cuba.

There are several important consequences of this model when applied to the Caribbean. First, archeological surveys in

---

13. These densities are far higher than the four per km² accepted by Keegan (1992) and Kelley (1992) as a model; but they were adopting the minimum value of Johnson and Earle (1987), which Keegan (1992) was careful to note as a falsifiable assumption.

14. Samuel M. Wilson, "Taino and Carib Strategies for Survival." Paper presented at the conference "Non-Imperial Polities in the Lands Visited by Christopher Columbus During His Four Voyages to the New World."

15. Keegan (1992) 163.

the Caribbean have usually been confined to the coastal areas. The model suggests that inland surveys may be appropriate on the larger islands of the Greater Antilles, and perhaps even Andros in the Bahamas.

More importantly, the model gives us a handle on one of the more vexing questions in historical demography: the pre-contact population of the Caribbean. Since the model seems to work well with Caribbean islands both large and small, we can have some confidence in applying the model to the Caribbean as a whole. Table 5.3 lists the Caribbean islands, along with model predictions of their likely populations. Although the model's limits are broad for any given island, the model may focus the range of debate more narrowly than in the past.

The model assumes that at the time of European contact, each island had reached its carrying capacity under a subsistence economy. Since the Bahamas were settled late, and in a south-to-north fashion, Bill Keegan has suggested on the basis of archeological evidence that islands in the northern Bahamas would not have reached this level at the time of contact.[16] Therefore, the population of the northern Bahamas could well have been lower than model predictions. To reflect this, I have arbitrarily reduced the populations for islands north and west of Cat Island by half, and of Abaco and Grand Bahama by two-thirds. This reduces the likely pre-contact Bahamian population total to around 140,000, which (considering the effects of disease) is consistent with the report by Peter Martyr that the Spanish depopulated the islands by taking 40,000 slaves from there in the period 1509-1513.

The final consequence of this model is that we can get some idea of the likely populations of first landfall candidates by knowing their size and, in turn, the likely size of Columbus's landfall island by knowing its population.

During the time that I was doing this research, Alex Pérez had been taking another tack entirely on the population question. Working from Columbus's report (unnoticed by many) that the entire population of Guanahani could be subjugated by 50 men, Pérez argued to the Round Robin that this description

---

16. Keegan (1992).

TABLE 5.3. Model predictions of pre-contact Caribbean Island Populations.

Island	Total Area	#	Mean Area	Population Range Mean	Low	High
Grand Bahama	1,373	1	1,373	6,020	2,855	12,694
Abaco	1,681	1	1,681	6,972	3,307	14,701
Berry Is.	31	19	2	1,295	614	2,731
Eleuthera	518	1	518	4,452	2,112	9,387
New Providence	207	1	207	2,288	1,085	4,825
Andros	5,957	2	2,979	31,677	15,024	66,791
Little San Salvador	13	1	13	307	146	648
Exuma Cays	104	35	3	3,685	1,748	7,771
Cat	389	1	389	7,234	3,431	15,252
Watlings	101	1	101	2,719	1,290	5,734
Conception	4	1	4	261	124	551
Rum Cay	78	1	78	2,255	1,069	4,754
Exuma	186	1	186	4,235	2,009	8,930
Long	448	1	448	8,014	3,801	16,898
Samana Cay	39	1	39	1,363	647	2,875
Crooked	238	1	238	5,065	2,402	10,679
Fortune	23	1	23	930	441	1,960
Acklins	389	1	389	7,234	3,431	15,252
Plana Cays	16	2	8	864	410	1,822
Ragged Is.	23	13	2	1,879	891	3,963
Mayaguana	285	1	285	5,772	2,738	12,171
Great Inagua	1,203	1	1,203	16,409	7,782	34,599
Little Inagua	127	1	127	3,211	1,523	6,771
West Caicos	40	1	40	1,389	659	2,928
Providenciales	75	1	75	2,191	1,039	4,620
N-M-E Caicos	355	1	355	6,769	3,210	14,273
South Caicos	70	1	70	2,084	989	4,395
Grand Turk	15	1	15	682	323	1,437
Total Bahamas	13,988	94	149	137,259	65,098	289,410
Cuba	111,468	1	111,468	438,656	208,027	924,842
Isle of Pines	3,056	1	3,056	32,273	15,306	68,048
Grand Cayman	197	1	197	4,415	2,094	9,310
Little Cayman	52	1	52	1,680	797	3,542
Cayman Brac	57	1	57	1,796	852	3,786
Jamaica	11,424	1	11,424	84,008	39,842	177,130
Hispaniola	75,876	1	75,876	331,818	157,372	699,638
Tortuga	180	1	180	4,136	1,961	8,720
Vache	40	1	40	1,389	659	2,928
Beata	40	1	40	1,389	659	2,928
Saona	65	1	65	1,975	937	4,165
Mona	56	1	56	1,773	841	3,738
Puerto Rico	8,768	1	8,768	69,334	32,883	146,190
Vieques	138	1	138	3,411	1,618	7,191
Culebra	27	1	27	1,044	495	2,202
Total Greater Antilles	211,444	15	14,096	979,064	464,342	2,064,357

TABLE 5.3. Model predictions of pre-contact Caribbean Island Populations. (cont.)

Island	Total Area	#	Mean Area	Population Range		
				Mean	Low	High
St. Thomas	83	1	83	2,358	1,119	4,973
St. John	53	1	53	1,703	808	3,591
St. Croix	218	1	218	4,752	2,254	10,020
Tortola	64	1	64	1,953	926	4,118
Virgin Gorda	20	1	20	840	398	1,771
Jost Van Dyke	7	1	7	392	186	827
Anegada	34	2	17	1,493	708	3,148
Sombrero	2	1	2	158	75	333
Anguilla	91	1	91	2,521	1,196	5,316
St. Martin	89	1	89	2,481	1,177	5,231
St. Barthelemy	21	1	21	870	413	1,835
Saba	13	1	13	614	291	1,296
St. Eustatius	21	1	21	870	413	1,835
St. Christopher	176	1	176	4,069	1,930	8,579
Nevis	130	1	130	3,266	1,549	6,886
Barbuda	163	1	163	3,848	1,825	8,114
Antigua	280	1	280	5,698	2,703	12,015
Montserrat	104	1	104	2,778	1,317	5,857
Total Leeward Is.	**1,569**	**19**	**83**	**40,666**	**19,287**	**85,745**
Guadeloupe	1,510	1	1,510	19,351	9,178	40,802
Marie Galante	153	1	153	3676	1,743	7,750
Dominica	790	1	790	12,094	5,736	25,501
Martinique	1,116	1	1,116	15,539	7,370	32,765
St. Lucia	616	1	616	10,097	4,789	21,290
St. Vincent	362	1	362	6,866	3,256	14,477
Grenadines	44	19	2	3,339	1,584	7,041
Carriacou	13	1	13	614	291	1,296
Grenada	344	1	344	6,616	3,138	13,951
Barbados	431	1	431	7,792	3,696	16,430
Tobago	300	1	300	5,991	2,841	12,632
Trinidad	4,828	1	4,828	44,972	21,329	94,823
Bonaire	288	1	288	5,816	2,758	12,263
Curacao	448	1	448	8,014	3,801	16,898
Aruba	184	1	184	4,202	1,993	8,860
Total Windward Is.	**11,427**	**33**	**346**	**154,981**	**73,503**	**326,776**
Total Caribbean	**238,428**	**161**	**1,481**	**1,311,970**	**622,229**	**2,766,289**

suggested a population for San Salvador in the hundreds, but not in the thousands. Pérez reasonably suggested a maximum population range of 500 to 1,000 on that basis. This estimate fit quite well with Jim Kelley's minimum of 634 to 935. So the *Diario*

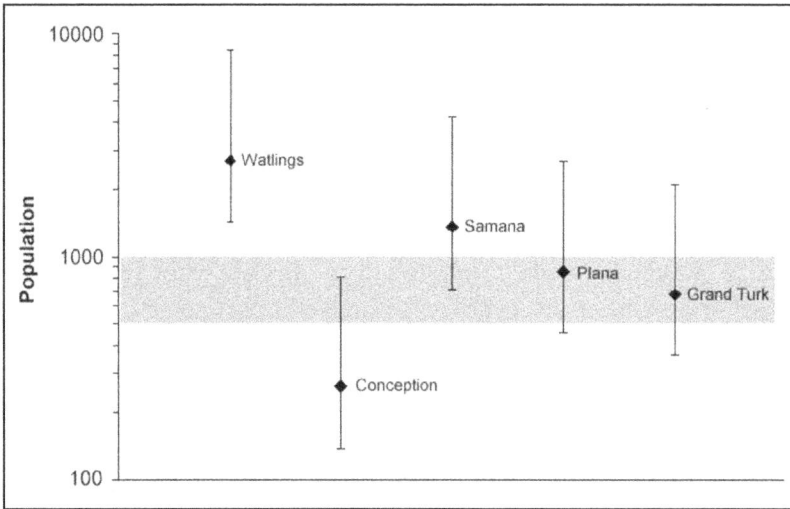

FIGURE 5.2. Population ranges of landfall candidates, as predicted by the Pacific model. Gray area is the expected population range from historical data.

contains two separate statements of Columbus from which the population of San Salvador can be inferred, and unsurprisingly, these statements confirm each other.

When I presented my analysis to the Round Robin in March 1995, I plotted the model predictions for the populations of some landfall candidates, as shown in Figure 5.2. The gray area in the figure represents the range between the Kelley minimum population and the Pérez maximum population for the landfall island.

If we assume that the population of the islands had reached carrying capacity at the time of discovery, which likely was true in our area of interest, the model predicts that, to fall within the expected San Salvador population range of 634 to 1,000, the size of single-island San Salvador would most likely be in the range of 13 to 25 square km, with one-sigma limits of 5 to 71 square km. These ranges are a little lower for a multiple-island San Salvador. Counting only dry-land areas, Conception is 3.7, Grand Turk is 15, the Plana Cays are 16, Samana Cay is 39, and Watlings is 101.

Considering the uncertainties inherent in a model of this kind, it would be overstating the case to claim that any islands, even those as small as Conception or as large as Watlings, should be eliminated from consideration on the basis of population alone. However, we can say that on the basis of population alone that the Plana Cays and Grand Turk have the strongest case for being Columbus's first landfall.

In the time since I presented this analysis to the Round Robin, Bill Keegan has done extensive archaeological field work on Grand Turk and the surrounding islets, and has found evidence of pre-Columbian habitation on some rather small islets in that vicinity. Keegan's work confirms that tiny islands can be quite densely populated, and lends further support to my population analysis (and indirectly to the Plana Cays landfall theory).

The population research was the first solid piece of scientific analysis that I had presented to the Round Robin on the Plana Cays theory, and as such marked a kind of coming of age for me in that group. But I soon found that there was a lot more interesting analysis that could be done with that wonderful, number-filled primary document, the *Diario* of Columbus's first voyage. And it would soon prove to be strong enough to drive a stake through the heart of the Columbus Round Robin.

6.

The Sign of the Four

SOMETIMES, if you're very lucky, an inspiration will strike you like a brick on the head. It happened to me in the spring of 1995, while I was reading a book on ancient Greek astronomy. The book was *The Crime of Claudius Ptolemy* by Robert R. Newton, and it, too, dealt with a historical controversy. Newton had analyzed the astronomical works of the second century Greek astronomer Ptolemy and had determined that most of his astronomical "observations" were faked—derived from theory, rather than actually observed outdoors.

Although Newton's book had stirred up a hornet's nest of criticism when it appeared in 1977, it was clear to me that his mathematical analysis was fundamentally sound. I had been reading Newton's analysis of Ptolemy's star catalog when the brick fell from the sky.

The star catalog in Ptolemy's great astronomical treatise[1] *Almagest* has long been suspected by astronomers of being simply a copy of an earlier (but now lost) catalog compiled by Ptolemy's predecessor, Hipparchos of Nicaea, more than a century before Christ. According to this hypothesis, Ptolemy copied Hipparchos's star coordinates with a simple addition of 2 2/3 degrees to the stars' longitudes, to account for their changed positions in the 265 years since Hipparchos's original observations.

Newton's brilliant idea was to note how the fractional endings of the longitudes would have been skewed out of kilter by

---

1. G. J. Toomer ed., *Ptolemy's Almagest.*

this process. Normally, when people measure things, there is a natural tendency to round numbers toward integers—to use whole numbers rather than fractions. But in the longitudes of the ancient star catalog, the integers are outnumbered by longitudes with 2/3 degree endings; and there are many other odd fractional distributions as well, which cannot be explained by any mechanism other than Ptolemy (or someone) fiddling with observations after the fact. In later years, Newton's thesis and methods had been extended by my friend Dennis Rawlins.

It struck me that a similar line of thinking might allow a historian to determine whether any set of numerical observations had been manipulated at some later time. And of course the log of Columbus is full of such numbers: nearly every daily entry contains some measurement of the ships' progress, usually given in leagues, occasionally in miles. And some theorists have long suspected that most or all of the league measurements had been converted from miles sometime after Columbus's original writing. As we saw in chapter 2, the Watlings Island theory heavily depends on the idea that Columbus's original measurements were in miles, and that the league measurements in the *Diario* were unit conversions. This miles-to-leagues conversion hypothesis is needed by the Watlings theory to account for the many distance discrepancies between the theory and reality. Allegedly, they are mistakes that Las Casas made in copying the *Diario*.

So I began my own analysis of the *Diario*'s distances, and following Newton's lead it soon became clear to me that unit conversions had indeed occurred; but more importantly, I could also prove the direction in which this conversion was done. I summarized my findings in a letter to the Columbus Round Robin in 1995, and followed it up with a lecture to the annual meeting of the Society for the History of Discoveries that November.

When Columbus returned triumphantly to Spain in 1493 following his first voyage, he immediately wrote to the Spanish Sovereigns of his success. At their command, he reported to the royal court, which was then meeting at Barcelona, and he gave his original log to the Sovereigns. Queen Isabella ordered the log to be copied, resulting in the so-called Barcelona Copy.

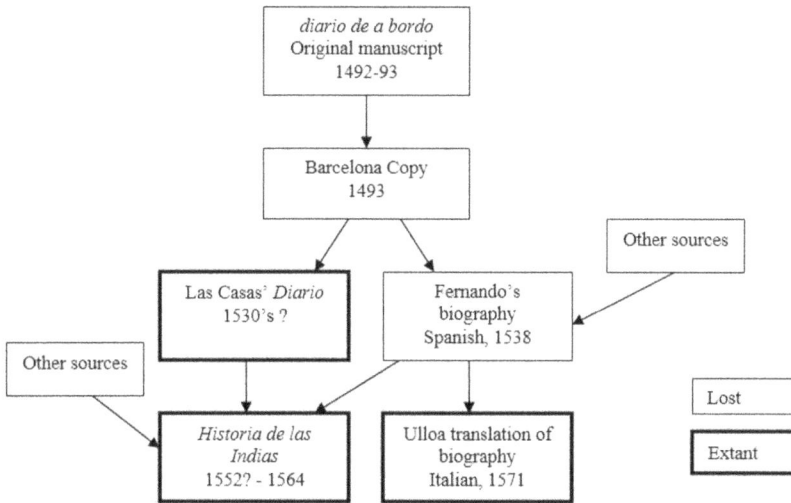

FIGURE 6.1. The log and its derivatives.

(We have a letter from the queen to Columbus in which she says that she has added a second scribe to the job, so that the copy will be done before Columbus's second voyage is due to set sail.) The queen kept Columbus's original, and as far as anyone knows it has not been seen since. But the Barcelona Copy was returned to Columbus in the autumn of 1493, and it remained in his possession until his death in 1506. It then passed into the hands of his heirs, but the copy, too, was lost sometime after 1554. It may have been sold by Columbus's ne'er-do-well grandson, Luis Colón, to pay his gambling debts.

Luckily for us, before being lost, large parts of the Barcelona Copy were abstracted by Las Casas into the *Diario,* in a manuscript that still exists in the National Library in Madrid. This document is popularly referred to as the "log" of Columbus. Las Casas's abstraction may have been part of the research program that eventually led to his massive tome, the *Historia de las Indias* (see Figure 6.1).

The *Diario* contains about 350 distance measurements in total. About two thirds of them are given in leagues exclusively, while the rest are about evenly divided into those distances given in miles exclusively and those given in both units. Significantly, there are about a dozen places where Las Casas had written

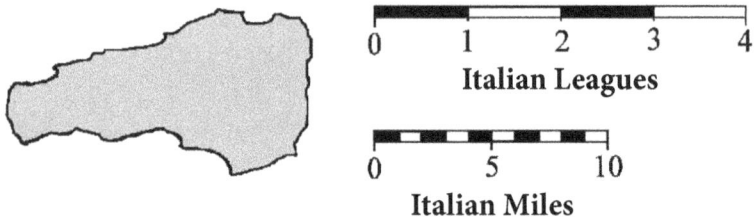

FIGURE 6.2. The size of Rum Cay.

the word "leagues," then crossed out leagues and substituted "miles." This implies that in at least some cases, Las Casas was not copying these distances directly from his source, but rather must have been converting from one unit to the other as he wrote. The distances given in both units show that this conversion was done at a ratio of four miles to one league.

In chapter 2, we saw that there are three or four places where the Watlings theory must rely on the hypothesis that Columbus actually wrote distances in miles, and that a mistaken conversion from miles to leagues exaggerated an actual distance by a factor of four. For example, the *Diario* tells us that Island II had a coastline running north-south for five leagues, and another running east-west for more than 10 leagues. The Watlings theory uses Rum Cay as Island II, and Rum Cay is only about five miles north-south and 10 or more miles east-west (see Figure 6.2). In addition to the Island II problem, Columbus gives the distance on Island III from the harbor to the end of the island as two leagues, while the Watlings theory requires this to be two miles—so once again, the Watlings theory must invoke the miles-to-leagues conversion hypothesis.

The hypothesis runs like this: if Columbus wrote in leagues, then the league dimensions given in the *Diario* are presumably original with him and therefore correct. But if Columbus wrote in miles in the first place, then it's possible that he could have written "five miles" and "ten miles" in the original, and that Las Casas, while habitually converting from miles into leagues, wrote "leagues" by mistake without changing the numbers. This supposition has allowed Rum Cay to be used as Island II by various historians for more than a century, in support of both the Watlings and Conception Island theories.

First person sections   **Third person sections**

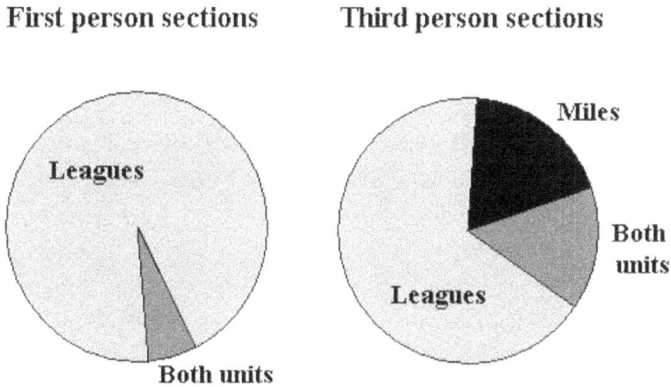

FIGURE 6.3. Difference in types of units when quoted directly, or when abstracted by Las Casas.

One line of evidence against this hypothesis is that the *Diario* speaks in two voices: in most of the text, Las Casas writes in third person, referring to Columbus as "the Admiral." So it is clear that Las Casas is paraphrasing, not quoting, as he is reading the Barcelona Copy. But in about 20 percent of the *Diario*, Las Casas does quote Columbus directly (or at least he claims to do so), switching to Columbus's first-person narrative. That portion of the log that describes Columbus's trip through the Bahamas is entirely in first person, and Las Casas claims that the Bahamian portion is a direct quote from Columbus. But none of those canceled "leagues" cases occur in the first-person (direct-quote) portions. This implies that the unit conversions were occurring only in the abstracted third-person portions.

In the first-person portions, there are fifteen distances given in leagues only, one distance given in both units, and none given in miles only. So if the first-person portions are indeed direct quotes, Columbus's original writing must have been predominantly in leagues.

Furthermore, if you refer back to Figure 6.1, you will see that there were actually two people who both saw the Barcelona Copy and reported on its contents. The first was of course Las Casas; the second was the admiral's son Fernando Colón, who wrote a biography[2] of his father in about 1538. Although Fernando's Spanish manuscript has not survived, it was rendered into Italian by Alfonso Ulloa, a Spaniard making his living as a professional translator. The Ulloa translation was published in Venice in 1571.

We know that Fernando also used the Barcelona Copy (and not the *Diario*) as his original source, because the biography contains a number of details of the first voyage that could only have come from Columbus himself, and which are absent from the *Diario*. For example, on September 15 the *Diario* reports that a bright meteor was seen by the men of the fleet. Fernando's biography adds the detail that the meteor was seen in the southwest. In general, though, the *Diario* contains much greater detail than the biography, which is why it is rightly considered a more important historical source.

Like the *Diario*, Fernando's biography also reports that the coastlines of the second island were five leagues north-south and 10 or more leagues east-west. Since it is beyond belief that both men could have made exactly the same errors in exactly the same places, it is certain that the Barcelona Copy itself must have contained these dimensions as given in leagues, and that they were copied correctly in both cases.

Interestingly, in Fernando's biography there are over 50 distance measurements in the first voyage chapters (including some given in direct quotes from the Barcelona Copy) and they are all in leagues. And since the biography, unlike the *Diario*, contains no evidence of unit conversions, this also indicates that the Barcelona Copy itself was written in leagues.

Of course, even if the Barcelona Copy was written in leagues as the evidence indicates, there remains the possibility that Columbus himself wrote in miles, and a conversion into leagues was done by the court copyists at Barcelona. Even at first glance, this speculation seems feeble: these copyists were the human Xerox machines of their day. Most would have been clerics who would have sworn an oath to copy what was given them exactly. Further, the Barcelona Copy contained navigational data vital to

---

2. Fernando Colón, *The Life of the Admiral Christopher Columbus by His Son Ferdinand*, Benjamin Keen, trans. and ed. Keen anglicized Fernando's name as "Ferdinand," which few would do these days.

the safety of the second voyage. Tampering with that data would have been not merely dishonest, it would have been dangerous.

And there are two other ways we can attack the problem of original units. First, when we examine other writings of Columbus (outside of the first voyage log and its derivatives) we find that he had a distinct personal preference for using leagues rather than miles, by a huge margin.

Table 6.1 shows every document that Columbus wrote in his lifetime and that contains distance measurements. In the table, I simply counted the times that Columbus uses one unit or the other. Of the five times "miles" are used in the 1498 letter, two merely tell how long a league is (e.g. "sixty-eight leagues of four miles each"). Additionally, one reference in the 1498 letter and one in the 1503 letter are descriptions of the length of a degree as 56 2/3 miles—which are quotes lifted from the Arabic astronomer Alfragan. So the actual ratio is at least 10 to 1 in favor of leagues, and may be as high as 18 to 1.

TABLE 6.1. Mile and league measurements by Columbus, excluding the _Diario_.[3]

Source[3]	Leagues	Miles
Letter to Santangel of 1493-2-15	8	0
Letter to Sovereigns of January 1495	1	0
Memorandum of July 1497	19	0
Testament of 1498-2-22	4	0
Journal of the Third Voyage, 1498	33	1
Letter to the Sovereigns of 1498-10-18	13	5
Letter to De la Torres of 1500	1	0
Letter to Pope Alexander VII, 1502	2	1
Letter to the Sovereigns of 1503-7-7	9	2
Will of 1506-5-19	1	0
Totals	**91**	**9**

3. Sources for Table 6.1: for the Santangel letter, see: Samuel Eliot Morison, _Journals and other documents on the life and voyages of Christopher Columbus._ 182-186. For the letter of 1495 January see Cristóbal Colón, _Textos y documentos completos._ Consuela Varela, ed., 166-167. For the memorandum of July 1497, see Colón (1982) 170-176. For the testament of 1498-2-22, see Colón (1982) 190-199. For the journal of the Third Voyage, see Morison (1963) 259-283. For the letter of 1498-10-18, see Morison (1963) 285-288. For the letter of 1500, see Morison (1963) 290-297. For the Letter to Pope Alexander VII, see Colón (1982) 310-313. For the letter of July 7, 1503, see Cecil Jane, _The Four Voyages of Columbus_, 72-111. For the will of 1506 see Colón (1982) 359-363.

As it turns out, the first-person sections of the *Diario* have a quite similar 13 to 1 ratio of leagues to miles. We saw that the first-voyage sections of Fernando's biography, drawn from the Barcelona Copy, favors leagues by about 50 to 0. Only in the third-person (abstracted) portions of the *Diario* is this pattern broken, where Las Casas records a ratio of just two league measurements for each use of miles.

Second, there is a way we can firmly settle the question of the direction in which the unit conversions occurred: by following Newton's example and examining the distribution of numbers in the measurements themselves. Those distances given in both leagues and miles would seem to present a chicken-and-egg problem, but the miles-only and leagues-only measurements are pure gold: we can assume that only one of these two number groups is a set of original measurements and estimates, while the other is a set of calculation results. And numerical analysis can tell us which is which.

As noted above, when people measure things, there is a natural preference to use integers rather than fractions. But when fractions are used, there is a tendency to prefer the fraction 1/2 (and fractional numbers ending in 1/2) over all other fractions. So if the league numbers are original measurements, they should look something like the numbers in this list:

5, 8, 10, 11, 13, 15½, 16, 18, 19 (original measurements)

Most are integers, and of those that are fractions, most end in 1/2.

But suppose that the league numbers had been converted from miles by dividing the mile numbers by four. In that case, the original mile numbers would look like the numbers in the list above, and the converted league numbers—the miles divided by four—would look like this list instead:

1¼, 2, 2½, 2¾, 3¼, 3⅞, 4, 4½, 4¾ (original measurements ÷ 4)

No more than a quarter of the converted league numbers should be integers, because no more than a quarter of the original mile numbers would have been evenly divisible by four to

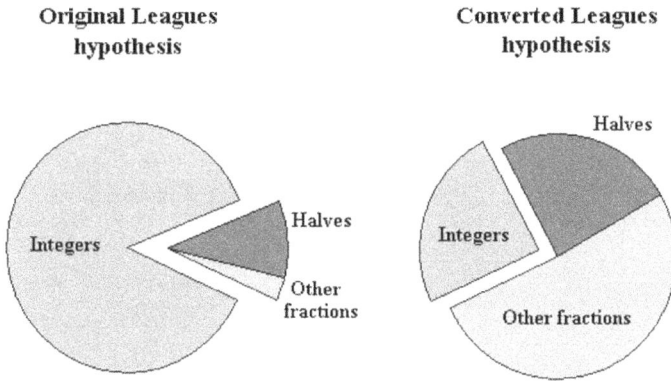

FIGURE 6.4. Predictions of the two hypotheses for the distribution of league numbers.

begin with. By the same reasoning, of those converted league numbers that are fractions, only a third (or less) should be fractions ending in 1/2, another third should be fractions ending in 1/4, and most of the rest should be fractions ending in 3/4.

In other words, these two hypotheses about the league measurements give vastly different predictions about the distribution of numbers in the measurements themselves. The original-measurement hypothesis predicts mostly integers, while the converted-from-miles hypothesis predicts mostly fractional endings. Further, among just the fractional numbers, the original-measurement hypothesis predicts mostly halves, while the converted-from-miles hypothesis predicts mostly fractions other than one-half.

When we examine the actual distribution of league numbers in the *Diario*, we find that 200 out of 236 are integers, and of the remainder, 28 out of 36 are fractions ending in 1/2. This is exactly what we would expect from a set of original measurements, but it does not meet our expectations of league numbers derived from miles.

We can apply a similar analysis to the miles-only numbers. Original mile number measurements should look like the numbers in the following list:

13, 16, 18, 19, 21, 23½, 24, 26, 27 (original measurements)

Actual Distribution

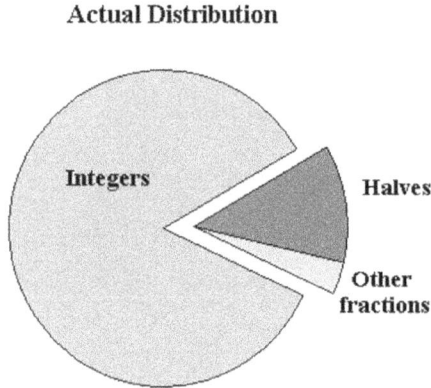

FIGURE 6.5. The actual distribution of league numbers in the *Diario*.

Most are integers, but they should also be evenly distrib-
uted. That means about a quarter should be multiples of four;
and the rest should be about evenly divided between numbers
one greater, two greater, and three greater than a multiple of
four. Multiples of four are always even numbers, and those
numbers two greater than a multiple of four are also even; while
numbers one greater and three greater than a multiple of four
are odd numbers. That means that of those numbers that are
not multiples of four, about two-thirds should be odd numbers
and about one-third should be even.

But suppose the mile numbers were derived from original
measurements in leagues, by multiplying the league numbers
by four. In that case, the original league numbers should look
like the list above, and the converted mile numbers should look
like the converted list below:

52, 64, 72, 76, 84, 94, 96, 104, 108 (original measurements × 4)

This is simply the previous list, with every number multiplied
by four. So if the miles are conversions, most of the converted
mile numbers are multiples of four, and of those not multiples
of four, most are even—because when you take a fraction ending in one-half and multiply by four, you get an even number.

Once again, the two hypotheses about the mile measurements give vastly different predictions about the distribution

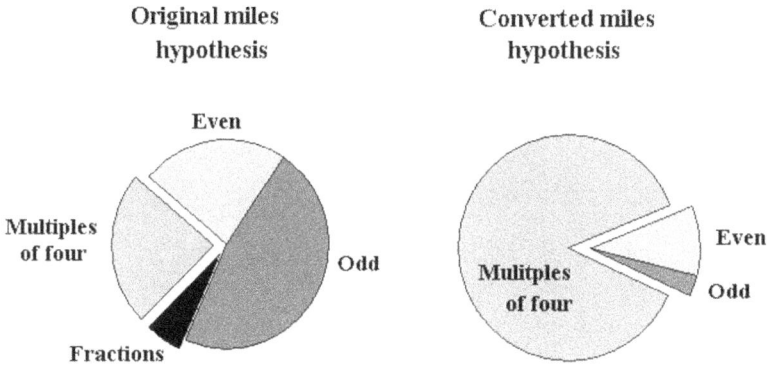

FIGURE 6.6. Predictions of the two hypotheses for the distribution of mile numbers.

of numbers in the measurements themselves. The original-measurement hypothesis predicts about 25 percent multiples of four, while the converted-from-leagues hypothesis predicts a large majority of multiples of four. Further, of those numbers that are not multiples of four, the original-measurement hypothesis predicts mostly odd numbers, while the converted-from-leagues hypothesis predicts mostly even numbers.

When we examine the actual distribution of mile numbers in the *Diario*, we find that *49 out of 62 are multiples of 4*, and of the remainder, *7 out of 13 are even.* This is exactly what we would expect if the mile numbers had been converted from original measurements in leagues. In fact, it cannot be explained in any other way. The reason the mile numbers are multiples of four is that they were multiplied by four; which means they were originally leagues. The probability that this distribution could occur by chance is less than one in a hundred quintillion.

But there is an important objection to this whole idea, one that Doug Peck had already raised in the Round Robin. Nearly everyone accepts the proposition that Columbus measured his speed in miles per hour. In fact, all of the speed measurements given in the *Diario* are in miles per hour. And in dead-reckoning navigation, you must find your distance run during the day by a time and speed calculation, based on your speed during the day. So wouldn't that require that Columbus find his distance in miles first, because the speeds were in miles per hour?

Actual Distribution

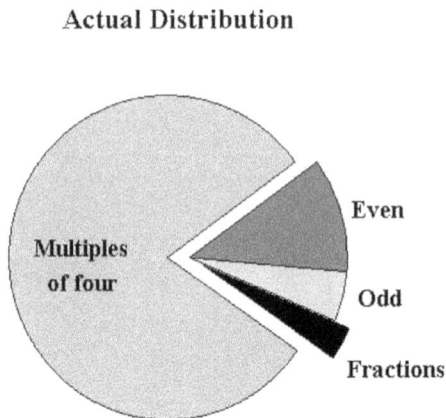

FIGURE 6.7. The actual distribution of mile numbers in the *Diario*.

The answer, surprisingly, is no. In thinking about this problem, I realized that there is a mathematical shortcut that Columbus could have used, which actually makes it faster and easier to reckon your distance in leagues when you start with speeds recorded in miles per hour. It's based on the fact that sailors do their work in watches of four hours and the convenient coincidence that there are also four miles per league. Let's see how this works.

Suppose on a given night the ship goes six miles per hour for three hours, then five miles per hour for five hours, then four miles per hour for four hours. What is the total distance run during the night?

To reckon in miles, you have a lot of math to do. First, you multiply six miles per hour times three hours, which is 18 miles, and you remember that number. Then you multiply five miles per hour times five hours, which is 25 miles, and remember that number. Then you multiply four times four, which is 16 miles, and remember that number. Then you add the remembered numbers: 18 plus 25 is 43 miles, and 43 plus 16 is 59 miles, which is the answer. But that's a long way around the barn to get there.

Reckoning in leagues is much easier. First, Columbus mentally divides the night into three watches of four hours each; it's

Leagues   Miles

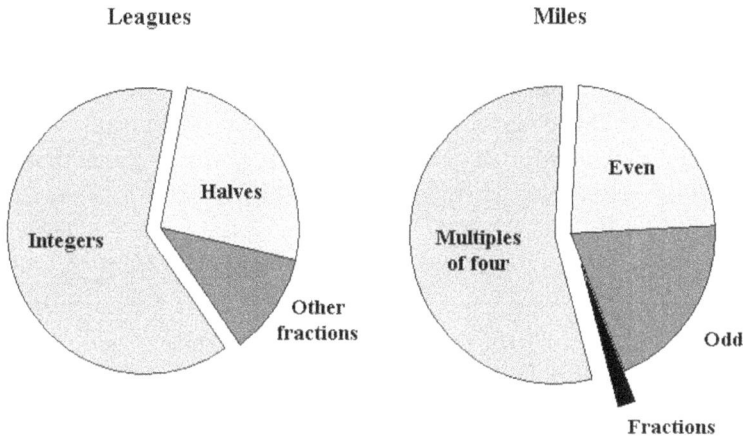

FIGURE 6.8. *Diario* measurements given in both units.

natural for Columbus to think in these terms. For each watch, Columbus makes a rough and ready estimate of the average speed during the watch. So for the first four-hour watch, Columbus estimates an average speed of six miles per hour. (It's really a fraction less, but Columbus ignores the fraction.) In the second watch, the speed is five miles per hour, and in the last watch the speed is four miles per hour. Then Columbus adds the speeds: six plus five plus four, to get fifteen. And that's the answer: fifteen leagues. Because of the happy coincidence that there are four hours per watch, just as there are four miles per league, miles-per-hour and leagues-per-watch will always be the same number.

Reckoning in leagues is easier than reckoning in miles, since there is no multiplication. The addition is easier, too, since the numbers are smaller when reckoning in leagues. And the results are predominantly integer number leagues, just as we expect, because rounding to integers is a natural part of the process.

There is one final point to consider. Recall that I previously excluded from my analysis those measurements that were given in both leagues and miles. When we look now at these measurements, we discover a curious fact (see Figure 6.8). First, we find the usual excess of multiples of four miles associated with the conversion from leagues into miles (although the excess is not as great as we saw in the miles-only measurements). But more interestingly, we also find an excess of fractional league numbers, especially non-half fractions, which we had previously said would show a conversion from miles into leagues.

Further, this excess of non-half-fractional league numbers is strongly clustered in the month of February 1493 on the return voyage. To be precise, there is a period in the log, from roughly January 29 through February 25, in which it appears that many of the league numbers were converted from miles—in the reverse direction of the usual conversion process. Further, this reverse conversion is done only on those distances that describe the length of the ship's daily or nightly run. Distances that are not associated with the ship's run appear to be original, in that they are given only in leagues and are never fractions.

There are at least two possible explanations for this. First, it may be that Columbus stopped measuring in leagues during this period, and began measuring in miles. But this fails to explain why those distances that do not describe the ship's run do not follow the pattern.

Second, it may be that during this period Columbus omitted many of his summaries of the ship's daily and nightly runs from his original log. If Columbus omitted these totals, it may have been possible for Las Casas to reconstruct the daily totals from hourly (or perhaps four-hourly) speed and time records in the original log. But Las Casas probably would not have known about the mariner's league computation shortcut. So his reconstruction, from miles per hour speeds, would have been computed in miles first, and then converted into leagues.

This would account for the mile-to-league conversions on the return voyage, and also explains why the non-ships-run distances look like original league numbers.

The reason that this anomalous period on the return voyage is important is that it shows clearly that all unit conversions are detectable phenomena, regardless of the direction of the conversion. The dirty fingerprints of unit conversion are obvious, when you know where to look. We can tell where unit conversions occur in the *Diario*, we can tell where they do not occur, and we can tell in which direction they go. And all evidence of unit conversions, in either direction, occurs entirely in the abstracted third-person sections of the log.

So we know from sources other than the log that Columbus had a personal preference for using leagues rather than miles by a huge margin. We know that both witnesses who saw the Barcelona Copy reported that the distance measurements in it were given predominantly in leagues. We know (from the multiples of four) that most of the mile distances in the *Diario* must have been conversions from original measurements in leagues. We know (from the general absence of fractional numbers) that most of the league measurements are original. And finally, we know that there is no evidence for unit conversion of any kind in the first-person sections of the log.

Given this weight of evidence, this seems like the most likely scenario: Columbus wrote his log of the first voyage almost entirely in leagues. Decades after Columbus's death, Las Casas abstracted the log, converting some of the league distances into miles, and computing some omitted distances in miles. But the first-person sections of the *Diario*, including the Bahamian portions, contain no unit conversions, because they are direct quotes from the Barcelona Copy, just as Las Casas said.

And that means that Rum Cay cannot be the second island visited by Columbus, unless a more credible explanation for the size discrepancies can be found. To date, no such explanation has been forthcoming.[4]

I knew that this analysis would be devastating to the Watlings theory when it became known. So after giving the lecture and summarizing its contents for the Columbus Round Robin, I hoped that some theorists, especially the more mathematically minded ones, might reevaluate their positions.

But the fallout from my 1995 lecture and its associated Round Robin letter was far from what I expected. One by one, over the course of the next few months, nearly all the Watlings Island advocates announced that they were no longer actively interested in pursuing the Columbus landfall problem, or that they were retiring from the Round Robin. Doug Peck, Jim Kelley, Bill Dunwoody, Neal Sealy, and even Alex Pérez all dropped

---

4. Even the redoubtable Bill Dunwoody, a Watlings diehard and relentless critic of all other theories, has deliberately avoided the issue in his recent writings.

by the wayside. Joe Judge sent me a letter with complementary comments on my analysis, but he passed away the following April; his letter to me may have been his final word on the Columbus landfall. Charlie Hoffman and David Henige had stopped contributing before I had even arrived on the scene in 1992. Arne Molander was still game, but he no longer seemed capable of meaningful discussion without insult, at least in his letters to me. When I presented my findings publicly in November 1995, the Columbus landfall Round Robin had been a going concern for more than a dozen years. Within six months it was effectively dead.

There seemed to be nothing else to do. I put the Round Robin behind me and continued working on the landfall problem alone. But I soon discovered that without the spur of others' thoughts (and, sometimes, nonsense) arriving in my mailbox and driving me forward, my own pace of work on the landfall problem slowed to a crawl. That didn't bother me, though. I was the youngest person in the group. I had time.

7.

The Longitude Frauds

THE first person to notice that the mile numbers in the *Diario* were mostly multiples of four was David Henige,[1] one of the original founders of the Round Robin. Henige has an uncanny ability to detect the oddities, errors, and inconsistencies with original source documents, and he ultimately concluded that these faults were so great in the documents of the first voyage that they might never be solved. The multiples of four oddity was one of those odd things about the *Diario* that Henige had noticed, but it was not the only one.

Perhaps the most obvious oddity is that instead of being a straightforward account of Columbus's dead-reckoning navigation, a daily record of courses sailed and distances made good, the *Diario* contains a double bookkeeping of the distances on most—but not all—days. The first hint of this occurs on September 9, 1492, when Las Casas writes, "He made 15 leagues that day and he decided to report less than those actually traveled so in case the voyage were long the men would not be frightened and lose courage." The following day, Las Casas is even more explicit: "They made 60 leagues . . . but he reported only 48 leagues so that the men would not be frightened if the voyage were long."

This double bookkeeping has been the subject of much commentary over the years. In the first place, it seems odd to the

---

1. David Henige, *In Search of Columbus: Sources for the First Voyage.*

point of incredible that Columbus would be able to hide the actual distance sailed from the crew. His men were experienced mariners like Columbus, and many of them were skilled dead-reckoning navigators in their own right. Another odd thing, first pointed out by Jim Kelley,[2] is that the ratio of the "private" leagues to the "public" ones tends to cluster around a ratio of six to five. This is exactly the ratio between one Roman mile of 1,000 paces and one Italian mile of 5,000 palms. It is well known that Iberian sailors of this era used the Portuguese Maritime League, which is composed of four Roman miles. Therefore, Kelley proposed that Columbus was using a different length league than his Spanish crew, a league composed of four Italian miles. The double bookkeeping then would simply be an artifact of Columbus converting from his own league length, probably learned in his boyhood, to a league measure that his crew would be familiar with.

Kelley's explanation made a lot of sense, but Henige had noticed yet another odd discrepancy about the double book-keeping. There are a few places in the *Diario* where Columbus gives us a recap, a running subtotal, of the entire distance that the voyage has made good from their departure in the Canary Islands. The first of these occurs on September 19. On that day, the *Diario* records the voyage subtotals for the pilots of the three ships, but it does not record Columbus's own personal subtotal. But on October 1 at dawn—the conventional beginning point of the day's run in the westbound portion of the *Diario*—the pilot of *Santa Maria* reported that the fleet had made 578 leagues from Hierro in the Canaries. Meanwhile, Las Casas tells us that the "smaller account that the Admiral showed to the men was 584 [leagues]. But the true account that the Admiral figured and kept to himself was 707."

The first problem here is that when we simply add up the daily figures as given in each day's log entry, we don't get 707 leagues or even close to it. At dawn on October 1, the "private" leagues (i.e., Italian Leagues) total is 657, a full 50 leagues short of Columbus's subtotal. The fleet did make 25 Italian Leagues on the day of October 1 itself, and Las Casas does not state

---

2. James E. Kelley. Jr., "In the Wake of Columbus on a Portolan Chart," 77-111.

specifically that Columbus's personal subtotal was made at dawn, as he did with the pilot. So by stretching a point we might get the sum of daily distances up as high as 682. But no matter how you figure it, there seems to be between 25 and 50 leagues missing from the daily totals between the Canary Islands departure on September 8 and the October 1 subtotal.

That amounts to a good day's run, and it is simply not credible that an entire day could be missing from the log. Doug Peck suggested in the Round Robin that the discrepancy might simply be an accumulation of rounding errors of the daily totals: in other words, perhaps Columbus had kept track of each day's run in leagues and fractions of a league, but had only written down the integer parts of each number in the daily figures, while retaining the exact fractions for the subtotal. But 25 leagues is more than one league's difference per day, so no accumulation of rounding errors can account for the difference.

Even more vexing, Henige had pointed out a problem with the "public" subtotal of 584 leagues. This total is more difficult to deal with, since there are 10 days or partial days in the *Diario* where there is only one league number given, a number that (everyone assumes) is Columbus's private figure. Therefore, there is no public figure in the *Diario* for those 10 days. When we add up the total public figures, we get 360 leagues at dawn on October 1, so the missing 10 days must account for 224 leagues to bring the total up to Columbus's subtotal of 584 public leagues.

The problem is that the number of private leagues on those same 10 days is only 212, which is less than the number of public leagues. But we know that the private league numbers must be higher than the public: that is invariably true as Columbus converts from Italian Leagues into Portuguese Maritime Leagues. To Henige, this seemed more evidence that the *Diario* was corrupt and unreliable. This problem lay festering in the back of my head as I tackled a completely different issue.

Right after joining the Round Robin, Arne Molander and I had gotten into a dispute over Columbus's alleged use of lunar longitudes. There was one item of historical interest in his favor from that same era. That was Amerigo Vespucci's use of celestial longitudes in 1499. Molander had run across a copy of

Thomas Davies's paper on the Vespucci longitude (see chapter 1) and used it to buttress his argument.

It's fairly easy for a celestial navigator to determine his latitude. In the daytime, you can measure the angle of the Sun above the horizon when it reaches its highest point. That, plus an almanac to tell you the Sun's daily declination (its angle from the celestial equator) and one simple computation, will do the trick. At night, a similar observation using any star with known declination will work just as well.

But determining your longitude is a different matter entirely: while latitude is absolute, determined relative to Earth's axis, longitude is determined relative to some arbitrary starting point. In order to find your longitude, you need to know the difference in time between where you are and the time at your arbitrary starting point. Longitude requires the use of an accurate clock. But chronometers were more than two centuries from being invented in the late fifteenth century. So how did Vespucci do it? The story comes from a letter[3] that Vespucci wrote to his patron, Lorenzo de'Medici of Florence. Here's the relevant passage from his letter of July 18, 1500:

> . . . I compared this against the *Almanac* of Regiomontanus, composed for the meridian of the city of Ferrara, and verified it against the calculations of the *Tables* of King Don Alfonso. And after many nights watching, on the night of 23 August 1499, there was a conjunction of the moon with Mars, which, according to the *Almanac*, was to occur at midnight or half an hour before. I found that, when the moon rose on our horizon, an hour and a half after the sun had set, the planet had passed into the east, which is to say that the moon was about a degree and some minutes east of Mars, and at midnight was five and a half degrees to the east, more or less. Thus, setting up the proportion, 'If twenty-four hours equal 360 degrees, what do 5 ½ hours equal?', I find the answer to be 82 ½ degrees; and such was my longitude from the meridian of Cadiz.

This rather opaque passage needs some background. The Prussian astronomer Johannes Müller took the pen name

3. Lester C. Edwards, *The life and voyages of Americus Vespucius*, 151.

Regiomontanus. When his *Ephemerides* was published in 1474, it became one of the only astronomical references[4] available in the fifteenth century. Like all astronomical almanacs, it is composed with a standard meridian of observation. For Müller, it was his adopted home of Nüremburg, which is nearly on the same meridian as the Italian city of Ferrara. Müller wrote his ephemeris because an earlier standard work, the so-called Alfonsine Tables, were by then two centuries old and badly erroneous in their predictions of the planets. So right away, Vespucci betrays some ignorance by suggesting that Müller's work needed to be "verified" against the earlier, obsolete Alfonsine Tables.

All celestial objects rise in the east and set in the west. The fixed stars do so in a very regular way, but there are seven visible objects that move around the celestial sphere, more or less among the constellations of the zodiac. These seven objects are the Moon, the Sun, Mercury, Venus, Mars, Jupiter, and Saturn. In those days before Copernicus, all seven of these (including the Sun and Moon) were called "planets." The Moon and the Sun always move from west to east, compared to the fixed stars. The other planets move generally from west to east, too, but they sometimes stop and move "backwards" toward the west, before resuming their easterly courses. The Moon is the most important for our purposes: just remember that although the Moon moves toward the west compared to the horizon, as do the stars, the Moon moves toward the east compared to the fixed stars and the slower planets.

There was indeed a conjunction of the Moon and Mars on August 23, 1499. A lunar conjunction occurs when the speedy Moon, moving easterly along the zodiac, passes one of the slower-moving planets. When Vespucci writes that "the planet had passed into the east," the "planet" he refers to is the Moon, not Mars. So Vespucci is saying that the conjunction had already occurred when the Moon and Mars rose that night; the Moon was already east of Mars when they first became visible.

But from that point on, the whole passage seems like nonsense to an astronomer. According to Vespucci, the Moon rose an hour and a half after sunset, or at 7:30 p.m. from his location

---

4. Johannes Müller, *Ephemerides sive Almanach perpetuum.*

near the equator. At that time, the Moon was a degree and some small fraction east of Mars. Four and a half hours later, at local midnight, the Moon had moved to a position five and a half degrees east of Mars. (The motion of Mars in four hours is negligible.) If Vespucci is right, the Moon moved nearly four and a half degrees in four and a half hours.

But that's twice as fast as the Moon really moves. There is simply no way that anyone actually observing the Moon and making measurements of its position could make that kind of mistake. After doing some further research, I found that nearly everything that Vespucci reported about this computation was false. Indeed, the German historian Hermann Wagner had pointed out the fraudulent nature of Vespucci's "longitude determination" as early as 1917. Yet even today it is easy to find references both in print and on the web of the alleged high accuracy of this "observation," while the fact that it is an utter fabrication goes unrecognized.

Let's compare what Vespucci wrote to the true state of events. To simplify matters, we will adopt the assumption that Vespucci was at the mouth of the Oyapac River, the border between Guyana and Brazil. His actual position may have been somewhat different than that, but not by enough to make much difference in our calculations.

Vespucci says that according to Müller's almanac, the conjunction is predicted to occur at midnight Nüremburg time. But that's not true at all: the *Ephemerides* actually predicts the conjunction to occur at 4:23 a.m. Vespucci says that from his location, the Moon rose an hour and a half after sunset; the Moon actually rose two hours and fifteen minutes after sunset. Vespucci says that at moonrise, the Moon was a degree and some minutes east of Mars; it was actually almost three degrees east of Mars, 2.85 degrees to be exact. Vespucci says that at midnight, the Moon was five and a half degrees east of Mars; it was actually just less than four degrees east of Mars at midnight. And after all that, Vespucci computes his longitude to be five and a half hours west of Cádiz, or 82.5 degrees; his actual longitude was about 45 degrees west of Cádiz.

After a little analysis, I had worked a probable explanation of what Vespucci had done, and how he had arrived at the figures he did. It's possible that Vespucci actually saw the Moon and Mars rise together on the evening of August 23, 1499. He may even have made a note of it in his diary; Mars was particularly bright and particularly close to the Moon that night. But he could not have made any real measurements using real instruments; the errors are simply too great. And he did not determine his longitude from the event. The fraud probably occurred about a year later, when he was back in Spain composing his letter to de'Medici. Perhaps he ran across a note or diary entry about the event, or perhaps he recalled the event from his memory. Either way, he seized a perfect opportunity to deceive his patron about his navigational expertise.

In constructing his fraud, Vespucci made four key mistakes. First, Vespucci plagiarized Columbus. On his second voyage, Columbus had determined his longitude using the well-known method of timing an eclipse. In his *Libro de las Profecías*, or *The Book of Prophecies*, Columbus reported[5] that while off the coast of Hispaniola, he timed the eclipse of September 14, 1494, as five and a half hours west of Cape St. Vincent in Portugal. Columbus corresponded with Vespucci, and it may be that Vespucci had heard of Columbus's longitude measurement from the Admiral himself. If Vespucci already knew that the Indies were five and a half hours west of Europe, it would be no surprise that Vespucci's own Indies longitude "measurement" turns out to be five and a half hours west of Cadiz, essentially the same longitude that Columbus obtained. In other words, Vespucci started with a known longitude and then computed backwards to find the "observations" that would support that longitude. This is exactly the opposite of the way real navigators work. And since Columbus's longitude was badly wrong, Vespucci's longitude was equally wrong—and even more so, since Vespucci's location was east of Columbus's.

Vespucci's second mistake was that he trusted his memory. Angular distances can be deceiving for inexperienced observers, and Vespucci was no exception. The Moon was nearly three degrees east of Mars when it rose that night, but it very seldom comes closer than that, so in Vespucci's mind and memory, it

---

5. Delno C. West and August Kling, *The Libro* de las profecías *of Christopher Columbus*, 226, 227.

may have seemed quite close indeed. Vespucci guessed a separation of about one degree; and Vespucci guessed the time of the event as about an hour and a half after sunset. These guesses aren't bad for someone working without instruments. The problem is that if Vespucci had really been measuring his longitude that night, he *must* have been using instruments. Even when we consider the quality of instruments available in those days, neither of these guesses is close enough to be explained in the context of a real navigator making real measurements. But both are easily explainable in the context of deliberate fraud.

Third, Vespucci believed that the Moon moved one degree per hour. It's hard to say how Vespucci got this idea, since the geocentric speed of the Moon was only 31 arc-minutes per hour that night, about half the speed that Vespucci reported, and it never gets much faster than that. But given this error, Vespucci figured as follows: at some local time the conjunction occurs in Europe; so at the same local time in the Indies (five and half hours later, Vespucci thinks) the Moon should have moved along the ecliptic to a point five and a half degrees east of Mars at a speed of one degree per hour. Since Vespucci remembered the Moon as being one degree east of Mars at 7:30 p.m., it should take an additional four and a half hours to move an additional four and a half degrees eastward. That means the Moon should be five and half degrees east of Mars at midnight in the Indies. Therefore, the local time of the conjunction in Europe, five and a half hours away, should also be midnight. And these are exactly the fake observations that Vespucci reported.

Finally, Vespucci did not check the ephemeris. If Vespucci had really used the ephemeris to determine his longitude, he would have concluded that he was about nine hours west of Cádiz, not the five and a half hours he reported, and not the three he really was. Vespucci did not worry that de'Medici would actually check the ephemeris; such scientific works were (and still are) beyond the grasp of almost everyone, apparently including Vespucci himself, and also including the legion of modern historians who accept Vespucci's longitude as legitimate.

Recovering Vespucci's hoax computations brought me back to the issue of Columbus's own longitude determinations. While it seemed clear to me that Vespucci had plagiarized Columbus's longitude of five and a half hours, as reported in *The Book of Prophesies*, I was also aware that there are other accounts of this eclipse that gave different figures. And there was also a second reported eclipse longitude reported in the *Prophesies* that Columbus made in 1504.

Both of Columbus's longitudes were made using a technique known since ancient times. On September 20 in the year 331 BC, the army of Alexander the Great was encamped near Arbela in Mesopotamia (the modern city of Irbil, Iraq). The full Moon rose at sunset, and two hours later an eclipse of the Moon began. At the instant the Moon began to cross into Earth's shadow, the start of the eclipse was also seen in Carthage; but in Carthage, the local time was sunset, not two hours later as at Arbela. Ancient astronomers realized that this was because of a longitude difference of two hours, or 30 degrees, between Carthage and Arbela. This early eclipse longitude was widely known in the ancient world and was reported both by Pliny the Elder and by Claudius Ptolemy. Prior to the invention of the telescope, timing a lunar eclipse was the only reliable way to find a longitude difference between two points.

Columbus was a self-educated man and widely read in classical texts, so it is not especially surprising that he would try to use this method of determining longitude. Columbus also owned a copy of Müller's *Ephemerides*, and several sources report that on his second voyage, he observed the lunar eclipse on the night of September 14-15, 1494, and determined his longitude from it. But it turns out that the various sources disagree, often wildly, about the results of this observation. In a fragmentary text, written perhaps around 1497, the Genoese biographer Antonio Gallo reported:[6]

> He (Columbus) declared also from the observation of his people that when in the year of our Lord 1494 there appeared an eclipse in the month of September, it was seen in Española four hours before that it was visible in Spain.

6. John Boyd Thacher, *Christopher Columbus: His Life, His Work, His Remains*, 192, 195.

Columbus's son Fernando gives this report,[7] which may have been taken from the missing log of the second voyage:

> On September 15th by the mercy of God they sighted an island
> which lies off the eastern end of Española . . . in the middle of
> a great storm he anchored behind this island . . . That night he
> observed an eclipse of the moon and was able to determine a
> difference in time of about five hours and twenty-three minutes
> between that place and Cádiz.

In his own work *The Book of Prophesies*, Columbus himself[8] stated:

> In the year 1494, when I was at the island of Saona, which is at
> the eastern end of the island of Hispaniola, there was an eclipse of
> the moon on the 14th of September, and it was found that there
> was a difference from there to the Cape of St. Vincent in Portugal
> of five hours and more than one half.

But in a letter to King Ferdinand and Queen Isabela of July 7, 1503, Columbus contradicts himself,[9] and states: "In the year ninety-four I navigated in twenty-four degrees to the westward to the end of nine hours, and I cannot be in error because there was an eclipse."

In this quote, the "twenty-four degrees" refers to his approximate latitude. But Las Casas's great work, the *Historia de las Indias*, also quotes Columbus giving yet another accounting,[10] not just of his longitude but of his position while observing it:

> From the end of Cuba (that is seen in Hispaniola), which was called
> the End of the East, and by another name Alpha and Omega, he
> sailed westward from the southern part, until he passed the end
> of ten hours on the sphere, in such a way that when the sun set
> to him, it was two hours before rising to those that lived in Cádiz,

7. Keen (1992) 145.
8. West & Kling (1991) ibid.
9. Cecil Jane, ed, *The Four Voyages of Columbus*, 82.
10. Bartolome de Las Casas, *Historia de las Indias*, 390. Author's translation.

in Spain; and he says that there couldn't be any error, because there was an eclipse of the moon on the 14th of September, and he was well prepared with instruments and the sky was very clear that night.

And if that weren't enough, in a later chapter Las Casas repeats[11] the eclipse story, except, the second time around his position is at Saona and his longitude is 5 hours and 23 minutes west of Cádiz, exactly as reported in Fernando's biography.

As you can see, we have a problem here. In five primary sources by four authors, we have six reports of the longitude, giving five different results. And these results differ from each other by as much as six hours, or 90 degrees of longitude. Even worse, as it turns out, if Columbus had found his longitude by comparing the time of the eclipse to the prediction in the almanac, not one of these reports would be correct.

On that night, Columbus's correct longitude at Saona was 4 hours and 10 minutes west of Cádiz.[12] As it happens, Müller's prediction of the eclipse was 24 minutes late,[13] so Columbus should have found his longitude to be 4 hours and 34 minutes west of Cádiz. We know from modern experiments that an eclipse can be timed in this way to within five minutes or less; and the correct local time should be measurable to within 10 or 15 minutes using a sandglass or a nocturnal. So the total error should be no more than 15 or 20 minutes. But all of the longitude reports are off by 34 minutes or more, and in the worst case, by more than five hours. Indeed, it seems impossible to reconcile any of these longitudes to actual celestial observation, unless we resort to a series of mistakes or improbable procedures; and to account for all of the erroneous

11. Las Casas (1951) I, 395-396.
12. Actual longitudes of cited places: Nuremberg, 11° 5' E; Cádiz, 6° 16' W; Cape S. Vicente, 9° 0' W; Saona, 68° 39' W; St. Anne's Bay, 77° 12' W. Longitude differences are converted from degrees to hours by dividing by 15.
13. Johannes Müller, *Kalendar Maister Johannes Kunisperger*. unpaged. Müller's predicted time of mid-eclipse (19h 45m past noon) is converted to UT by correcting for convention (12h), longitude (44m), and equation of time (10m), so 19h 45m + 12h - 44m - 10m = 06:51 UT on the 15th. Actual mid-eclipse was 06:31 ET; applying 4m dynamical time correction gives 06:27 UT according to Jean Meeus & Hermann Mucke (1979) *Canon of Lunar Eclipses -2002 to +2526*. Vienna: Astronomisches Buro Wein. Müller's prediction of semi-duration (1h 48m) is 5m too great, but this is far too small to explain Columbus's discrepancies.

longitudes, the repertoire of such mistakes must be both huge and self-contradictory.

Our suspicions are raised even further when we read that Columbus anchored at Saona that night to take shelter from an approaching storm. Fernando even reports that the storm had already broken at the time of the anchorage. So how is it that celestial observations could have been made during a storm? Why does Columbus later report that the sky was clear that night? Perhaps most tellingly, why are there no actual observations in any of these reports, no time of the start or end of the eclipse? The only things we are given are computational results, which are easily faked. And how is it that according to both Fernando and Las Casas, Columbus was apparently able to time his observations to the nearest minute using an hourglass?

Indeed, the 10-hour longitude is so clearly at odds with reality that it, at least, has been viewed suspiciously for decades; Morison thought[14] it must have been cooked up somehow. But why would Columbus falsify such a result? A critical clue can be found in Columbus's *Book of Privileges*. Prior to both his second and third voyages, Columbus requested that the Spanish Sovereigns confirm his appointments as admiral of the Ocean Sea and viceroy of the newly discovered lands. The documents confirming these privileges confine Columbus's realm to "the Ocean Sea in the region of the Indies."[15] Therefore, if the newly discovered lands were not really in the region of the Indies (that is, in Asia) Columbus's entire personal fortune may have been at risk. Indeed, it may have been just such a thought that led Columbus to demand that his crew on his second voyage sign a document swearing that Cuba was the mainland of Asia.[16]

In his letter of 1503, which we quoted in part above, Columbus reminds the Sovereigns that according to the ancient geographer Marinus of Tyre, the combined landmass of Europe and Asia made up 15 hours of longitude,[17] or twelve hours according to Ptolemy. If true, the remaining longitude difference—in

---

14. Samuel Eliot Morison, *Admiral of the Ocean Sea*, II, 147.

15. Helen Nader and Luciano Formisano, *The Book of Privileges Issued to Christopher Columbus by King Fernando and Queen Isabel*, vol. 2 of the *Repertorium Columbianum*, 73, 74, 87, 151, 153.

16. Morison (1942) II, 140–141.

17. Jane (1988) II, 84.

Columbus's mind, the width of the Ocean Sea from Europe westward to Asia—must have been between 9 and 12 hours. In this context, it is easy to see is why Columbus claimed longitudes so clearly fraudulent as 9 or 10 hours between Spain and the West Indies: if the Ocean Sea were 9 or 10 hours wide, then according to Marinus his discoveries were firmly within Asia and his privileges were secure. Since he needed the Ocean Sea to be 9 hours wide, he simply claimed it as a fact and then added in the part about the eclipse to give his statements a fig leaf of scientific respectability.

But even if this is true, what about the other reported longitudes from the same eclipse? Where did they come from? And why are they less than nine hours? Such differences are commonly seen in cases of fraud. When a story is true, it is drawn from a real memory of actual events; but when a story is fabricated, the fabrication often changes over time, as the hoaxer seeks to make his story ever more unimpeachable. Ironically, these very changes are one of the best ways to detect a hoax.

But it was that impossibly precise "five hours and twenty-three minutes" longitude that most caught my eye. How could Columbus have arrived at just that figure? An argument between Columbus and the cosmographers of his day provides a clue. Both Eratosthenes and Poseidonios had measured the size of Earth fairly well in ancient times, but due to errors in translation of various units of measure, the uncertainty in Earth's size had grown larger by Columbus's day. Many believed that a degree of Earth's surface measured 66 2/3 miles; Columbus himself held for a smaller degree[18] of only 56 2/3 miles. He took this figure from the Arabic astronomer Ahmed ben Muhammed Al Fargani, but Columbus was unaware that the Arabic mile was much longer than his own Italian mile. Therefore, Columbus's degree measurement was far too short.

One consequence of knowing the size of Earth is that it allows you to convert between linear measurements, like miles or leagues, into angular measurements, like degrees of latitude or hours of longitude. So let's compute backwards: given that an hour of longitude is 15 degrees, and supposing that there are

---

18. Jane, ibid (1988).

56 2/3 miles for each degree, and four miles to a league, how many leagues does 5 hours and 23 minutes equal? The answer turns out to be about 1,143.9 leagues. And that number is suspiciously close—perhaps too close—to a number any Columbus scholar knows quite well.

On November 2, 1492, while Columbus is off the coast of Cuba, the *Diario* records: "And he says that by his account that he had gone 1,142 leagues from the island of Hierro."[19]

Once again the *Diario* seems to have a problem with addition, since up to this point Columbus has sailed over 1,230 leagues on the whole voyage. Most scholars have assumed that Columbus derived this number by measuring a chart, but if he had been measuring correctly, he should have found that his true distance from Hierro was only about 1,100 leagues. But note that Columbus does not say to where from Hierro the 1,142 leagues is measured. Once again, we have an unspoken assumption that his current position off Cuba is being measured. But this assumption may also be wrong.

This distance was so close to the one I had derived from the 5 hour 23 minute longitude that I found the whole thing suspiciously neat. So I converted the other way, perhaps following in Columbus's footsteps: 1,142 leagues converted back into an hours-and-minutes longitude gives 5 hours, 22 minutes, and 27 seconds. That is only three seconds difference from rounding up to the 5:23 of the eclipse. Just one more mile would do it: if the true distance was 1,142 1/4 leagues exactly, it would round down to 1,142 leagues of distance, as reported in the *Diario*, and also round up to Columbus's 5 hours 23 minutes of longitude, as reported both by Fernando and Las Casas.

That's interesting, and certainly significant. But where did that 1,142 leagues itself come from? The daily transatlantic distances only add up to 1,108 or 1,109 leagues (because of a few ambiguities there is some wiggle room) and that is 33 or 34 leagues short of 1,142. But then again, we have already seen that there appears to be between 25 and 50 leagues missing from the *Diario* between September 8 and October 1. And the needed 34 leagues would fill the bill nicely.

19. Dunn & Kelley (1989) 130, 131.

The key that unlocks both of these mysteries is found not in the *Diario*, but in the other major historical record of Columbus's lost log: the biography of Columbus by his son, Fernando. This biography also notes the double bookkeeping of distances, but there is a key discrepancy between the two accounts. According to Fernando, the double bookkeeping starts on September 9. On that day, Columbus sails 18 leagues and reports to the crew 15 leagues.[20] But Las Casas records only the publicly announced 15-league figure; he does not start the double figures until the following day,[21] September 10.

So by reading the *Diario* alone, we have simply *assumed* that the 15 leagues reported by Las Casas on September 9 is the number of "private" leagues, even though it is not explicitly labeled as such by Las Casas. In reading Fernando's account, we realize that our assumption was wrong. The unlabeled figure is actually the public figure, in Portuguese Maritime Leagues. By correcting this mistake, we have added three leagues to the voyage. But could this same mistake also have occurred elsewhere in the *Diario*?

Besides the case that we have just discussed, there are seven other cases[22] in the first two weeks of the voyage where Las Casas gives only one figure for the day's run, not explicitly labeled as being either a private or public figure. Up until now, all historians have assumed that these unlabeled singletons are Columbus's private figures in Italian Leagues. But suppose, as in the case of September 9th, that we have been wrong? What if we make the opposite assumption, that the unlabeled numbers are really Portuguese Maritime Leagues? In that case, we could reconstruct the correct figures in Italian Leagues by applying Jim Kelley's 6-to-5 ratio, and rounding to the nearest whole number. If we do this, as shown in Table 7.1 (see page 142), we will add 33 or 34 leagues to the voyage between September 9

---

20. Benjamin Keen, trans., *The Life of the Admiral Christopher Columbus by His Son Ferdinand*, 48.

21. Dunn & Kelley (1989) 28, 29.

22. There are eight unlabeled distances in the first two weeks of the voyage, followed by two weeks in which there are no such cases. Distances recorded in the last three days of the voyage are again unlabeled. Here we make the conventional assumption regarding the final three days, i.e., that they are "true" figures in Italian Leagues.

TABLE 7.1. Unlabeled league numbers in the Diario, assumed to be public figures.

Date	Las Casas	As corrected	Difference
September 9 day	15	18	3
September 9 night	30	36	6
September 11	20	24	4
September 15	27	32	5
September 20	"7 or 8"	9	1 or 2
September 21	13	16	3
September 22	30	36	6
September 23	27	32	5
Total			33 or 34

and October 1, which is the exact number we need, twice over. It is enough to account for the 25 to 50 leagues known to be missing from the *Diario* on that date; and it will account exactly for the 1,142 leagues from Hierro figure that the *Diario* quotes on November 2. And as an added bonus, it also explains David Henige's vexing issue with the missing public league numbers, since 8 of the 10 of the missing numbers are now shown to be private figures and not public ones. (On the other two days, Las Casas tells us that Columbus reported fewer leagues to the crew, but doesn't say how many fewer; so we know that those days are the private league numbers.)

As it turns out, all of the remaining longitude results from 1494 can be derived in a similar way. It is possible that Columbus wanted to view the eclipse, planned to view it, perhaps even promised to view it. But on the night itself, bad weather intervened. In his frustration, it must have occurred to Columbus that there was another method for determining longitude right at his fingertips: a method that had nothing to do with eclipses or celestial observation at all.

Las Casas records that on his second voyage, Columbus measured the transatlantic distance from Gomera to Dominica to be 850 leagues.[23] If we take this 850 league measurement

---

23. Las Casas (1951) I, 497.

and convert it into a longitude using Columbus's own size-of-the-Earth formula, it becomes exactly[24] four hours of longitude: the same longitude reported by Gallo in his biography.

Some readers will have noticed by now that in making this computation, we neglected to account for the fact that these distances were not measured along the equator, but at a somewhat higher latitude. There is some evidence[25] that Columbus had little or no knowledge of trigonometry, necessary to make this correction; and the conclusions that we eventually reach will provide additional justification for this position. If Columbus actually figured in this way, he probably would have rejected the four-hour result rather quickly, because it is not close enough to the desired nine hours that he needed to secure his position. He may have confided this result to his brother Diego, or one of the Genoese merchants on the second voyage, and perhaps that was where Gallo picked up the story.

Some time later, it probably occurred to Columbus that he had measured a longer transatlantic distance on his first voyage than on his second. If we include the missing 33 leagues, the first voyage transatlantic distance is 1,142 1/4 leagues, which fits the *Diario* entry of November 2. If we convert this into a longitude, it becomes exactly 5 hours and 23 minutes, the longitude reported in Fernando's biography and by Las Casas in the *Historia*.

But apparently, as the years passed, Columbus still wasn't satisfied. At some point, he must have realized that the transatlantic distance, taken by itself, was still too low. To increase the total, he added in the distance sailed westward within the Indies. In referring to the *Diario* of the first voyage, we find that some of the westerly distances along the north coast of Cuba have been omitted. But we saw in chapter 2 that the westerly distance

---

24. All longitude computations here are rounded to the nearest minute. There are 4 miles to a league and 15 degrees to an hour of longitude, so: leagues x 4 ÷ 56 2/3 ÷ 15 = hours. Or combining terms, $L ÷ 212.5 = h$, with remainders expressed sexigesimally.

25. Columbus timed the length of the daylight on December 13, 1492, the day after the winter solstice. This was clearly an attempt to determine his *klimata*, which was often used as a substitute latitude by Ptolemy and Marinus of Tyre. But Columbus did not then convert this measurement into an actual latitude, which he easily could have done by trigonometric or geometric means. See Curtis Wilson, "Hipparchus and Spherical Trigonometry," 14-15.

from the Bahamas landfall to the landfall in Cuba must have been at least 31 leagues: five or more west from Island I to Island II, more than 10 leagues west along Island II; eight or more west from Island II to Island III, then adding westerly vectors from the Cape Verde fix to the *Islas de Arena* gives an additional sixteen, and there is some additional westing from the *Islas de Arena* to Cuba that we're not counting. Adding this 29 leagues to the transatlantic total and converting to a longitude gives us at least 5 hours 31 minutes. This matches the longitude in *The Book of Prophesies*, given as more than five and a half hours. Interestingly, the lack of precision expressed by Columbus in this longitude may indicate that the omitted Cuban distances in the *Diario* are attributable to Columbus himself, and not to the abridgment of Las Casas.

In one of history's most amazing ironies, it is almost certain that Amerigo Vespucci had no idea that Columbus's five and a half hour longitude was itself fraudulent when he used it as a basis for constructing his own celestial longitude fraud.

As icing on the cake, let us consider one more lunar longitude. The eclipse of 1494 was not the only eclipse from which Columbus claimed to have derived a longitude. On his fourth voyage, Columbus observed the eclipse of February 29, 1504, while he was marooned at St. Anne's Bay, Jamaica.[26] Columbus wrote in *The Book of Prophesies* that he determined from the eclipse that his longitude was 7 hours and 15 minutes west of Cádiz. Columbus's actual longitude was 4 hours and 44 minutes west of Cádiz, so again there is a huge error that demands explanation. In 1992 astronomer Donald W. Olson proposed a series of mistakes that would explain most of the discrepancy. If Columbus made the mistakes Olson attributed to him, he would have computed a longitude of 7 hours 13 minutes west of Cádiz,[27] which is tolerably close to the 7 hours 15 minutes he actually recorded.

But since we know that the 1494 eclipse longitudes are fraudulent, and we know how they were constructed, naturally we are led to suspect another explanation entirely. In his letter to the Sovereigns of July 7, 1503, Columbus wrote the following description of his return from Central America: "When I set out

---

26. Keen (1992) 272-273.
27. West & Kling (1991) 226-227.

thence to come to Española, the pilots believed that we were going to reach the island of San Juan, and it was the land of Mango, four hundred leagues more to the west than they said."[28]

The island of San Juan is the modern Puerto Rico, and Mango is a part of western Cuba. The significance of this passage is that this is the longest east-to-west distance within the Indies that Columbus ever recorded in any of his writings. So let's take this and add to it the longest transatlantic distance that Columbus sailed in his lifetime, the 1,142 1/4 leagues from the first voyage. This gives us 1,542 1/4 leagues, the maximum westerly distance that Columbus could reasonably claim to have ever sailed from Spain. When we convert this maximum distance into a longitude, we get exactly 7 hours and 15 minutes: the same longitude that Columbus reported as being derived from the eclipse of 1504.

So starting with the vexing problem of the subtotal that wouldn't add up, we found a mechanism for resolving the discrepancy; and in so doing, we added about 33 leagues to the westward passage on the first voyage. For those who may have lost count, those 33 leagues can now explain, in whole or in part, no less than six previously unexplained navigational results in the annals of Columbus. These are:

1. The 707-league subtotal of October 1, 1492.
2. The Henige conundrum: missing public distances before October 1 are not really greater than the private distances, because it is often the private distances that are really missing.
3. The 1,142 league total of November 2, 1492, is the transatlantic distance rounded to the nearest whole number.
4. The 5 hour 23 minute longitude of September 14, 1494, is the transatlantic distance converted to a longitude.
5. The more than five and a half hour longitude of September 14 is the transatlantic distance plus the first voyage distance within the Indies, converted to a longitude.
6. And the 7 hour 15 minute longitude of February 29, 1504, is the transatlantic distance plus the fourth voyage distance within the Indies, converted to a longitude.

---

28. Jane (1988) II, 98.

In addition to these, we also found that the four-hour longitude report of Gallo is the second voyage transatlantic distance, converted to a longitude.

When I solved the mystery of the fraudulent longitudes in 1997, I also recognized that the missing 33 leagues in the log of the first voyage might play an important role in the one last great piece of the Columbus landfall puzzle: his transatlantic track.

8.

Across The Atlantic

THERE are two ways we can find Guanahani. In chapter 2, we traced Columbus's inter-island track backwards to Guanahani from Cuba. The other way is to trace Columbus's transatlantic track forward, starting from his departure in the Canary Islands and working our way day by day across the ocean. By following the courses and distances given daily in the log, we will finally arrive at Guanahani by dead reckoning, the same way Columbus did in 1492.

Although the method sounds simple, there are several major issues that must be addressed before we can proceed. The first of these questions is which way does the compass point? It may sound odd, since most people know that a compass points north. But at most times and places, the compass does not actually point true north; it points a few degrees east or west of true north. The difference between magnetic north (the direction the compass points) and true north is called magnetic declination.[1]

A few degrees may not sound like much to be concerned with, but it is absolutely crucial. The transatlantic track is some 3,000 miles long, and if you were to draw a one-degree angle with 3,000-mile-long legs, the gap at the end would be over 50 miles wide. That's greater than the distance between, say, the

---

1. In years past, magnetic declination was called magnetic "variation," but declination is the currently accepted term. This is not to be confused with *astronomical* declination, which is, on the celestial sphere, exactly the same as latitude is on the terrestrial globe.

Plana Cays and Samana Cay, or Caicos and Grand Turk. So even a one-degree error in declination might easily take you to the wrong landfall.

The second major issue that must be addressed is that of ocean currents. The ocean is a moving, living thing, and currents can and will move ships in directions other than the direction they're pointed. So even if Columbus records his course as west, and even if we know what the magnetic declination was at that time and place, we would still need to know which direction the ocean itself is moving, to know the aggregate direction that the ship is moving. Currents in the open ocean are generally weak, usually less than one knot; but even a half a knot current will move a ship 12 nautical miles in a day, and there are 33 days on the voyage to account for.

And there is yet another problem that should be addressed, the effect of leeway. Unless the ship is sailing directly downwind (which seldom happens) the wind is hitting the ship on one side, to a greater or lesser degree. This will cause the ship to shift a little bit sideways as it makes its forward progress. The exact amount of leeway depends on the form of the ship's hull underwater, as well as the shape and area of the sails and rigging, and the difference in direction between the wind and the ship's heading.

There have been at least six published attempts to trace Columbus's track across the Atlantic to Island I, and all of them are fraught with unmeasured (and usually unmentioned) errors.

Charles A. Schott of the U.S. Coast and Geodetic Survey was the first[2] to trace the track in 1880. Schott started with a guess at magnetic variation in the North Atlantic in 1492, which he got from a colleague of his. Then he simply took all of the daily courses and distances in the log of the first voyage and computed the daily positions Columbus should have been at if the courses and distances were correct. He applied a correction for magnetic variation to arrive at the true course sailed on a given day, but he did not apply any corrections for currents or for leeway.

_____

2. Charles A. Schott, "An Inquiry into the Variation of the Compass Off the Bahama Islands, at the Time of the Landfall of Columbus in 1492."

Since Schott assumed that Columbus used the Portuguese Maritime League of 3.2 nautical miles, the initial end-of-track position he arrived at was far west of the Bahamas. So he applied an arbitrary "fudge factor" of 11 percent to his daily distances to ensure that his mathematical Columbus would not run aground before sighting land. (If he had included the effects of currents, which generally set to the west in this part of the Atlantic, his fudge factor would have been even greater.) Schott's final end-of-track position was near Mayaguana Island. But since he was well aware that the magnetic declinations he used were quite speculative, he also suggested that any island between Samana Cay and Grand Turk was possible.

U.S. Navy lieutenant John McElroy, apparently unaware of Schott's work, published[3] his own trace of Columbus's track in 1940. McElroy followed the same procedure as Schott, and applied a similar fudge factor to the distances.

McElroy applied daily compass corrections from a chart drawn up by Willem Van Bemmelen in 1899. Van Bemmelen had done extensive research on old sailing ship records to reconstruct the magnetic field, and had published an isogonic chart (a chart that shows the pattern of magnetic declinations) during past centuries, going back as far as 1500.

But McElroy apparently did not realize that Van Bemmelen's chart for 1500 had used Columbus's first voyage data as a primary source—and Van Bemmelen had assumed that the landfall was at Watlings Island. Therefore, using Van Bemmelen's chart, McElroy's reconstructed track ended right at Watlings Island, in a classic piece of unintentionally circular reasoning. Two years later, Samuel Eliot Morison proceeded to use McElroy's transatlantic track as a cornerstone for his contention that the Watlings Island landfall had been conclusively proven; and Morison, too, was unaware of the circularity of the argument.

In 1986, Luis Marden traced the track again[4] as part of Joe Judge's attempt to prove the Samana Cay landfall. Although he still used Van Bemmelen's isogonic chart, and still used a fudge

---

3. John W. McElroy, "The Ocean Navigation of Columbus on His First Voyage," 209-240.
4. Luis Marden, "The First Landfall of Columbus," 572-577.

factor for distance overruns, Marden did correctly note that McElroy had not accounted for the effects of either current or leeway in his reconstruction. Marden attempted to fill this gap.

Using a pilot chart of the North Atlantic, Marden applied prevailing currents from the chart to each day of the track—but only for the first half of the trip. Marden excused the last half of the trip by claiming (incorrectly) that the currents on the last half of the trip were always westerly, therefore would have had no effect on Columbus's westerly course. In truth, currents are a little southerly in the eastern Atlantic and a little northerly in the western Atlantic, so Marden's procedure applied the southerly drift but not the northerly.

But leeway (in this region of prevailing northeast trades) would always push a little southward, so Marden applied an arbitrary leeway factor to the whole trip, again pushing Columbus southward. His track ended (who would have guessed?) right off Samana Cay.

Marden's effort did not go uncriticized in the scientific community. At the Woods Hole Oceanographic Institution, Roger A. Goldsmith and Philip L. Richardson pointed out that Marden's use of prevailing currents from pilot charts was incorrect: he should have been using vector averages, which can be computed from data collected by the U.S. Navy since the mid-nineteenth century. Vector averages give overall lower current speeds and are appropriate when the length of time studied is greater than a day or two. Goldsmith and Richardson properly applied current drift to the entire voyage and also applied a different type of leeway to their track. Again using Van Bemmelen's isogons, and again using a fudge factor for distance, their track returned the endpoint to the vicinity of Watlings Island.

In a sharp contrast to the previous purely mathematical studies, Round Robin member Douglas T. Peck, a retired Air Force officer from Bradenton, Florida, got in his boat and actually sailed across the Atlantic in 1991. Short, muscular, gray-bearded, earringed, and given to salty language, meeting Doug Peck in person gives you the impression that he has just stepped off the deck of a sixteenth century privateer. But beneath that colorful veneer is the mind of a serious historian. On his voyages, Peck made a notable advance on his predecessors by using the 2.67 nm Italian League, and thereby avoided the usual fudge factor for distance overruns. He also used an isogonic chart similar (but not identical) to Van Bemmelen's of 1899. Peck ended up 44 nautical miles west of Watlings Island, supporting a landfall theory he had long advocated. His report of the trip has not been published, but was widely circulated in the Round Robin.

Meanwhile, supporters of more southerly landfalls in the Turks and Caicos Islands were impressed with Goldsmith & Richardson's first study, but noticed some flaws of their own. Accordingly, with the financial support of the government of the Turks and Caicos Islands, Richardson and Goldsmith reran their computer simulations but with two notable improvements.

First, following Peck's lead, they dropped the Portuguese Maritime League and adopted the more sensible Italian League of 2.67 nautical miles, avoiding the fudge factor. Second, they dropped the use of Van Bemmelen's isogonic chart. Instead, they derived their own isogons, which depended primarily on analysis of the transatlantic tracks sailed by Columbus's *eastbound* first voyage, and westbound second voyage. These changes resulted in a more southerly and shorter track, ending between Grand Turk Island and East Caicos Island. Goldsmith and Richardson also verified their magnetic declinations by simulating the eastbound first voyage and the westbound second voyage, to insure that those tracks also ended in the correct places.

As for myself, in the mid-1990s I was skeptical of all the transatlantic track work, because I was aware that the magnetic data on which it all rested was so slender. After 1600, there were enough historical records to reasonably determine magnetic declination in the Atlantic, but before then, the historical records were simply too sparse to support anything more than guesswork.

But by 1998 significant advances had been made in modeling the geomagnetic field during historical times. Scientists had made a rough (but scientifically valid) model of the earth's magnetic field for the years between 0 and 1700 AD, based on data from archaeological and geological sources, using a method known as spherical harmonic analysis, or SHA. To understand this method better, consider a guitar string as it vibrates.

FIGURE 8.1. Fundamental Wave.

FIGURE 8.2. First harmonic wave.

When you pluck the string in the center, you get a tone, called a fundamental tone (see Figure 8.1).

If you constrain the center of the string from moving, you get a different tone, one octave higher. This tone is called the first harmonic (Figure 8.2). There is also a second harmonic, and a third, and so on, for as high as you want to go.

If you add together some of these harmonics, you get a repeating wave that looks disordered and chaotic (Figure 8.3). Although it's easy to create chaos out of order, one of the neat things about math is sometimes you can also create order out of chaos. In particular, it has been shown that any wave that repeats itself, no matter how chaotic or random-looking, can be broken down into a set of simple fundamental components. This process of finding the simple components from a complex wave is called harmonic analysis, or Fourier analysis after the mathematician who invented it.

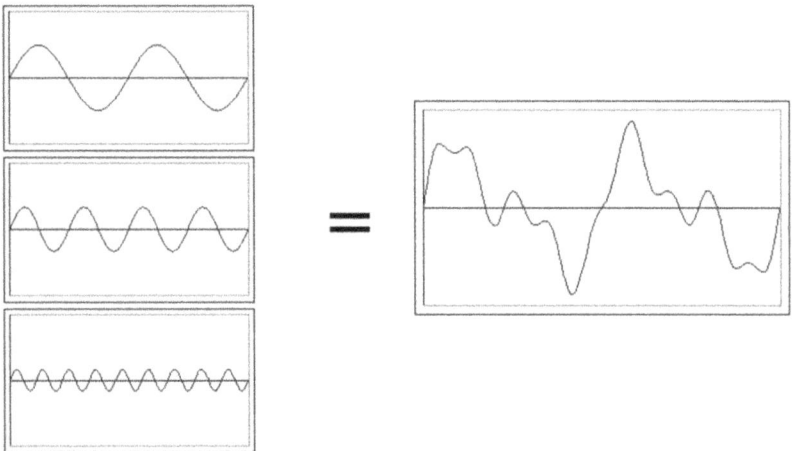

FIGURE 8.3. Adding Harmonics.

One way to insure that a wave repeats itself is to wrap it around a circle, as in Figure 8.4. Here, the thin black line represents the axis, now wrapped in a circle. It's easy to see that any wave that can be wrapped around a circle like this will always repeat as it meets itself.

But it's even more useful to take our one-dimensional wave and make it two-dimensional, like the waves on the surface of a pond. Then, instead of wrapping a one-dimensional wave

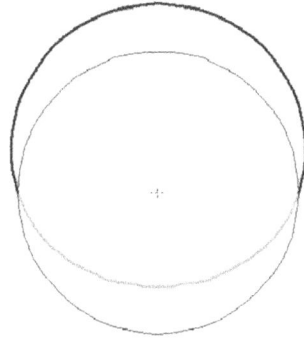

FIGURE 8.4. The first harmonic, wrapped around a circle.

around a circle, we can wrap our two-dimensional wave around a sphere, like Figure 8.5, to insure that it will always repeat. Spherical waves also have component harmonics. And like one-dimensional waves, any spherical wave, no matter how chaotic or random looking, can be broken down into its simple fundamental components. This is the process known as spherical harmonic analysis, or SHA.

As it turns out, a lot of interesting phenomena can be modeled with spherical waves. Like the small variations in Earth's gravitational field, for instance. Or, more to the point, the variations of Earth's magnetic field.

If Earth's magnetic field were a perfect dipole—that is, a perfect bar magnet perfectly aligned with the axis of Earth—the spherical wave representing it would look like Figure 8.5, and every compass would always point true north. Since the magnetic field is not a perfect dipole, the direction of the compass does not point exactly north in most times and places; it is usually a few degrees off, one way or

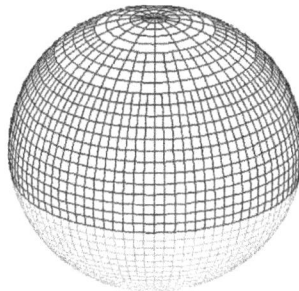

FIGURE 8.5. A simple spherical wave: degree 1, order 0.

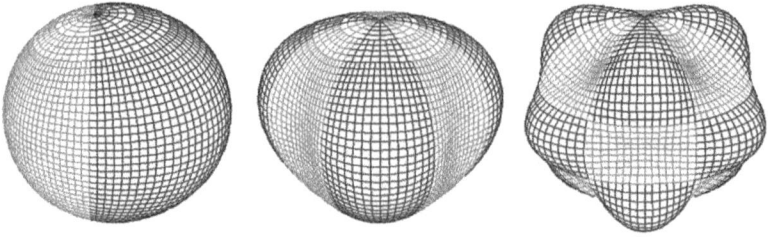

FIGURE 8.6. Higher order spherical waves.

another. The difference between true north and magnetic north is called magnetic declination.

This simple wave in Figure 8.5, representing the dipole, comprises 90 percent of Earth's magnetic field. It's the other 10 percent that's troublesome. If we want to model the magnetic field using spherical waves, we have to add small parts of a lot of other waves to the model.

This dipole wave is called a first-order wave. As we continue to add higher-order spherical waves (Figure 8.6) each successive wave generally adds less and less information to the final model—or we might say that successive waves tend to have smaller amplitudes. Most of the information in the model lies within the first few orders. For the last 20 years or so, geophysicists have used this technique to develop a standard model of Earth's current magnetic field. This model, called the international geomagnetic reference field, or IGRF, is a tenth-order model, composed of 120 spherical waves. The IGRF has been shown to predict magnetic declination to within a half-degree of accuracy over oceanic areas—even over those areas too remote to be easily visited.

Earth's magnetic field changes slowly over time and magnetic declination changes with time, too, over periods of several decades. Every five years, the IGRF is updated to reflect these changes (see Figure 8.7).

Having learned that SHA is an efficient way of modeling the geomagnetic field, scientists began to apply the same technique to historical magnetic observations, eventually developing models going back as far as the seventeenth century.

In 1995 I developed a web site devoted to the navigation of Columbus and to the problem of determining the location of his

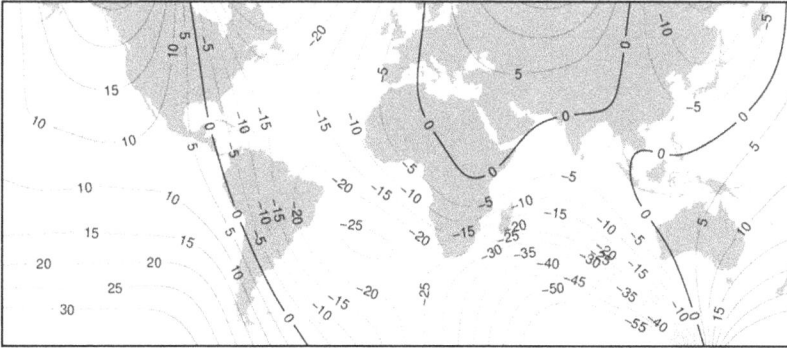

FIGURE 8.7. Isogonic chart from the IGRF for year 2000.

first landfall in the New World. When I wrote about this issue of tracing the transatlantic track, I proposed that any such tracing, to be scientifically acceptable, should meet the following criteria:

- It must use a consistent league length throughout, and this league length must also be consistent with the inter-island track. Such a league length should also be historically supportable. Currently, only the 2.67 nautical mile Italian League has been shown consistent with Columbus's reported distances along Cuba and Hispaniola.
- It must account for the effects of current and leeway using vector averages. Simulations based on by-guess and by-gosh eyeballing of currents shown on pilot charts are simply inadequate.
- The isogonic chart used for the track should be based on an SHA model of Earth's magnetic field.
- The magnetic model used must be able to recreate Columbus's return voyage (using currents and league length as described above) from Samana Bay, Hispaniola, to Santa Maria Island in the Azores, using the courses and distances in Columbus's log. Richardson and Goldsmith had used a similar check in their 1992 study, and it seemed an admirable idea to me.
- The magnetic model used must also be able to recreate Columbus's second voyage from the Canary Islands to Dominica in the West Indies, following a constant west-by-south course, as Columbus stated in his instructions

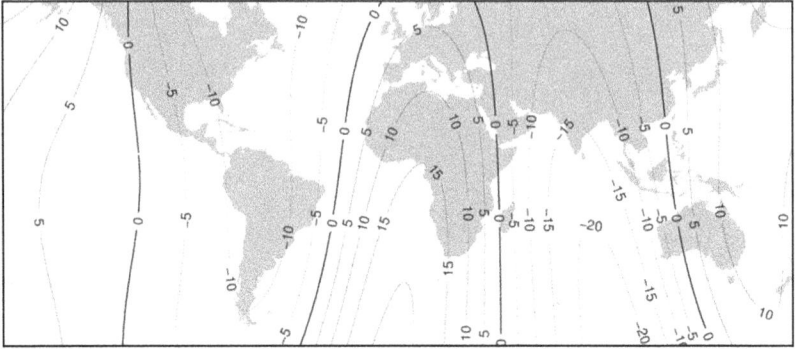

FIGURE 8.8. Isogonic chart from the Hongre model.

to his captains. Richardson and Goldsmith had missed this check, but since the voyage could be reconstructed, it certainly should be.

- Sources of error must be clearly stated and properly accounted for.

Back in 1995 I had my doubts that any such scientifically valid study could be done. At the time, there were no SHA models of the magnetic field for the fifteenth century, and there appeared to be no hope of getting any. Historical geomagnetic observations simply do not go that far back.

But over the past 20 years, new data about the magnetic field in historical times have emerged. Not historical data, but archaeomagnetic data. When a fire burns over a hearthstone, the heat softens the stone's grip on tiny magnetic regions within the rock, allowing them to rotate in response to the local magnetic field. When the site is abandoned, the cold rock retains the magnetic alignment of the last time it was heated. Such hearthstones can be dated by conventional archaeological methods, and they can be used as markers for the magnetic field at those particular times and places.

Volcanic eruptions often trap the remains of organic material, such as trees, within lava. If the eruption is recent (in geologic terms) the date of the eruption can be determined using carbon-14. As the lava cools and solidifies, tiny magnetic regions within the lava solidify in the direction of the magnetic field at the time of the eruption.

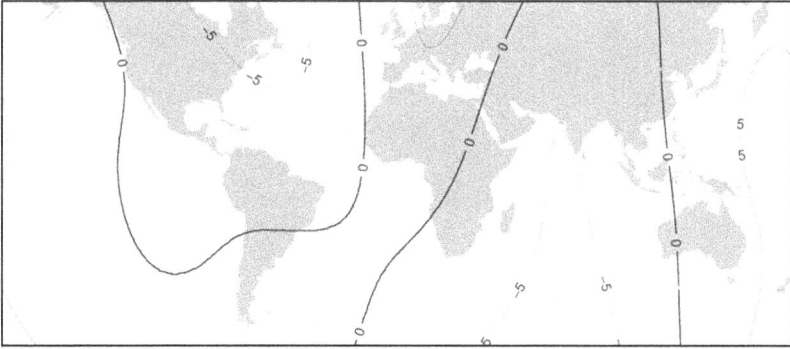

FIGURE 8.9. Isogonic chart from Constable (2000).

In the spring, melting water flows into temperate lakes, bringing a load of silt. Usually, some of these particles are composed of ferrous minerals, and therefore have tiny magnetic regions within them. As the silt particles slowly descend to the bottom, these magnetic regions align themselves with the local magnetic field. When this year's silt becomes trapped underneath successive layers, their alignments are preserved. Such annual deposits are called varves, and they can be dated by carbon-14 from organic material within the same layer. Lake varve deposits can provide a continuous record of magnetic field alignments for several millennia in some locations.

Pile up enough hearthstones, enough volcanic eruptions, and enough lake varves from enough times and in enough places around the world, and you can create magnetic models.

In recent years, several such models have been created. In 1998 Hongre, Hulot, and Khokhlov published[5] a third-order SHA model based on an archaeomagnetic dataset that relied primarily on hearthstone data. Like any third-order model, it was crude, but even a crude model is better than nothing. This model confirmed that magnetic declination at the time of Columbus was easterly in Western Europe, and westerly in the North Atlantic.

Two years later, Constable, Johnson, and Lund published another third-order magnetic model[6] for historical times. This

---

5. L. Hongre, G. Hulot, and A. Khokhlov, "An Analysis of the Geomagnetic Field over the Past 2000 Years," 311-335.

6. C. G. Constable, C. L. Johnson, and S. P. Lund, "Global Geomagnetic Field Models for the Past 3000 Years: Transient or Permanent Flux Lobes?," 358 991-1008.

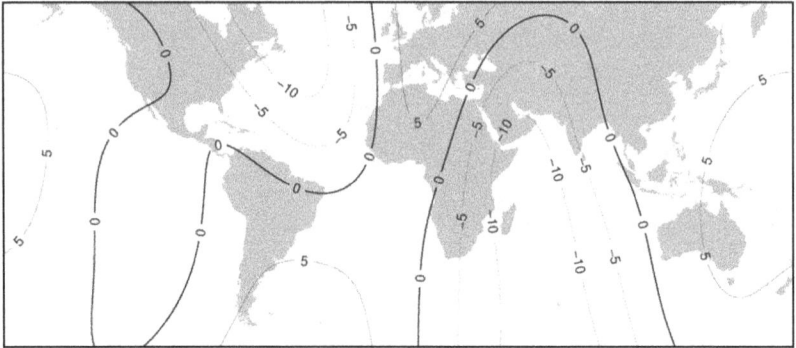

FIGURE 8.10. Isogonic chart from the CALS3K.1 model for 1493.

model was based on a different archaeomagnetic dataset, drawn primarily from lake varves. It confirmed the westerly declination in the North Atlantic, but the magnitude of this declination was considerably different from the earlier model of Hongre.

I was excited by the prospect of both of these new magnetic models. Could they at last be used to trace the transatlantic track in an acceptable manner? Alas, it turns out that neither of these models was capable of meeting the criteria that I had laid out in 1995. The Hongre model was not able to replicate the first voyage eastbound, while the Constable model was not able to recreate the second voyage westbound.

However, new lake varve data from all over the world continued to be published, and by 2003 a new SHA model of the magnetic field in historical times, using this new data, was published by Korte and Constable. The model is called the Continuous Archaeomagnetic and Lake Sediment model for 3,000 years, or CALS3K.1 for short (see Figure 8.9). This model took its data from many more sites and epochs than anything that had come before. And unlike the earlier attempts, CALS3K.1 was a full tenth-order model of the magnetic field, like the modern IGRF.

So how accurate is the CALS3K.1 model? As a tenth-order model, the spatial detail is as good as one could wish; but you cannot expect that CALS3K.1 will be as accurate as the IGRF, since the archaeomagnetic data that underlie CALS3K.1 are generally considered accurate to only about 2 degrees or so. Nevertheless, it is *possible* that at some epochs and in some

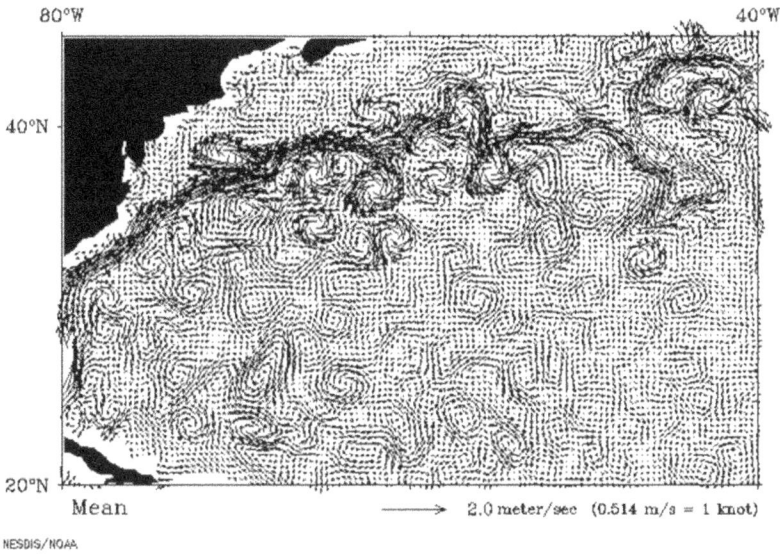

80°W   40°W

40°N

20°N
Mean   ⟶ 2.0 meter/sec (0.514 m/s = 1 knot)

NESDIS/NOAA

FIGURE 8.11. Satellite derived surface currents in the western North Atlantic, showing meso-scale eddies.

places, it might approach the half-degree accuracy of the modern IGRF. To know whether it does or not during the time of Columbus and in the North Atlantic, we will have to test the model. And in fact, we will use the same tests that I proposed in 1995: the two transatlantic crossings made by Columbus in the year 1493. And following those same criteria, we will have to accurately account for ocean currents.

In the open sea, far from the land, ocean currents behave a lot like winds in the atmosphere. Like winds, currents have a prevailing direction, in which they can be expected to move. And like winds, the actual direction experienced on any particular day might be quite different from, or even opposite to, the prevailing direction. This is because daily current direction is dominated by medium-scale structures called mesoeddies, which, like large high and low pressure systems in the atmosphere, form, move, and die over periods of several weeks. (You can see some of these eddies on Figure 8.11.) Further, there is a seasonal component to the formation of these eddies and currents. Therefore, it is impossible to determine the actual currents that Columbus's fleet experienced in 1492.

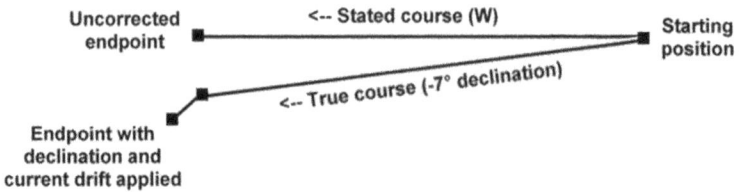

FIGURE 8.12. One hour's computation.

When we simulate an ocean voyage, it is very important to keep track of the errors inherent in the process. By far, the largest source of error is the drift of the ship due to the variability of ocean currents. If Doug Peck were to retrace Columbus's voyage a dozen different times, he would come out at a dozen different locations. Would these locations be clustered tightly or scattered widely? How can that be determined with confidence? Well, we could cross the ocean a dozen times to find out. But we don't have to. The Atlantic has already been crossed, not merely dozens of times, but thousands of times, by skilled navigators who have kept careful track of their daily positions. And those records still exist.

In the 1850s Matthew Fontaine Maury, remembered today as the U.S. Navy's first oceanographer, began collecting daily drift reports from American and Dutch navigators. Every day at noon, a nineteenth-century navigator would shoot the sun to give him his true position. He would then compare his true position to his dead-reckoning position, as computed by the ship's course and speed sailed from the previous day's noon fix. The difference in the two positions, if any, is due mostly to the set of the current—although the ship's leeway also plays a part. So by using the ship drift data, we account for the average effects of both current and leeway at a stroke.

Up until 1975, the U.S. Navy, and later the National Oceanographic and Atmospheric Administration, kept a running collection of this ship drift data, eventually growing to comprise some four million daily drift observations, about half of them taken in the North Atlantic. These are available on CD-ROM.[7]

---

7. http://www.nodc.noaa.gov/General/NODC-cdrom.html#oceandrft.

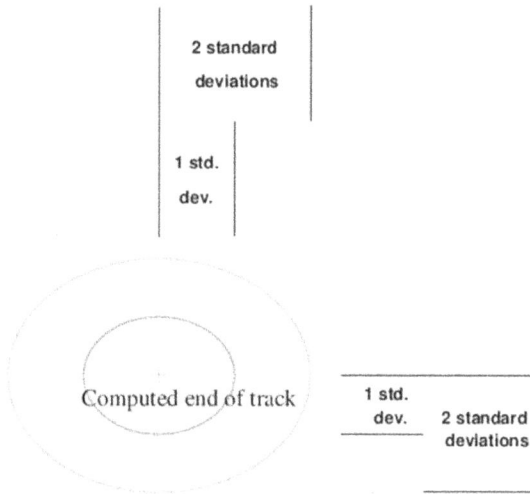

2 standard
deviations

1 std.
dev.

Computed end of track

1 std.
dev.   2 standard
        deviations

FIGURE 8.13. The error ellipse.

In order to compute the expected current drift at any position, I took all observations that are within one degree of the position in both latitude and longitude. To insure that I did not neglect the seasonality of currents, I also looked only at observations within thirty days of the desired date regardless of year. That gave me a subset of observations for that specific location and time of year, containing between several dozen and several hundred individual ship drift observations.

These individual observations are averaged, and the variance of the observations is determined both on the north-south axis and the east-west axis.

Here's how a typical computation works (see Figure 8.12). In my simulations, I recomputed Columbus's position for every hour of the voyage. Starting with the stated magnetic course and speed, as given in the log, I compute the magnetic declination at each hourly position according to the CALS3K.1 model to determine the true course sailed. Then I move the ship along the true course for its known speed. Finally, I compute the currents and apply one hour's worth of average drift for this date and location, while retaining the variances of the drift for later use. Then I repeat the whole process for the next hour, with the new starting position.

At the end of the voyage, we have two results: a final position, and a sum of all the current variances for the voyage (see Figure 8.13 on page 161). From the current variances we can compute the standard deviation of the current drift on both the north-south axis and the east-west axis. Because of the variability of currents, we cannot claim that the computed final position is exactly where one would end up if such a voyage were actually sailed. The best we can claim is that one would end up near the final position, and we can draw an error ellipse around the final position that shows the standard deviation that we determined from the variance of the currents. If the magnetic model is correct, it is quite likely that any actually sailed voyage would end up within, or pretty close to, this error ellipse.

To validate Korte's CALS3K.1 model of the magnetic field, let's look at Columbus's second voyage westbound, which, he told us, was sailed on a constant west-by-south magnetic course from Hierro in the Canary Islands. Since we do not have a log for this voyage, we have no idea of the speeds sailed on each day. Therefore, we will assume a constant average speed adequate for the fleet to arrive at Dominica in the West Indies after a remarkably fast 21-day crossing. Figure 8.14 is the computed end of the transatlantic track using the CALS3K.1 magnetic model. The error ellipse is 60 nautical miles wide north-south, and 90 nautical miles wide east-west. The black Maltese cross is the known landfall of Columbus on the second voyage. We know that the landfall was at this point, because Diego Alvarez Chanca tells us, in a letter written after the voyage, that Dominica was the first island seen on the morning of November 3, 1493, and shortly thereafter the island of Guadeloupe was seen. This specific order of seeing these islands as they rise above the horizon can only occur in a very small patch of the ocean, marked here.

After ten years of trying probably dozens of isogonic charts as the basis for such simulated voyages, it was extremely gratifying to see that the CALS3K.1 model actually got to the Dominica landfall. Of all the voyages, this second voyage westbound is in my experience by far the simulation most likely to fail. This is partly due to the fact that the error ellipse for this voyage is smaller than the ones for the first voyage, as we will see.

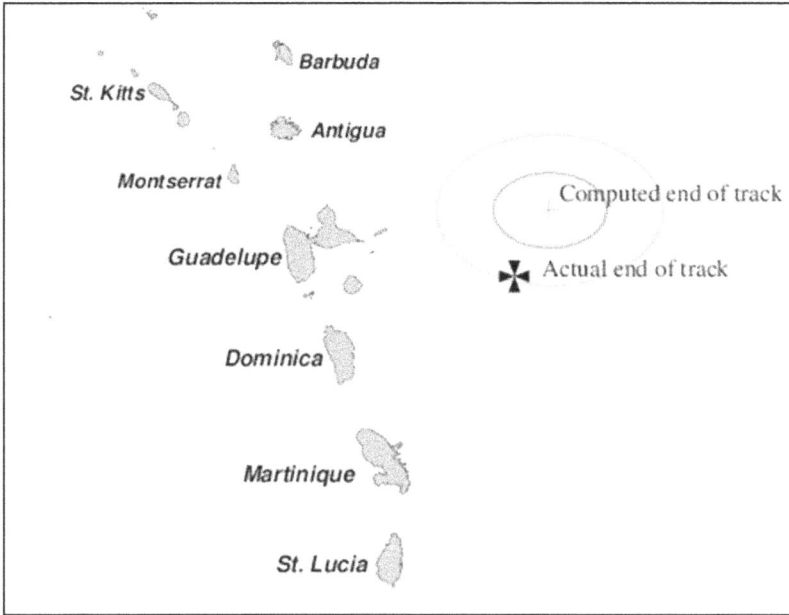

FIGURE 8.14. Endpoint of second voyage, using CALS3K.1 model.

Note also that the final computed position is a little to the north of the actual landfall. If we wanted to tinker with the model, we might be tempted to crank in a little extra westerly declination at this point. Since westerly declination draws you leftward regardless of your direction of travel, doing that would make the computed final position fit the actual landfall better. But as we shall see, there is a very good reason for not engaging in such tinkering—even beyond the obvious one of invalidating the science behind the model.

For our next validation test, let's look at the eastbound passage of Columbus's first voyage. In this case, we are blessed with the log of the first voyage, which records the actual courses and speeds sailed on each day. Following the same procedure, we can compute the end of the simulated voyage and see if it arrives at the Azores, as Columbus did on February 15, 1493. And in fact, it does, within the known limits of current variability (see Figure 8.15 on page 164). The first thing to notice is that the error ellipse is larger than it was for the voyage to Dominica; it's 83 nautical miles north-south and 104 nautical miles east-west. This is because this voyage passes through the middle of the North

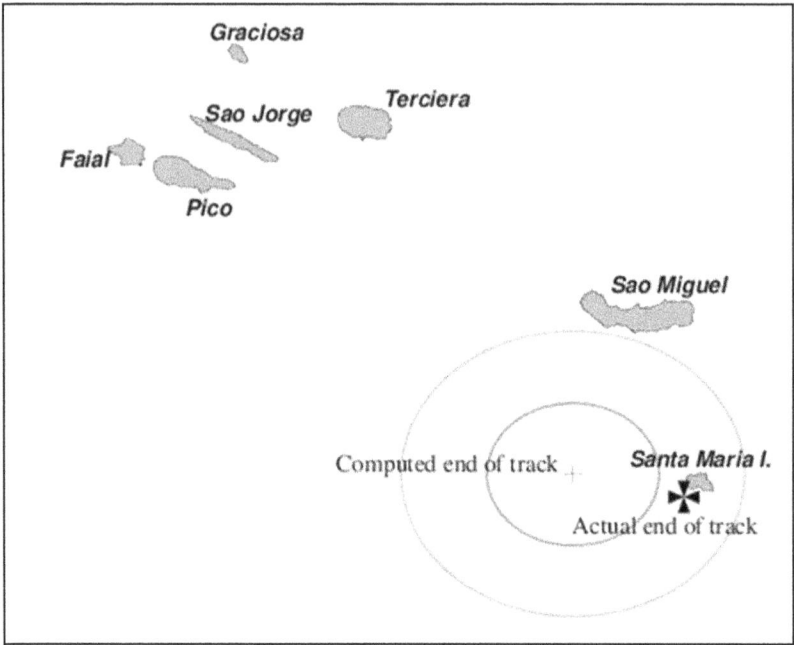

FIGURE 8.15. Endpoint of first voyage eastbound, using CALS3K.1

Atlantic gyre, a region of the sea long known for its fickle winds and unpredictable currents. Accordingly, our computed current variances are rather large, and the error ellipse reflects this.

Note that here the computed final position is remarkably close to the actual landfall at Santa Maria Island. Here we are not tempted to tinker with the model at all, since there seems to be no change that will make the computed position fit the actual landfall any better. But that also means that if we tinker with the model to improve the final position of the second voyage, we will inevitably make the final position of this simulated voyage fit worse. In other words, tinkering will not improve the overall situation one bit.

In my experience, it has been extraordinarily rare to find any magnetic model that can successfully recreate both of these voyages at the same time. That the CALS3K.1 model of Korte & Constable has done this is a stunning achievement and a tribute to twenty-first century science.

Finally, this magnetic model is not only successful, it is also strongly constrained. If the average magnetic declination in the

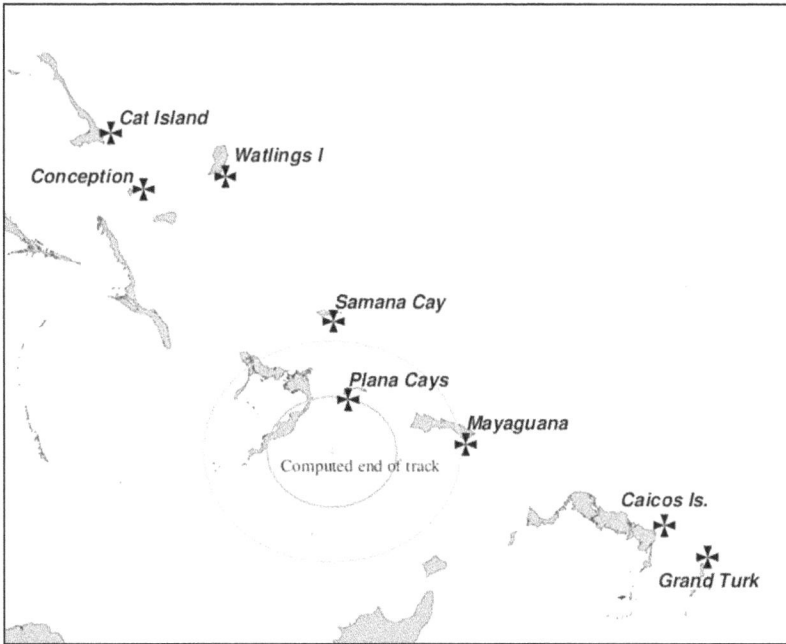

FIGURE 8.16. Endpoint of the first voyage westbound, using CALS3K.1.

North Atlantic at this epoch were different from the model by even a degree, one way or another, one or both of these two validation tests would fail. The actual average magnetic declination in the North Atlantic at the time of Columbus must have been very close to the CALS3K.1 model prediction.

Having validated the model, and having shown that the model is strongly constrained, naturally we want to know what the model predicts for the first voyage westbound. Can we, at long last, determine the location of the first landfall of Columbus in the New World? The model prediction is shown in Figure 8.16. The error ellipse is 83 nautical miles north-south by 100 nautical miles east-west.

In the previous chapter, we saw from multiple lines of evidence that there were some 33 leagues missing from the log of Columbus in the westbound passage. We also saw where the missing leagues were hiding and how they might be restored. In my simulation here, I have included those missing leagues. If I had not done so, the center of the error ellipse would have ended up just north of North Caicos Island, and Caicos would have been the only landfall island within the ellipse, although Mayaguana would have been a marginal case.

The Maltese crosses show 8 of the 10 landfall islands that have been proposed by various theorists. Given the variability of currents, it is not surprising that we cannot pin down the landfall to a single island on this basis alone. But although we may not be able to say where the landfall is, we can say with some confidence where the landfall isn't. Grand Turk was the favored landfall for much of the nineteenth century, and Watlings Island was the favored landfall for much of the twentieth century. Both of these are hard to support using the CALS3K.1 model.

Samana Cay lies just outside the error ellipse, yet close enough that it can't be eliminated on this basis alone. The two landfalls inside the error ellipse are Mayaguana, a theory that has never quite caught on for reasons that I can't fathom (since I've always thought it could make a pretty good theory) and closest of all, the Plana Cays.

From a personal perspective, I find this quite gratifying. In 1991 I first examined the courses and distances Columbus sailed through the Bahamas. On the basis of that inter-island track, I showed that the Plana Cays had by far the best inter-island track of all proposed landfalls. And now I can also say that Plana has the best transatlantic track of all proposed landfalls. So now I feel justified in saying that from a scientific perspective, the Columbus landfall debate is probably over. The CALS3K.1 model has very likely pounded the final nail in the dispute. At this point, there is simply no other theory that fits so much of the evidence so completely as the Plana Cays, Columbus's first landfall in the New World.

Afterword

THROUGHOUT this book, I have been writing with the assumption that the mystery of Guanahaní has been solved. In one sense, this is quite true. The Plana Cays theory is so clearly superior to all others in so many respects that it seems unlikely (to me, at least) that the issue will continue to be controversial for much longer. But if I am wrong about this, I stand ready to debate any who might support another theory. I can say this only because the Plana Cays theory has already been through the fire of informed criticism, thanks to the Round Robin, and because it has succeeded on the merits of the evidence.

Yet in a broader sense the problem is not solved, for there is still much work to do. As Thomas Kuhn wrote in *The Structure of Scientific Revolutions*, a new status quo cannot be reached until after a state of crisis has been reached, and after that crisis has been resolved. The crisis in the landfall problem came when the leagues-miles issue was settled in 1995, bringing about the falsification of the old status quo, the Watlings Island theory. But the resolution of a crisis requires that a new status quo be created in place of the old. This book is one step toward creating the new status quo.

When current history books address the Columbus landfall, they usually give Watlings Island, the official San Salvador, as the location. Old books cannot be changed, nor should they be. But new books need to be written reflecting the new reality. This process has already begun. Some years ago I stumbled across the article in Wikipedia, the online encyclopedia, about Guanahani and the landfall problem. I was surprised and pleased to discover that the article names the Plana Cays as the most likely landfall, and cites my research.

Recently, I received an e-mail from Dr. James E. Wadsworth, professor of history at Stonehill College in Easton, Massachusetts. Although his nominal reason for writing was to ask permission to use my map of Columbus's first voyage in his upcoming book, *Columbus and His First Voyage: A History in Documents*, his main point was, that after doing his own research and review of the literature, he had become convinced that the Plana Cays route was the one that made the most sense. So the tide is now turning. It has always been this way in science: when the revolution comes, the cumulative efforts of many fine and intelligent people are rendered obsolete at a stroke. This is the price of progress, and the price is high.

But there is a good reason to pay the price. Knowledge does not belong to any single person. It is the highest aspiration and the richest legacy of all humanity. If the mystery of Guanahani has not been solved, then we have all failed, every one of us—even those of us who pursued the most promising ideas. Because that means we will have created no new knowledge; our only legacy will be greater doubt and confusion than we had when we started. But if a new status quo does emerge, then we have all succeeded, every one of us—even those who advocated the false trails and the dead ends. Each failure carries with it the seeds of success, and each dead end limits the area in which success might finally be found. And every one of us—Molander and Dunwoody, Peck and Pérez, Henige and Kelley, and so many others—is the author of that success. It is a legacy of which we can all be proud.

And it may yet be that I will have to pay that price myself. In 2005 Korte and Constable updated the CALS3K.1 model with new data and used a new methodology to produce a new model covering 7,000 years, which they called CALS7K.2. The isogonic chart for 1493 under CALS7K.2 looked surprisingly familiar: it was a fairly good match for Van Bemmeln's chart of 1899, with an agonic line—a line of zero magnetic declination—sweeping east and west across the southern North Atlantic. When I ran the model against Columbus's voyages, the result was therefore not surprising: the track of the second voyage westbound strayed north, just as it had for the Van Bemmeln chart. And, just like Van Bemmeln, the track of the first voyage westbound ended up in the vicinity of Watlings.

But CALS7K.2 is not the end of it either. Already, one scientist has noted that CALS7K.2 is not as accurate as the earlier CALS3K.1 model in predicting magnetic declinations in the first millennium BC, apparently due to the rather different methodology that the two models employ; some scientists have advocated going back to CALS3K.1 for work during those time periods. Archaeomagnetism is a rapidly changing science, with new results being published constantly and new data constantly being taken in the field. The final word on the subject is yet to be spoken. But for now, only CALS3K.1 has been validated against both of Columbus's 1493 voyages; and I suspect, given the rather sharp constraints of those known voyages, that any future model that can meet those tests will turn out to look a lot like CALS3K.1.

The Plana Cays do not officially have individual names; they are called East Plana and West Plana by convention only. If the Bahamian Parliament ever sees fit to name the islands themselves, it seems to me that *Guanahani Cay* is the only reasonable name for the western cay, where Columbus first came ashore near the southern tip of the island. Some might think that presumptuous, but it seems to me that renaming Watlings Island as "San Salavdor" was already rather presumptuous, so there is no reason not to continue that trend, albeit in a more historically correct manner.

According to research by Ramón Didiez Burgos, the eastern cay was called Mayaguaín by the Lucayans; but it hardly seems likely that this name would be resurrected, given the close proximity of Mayaguana Island. If it were up to me, I would call the eastern cay either *Triana Cay* or *Rodriguez Cay*, after Rodrigo de Triana, the sharp-eyed sailor aboard the *Pinta* who was the first to sight land. He is also known as Juan Rodriguez Bermejo in some sources; but names in the fifteenth century were not as fixed as they are today, and according to Alice Bache Gould, they are the same person. (Triana is a town in Andalusia near Palos. If "Juan Rodriguez Bermejo" follows modern form, Rodriguez would be his father's family name, and it seems likely that Triana was his hometown.) The European Space Agency has already named a space probe *Triana* in his honor, and a permanent geographical name seems an even more appropriate tribute.

If these suggestions are ever adopted, the two Plana Cays would carry one Taino name and one European name, a permanent reminder of the first encounter between those two cultures that changed the world forever.

Appendix A
The Westbound Voyage: Log and Track

FOLLOWING is the output from my simulated voyage from Hierro in the Canary Islands to Guanahani, using the CALS3K.1 model. Leagues are from the log (but with corrections as explained in chapter 7) and converted to modern nautical miles at the rate of 2.67 Leagues per nmi.

THE WESTARD VOYAGE: LOG AND TRACK

Date	Leg	Lat.	Long.	Course	Lgs.	North current set (m/hr)	East current set (m/hr)	N-S current variance total (A) (nmi)	E-W current variance total (A) (nmi)	Magnetic Decl. (degrees)	Notes
Sep 8		28.000	-17.000	0	0					-2.62	
Sep 8	1	27.929	-17.478	270	9	-395	-169.8	73.5	73.3	-3.02	B
Sep 9	1	27.853	-18.402	270	18	-335.9	-176.1	147.1	144.9	-3.82	B
Sep 9	2	28.046	-20.220	281.5	36	-293.5	-221.4	147.1	144.9	-5.12	
Sep 10	1	27.801	-23.288	270	60	-158.6	-255.7	197.2	227.8	-5.6	
Sep 11	1	27.675	-24.531	270	24	-231.3	-366.8	263.4	285.3	-5.98	B
Sep 11	2	27.555	-25.557	270	20	-275.8	-243.2	263.4	285.3	-6.53	
Sep 12	1	27.348	-27.240	270	33	-214.2	-172.7	302.9	348.1	-7.02	
Sep 13	1	27.099	-28.924	270	33	-345.4	-198.9	341.5	443.2	-7.29	
Sep 14	1	26.944	-29.971	270	20	-199.2	-240	379.3	529.7	-7.64	B
Sep 15	1	26.716	-31.591	270	32	-196.5	-172.9	409	580.1	-7.99	
Sep 16	1	26.460	-33.583	270	39	-85.7	-306.6	452.3	688.9	-8.29	
Sep 17	1	26.112	-36.072	270	50	-144.3	-159.3	498.9	761.6	-8.43	
Sep 18	1	25.739	-38.798	270	55	-72.3	-166.7	539	803.7	-8.43	
Sep 19	1	25.583	-40.079	286.88	25	33.9	-267.2	570.3	855.1	-8.45	
Sep 20	1	25.647	-40.572	270	9	25.6	-228.6	604.7	947.1	-8.43	B
Sep 21	1	25.546	-41.402	270	16	16.8	-211.6	644.8	1040	-8.43	B
Sep 22	1	25.942	-43.140	292.5	36	28	-69.6	683.3	1138.1	-8.47	B
Sep 23	1	26.752	-44.498	315	32	-177.6	-350.1	710.9	1205.4	-8.59	B
Sep 24	1	26.651	-45.248	270	15	-22.4	-154	758.1	1283.1	-8.51	
Sep 25	1	26.617	-45.475	270	4.5	-42.3	-50	809.7	1374	-8.48	
Sep 25	2	26.004	-45.980	225	17	-35.2	-18.5	809.7	1374	-8.28	

Date	Leg	Lat.	Long.	Course	Lgs.	North current set (m/hr)	East current set (m/hr)	N-S current variance total (A) (nmi)	E-W current variance total (A) (nmi)	Magnetic Decl. (degrees)	Notes
Sep 26	1	25.951	-46.385	270	8	-39.8	-236.2	872.3	1455	-8.22	
Sep 26	2	25.758	-46.548	225	6	-53.6	-150.8	872.3	1455	-8.15	
Sep 26	3	25.653	-47.375	270	17	-24.7	-219.8	872.3	1455	-8.02	
Sep 27	1	25.501	-48.597	270	24	-21.4	-216.2	920.3	1510	-7.8	
Sep 28	1	25.458	-49.307	270	14	190.3	-116.1	974.1	1583.8	-7.67	
Sep 29	1	25.340	-50.526	270	24	106.9	-210.3	1035	1649.8	-7.44	
Sep 30	1	25.248	-51.282	270	14	-56.6	-310.3	1069.2	1722.3	-7.27	
Oct 1	1	25.114	-52.540	270	25	18	-172.8	1108	1790.3	-6.99	
Oct 2	1	24.923	-54.489	270	39	63.3	-217	1153.5	1863.5	-6.52	
Oct 3	1	24.697	-56.806	270	47	8.1	-131.6	1229	1934.8	-5.93	
Oct 4	1	24.463	-59.901	270	63	167.2	-143.5	1276.8	2018.2	-5.12	
Oct 5	1	24.273	-62.719	270	57	93.2	-209.4	1322.9	2087	-4.37	
Oct 6	1	24.163	-64.735	270	40	77	-310.7	1384.4	2148.5	-3.85	
Oct 7	1	24.093	-65.877	270	23	-33.6	-235.3	1429.1	2219.9	-3.57	
Oct 7	2	23.998	-66.122	247.5	5	26.7	-210.5	1429.1	2219.9	-3.47	
Oct 8	1	23.780	-66.659	247.5	12	24.2	-144.9	1485.3	2264.3	-3.3	
Oct 9	1	23.618	-66.829	225	5	91.9	-153.1	1543.3	2317.9	-3.23	
Oct 9	2	23.647	-67.027	281.25	4	107.9	-157.5	1543.3	2317.9	-3.19	
Oct 9	3	23.229	-68.032	247.5	23	122.9	-160.5	1543.3	2317.9	-2.89	
Oct 10	1	22.146	-70.652	247.5	59	140	-202.1	1609.2	2380.8	-2.16	
Oct 11	1	21.657	-71.890	247.5	27	101	-534.8	1669.1	2461.1	-1.85	
Oct 11	2	21.636	-72.992	270	23	145.6	-410.6	1669.1	2461.1	-1.67	
Oct 12	2										C

Total Voyage: 1142.5 leagues

Notes.

A. Currents are given in meters per hour; to get knots, divide by 1,852. Currents are measured once per leg (which is usually less than a whole day) but current variances are only measured once per day, because the underlying data was only collected once per day. Variances always increase during the voyage, but only on the first leg of any given day. Current variances are given in nautical miles per day. To get the standard deviation on any given day, take the square root of the variance. At the end of the voyage, the standard deviations are 40.9 nmi north-south, and 49.6 nmi. east-west. Positions and magnetic declinations are given for the end of each leg's run.

B. The given distance is a correction from the *Diario* of Las Casas, as the evidence in chapter 7 shows.

C. After sighting land, Columbus wrote that the land was two leagues distant, but he does not say in which direction. In the Plana Cays scenario, the most likely direction would have been north or northwest. Including that datum would have put the final endpoint for the simulation at 21.726 N, 73.000 W. This would not alter the conclusion of the analysis in any way.

Appendix B
The Eastbound Voyage: Log and Track

FOLLOWING is the output from my simulated return voyage from Samana Bay, Hispaniola, to Santa Maria in the Azores using the CALS3K.1 model. Leagues are (generally) from the log, and converted to modern nautical miles at the rate of 2.67 Leagues per nmi.

THE EASTWARD VOYAGE: LOG AND TRACK

Date	Leg	Lat.	Long.	Course	Lgs.	North current t set (m/hr)	East current t set (m/hr)	N-S current variance total (A) (nmi)	E-W current variance total (A) (nmi)	Magnetic Dec. (degrees)	Notes
Jan 15		19.167	-69.325	0	0						
Jan 16	1	19.154	-69.238	101.25	2	160.8	-582	112.1	139	-1.81	
Jan 16	2	19.327	-68.546	78.75	16	152.6	-543	112.1	139	-1.96	
Jan 16	3	19.268	-68.482	135	2	168.3	-466.7	112.1	139	-1.98	
Jan 16	4	19.591	-68.050	56.25	12	174.8	-453	112.1	139	-2.1	
Jan 17	1	20.165	-67.314	56.25	21	175.2	-463.5	216.1	262.1	-2.36	
Jan 17	2	20.196	-66.829	90	11	117.8	-403.1	216.1	262.1	-2.47	
Jan 18	1	20.137	-66.391	101.25	10	125.9	-390	277	346.4	-2.55	
Jan 18	2	19.968	-66.102	123.75	7.5	134.6	-378.6	277	346.4	-2.57	
Jan 18	3	20.646	-66.040	11.25	15	137.9	-386.6	277	346.4	-2.72	
Jan 19	1	21.274	-65.967	11.25	14	149.5	-360.2	332.8	442.4	-2.86	
Jan 19	2	21.898	-65.599	33.75	16	168.2	-339.6	332.8	442.4	-3.07	
Jan 19	3	22.237	-65.294	45	10	140	-308.9	332.8	442.4	-3.22	
Jan 19	4	22.667	-65.042	33.75	11	146.7	-319.4	332.8	442.4	-3.37	
Jan 20	1	22.840	-64.903	45	5	80.3	-300.3	414.2	526.3	-3.46	
Jan 20	2	22.760	-64.815	135	2.75	63.2	-292.7	414.2	526.3	-3.48	
Jan 20	3	23.149	-64.712	22.5	9	70.9	-299.9	414.2	526.3	-3.58	
Jan 21	1	23.773	-64.643	11.25	14	66.8	-298.8	497.2	599	-3.73	
Jan 21	2	24.279	-64.471	22.5	12	-13.7	-241	497.2	599	-3.89	
Jan 21	3	25.170	-64.157	22.5	21	9	-103.1	497.2	599	-4.19	
Jan 22	1	25.510	-64.036	22.5	8	26.5	-46.8	558.2	667.4	-4.3	
Jan 22	2	25.711	-64.011	11.25	4.5	74.9	-62.1	558.2	667.4	-4.37	
Jan 22	3	25.814	-63.918	45	3	80.5	-127.8	558.2	667.4	-4.41	

Date	Leg	Lat.	Long.	Course	Lgs.	North current t set (m/hr)	East current t set (m/hr)	N-S current variance total (A) (nmi)	E-W current variance total (A) (nmi)	Magnetic Dec. (degrees)	Notes
Jan 22	4	26.124	-63.272	67.5	15	69.5	-154.9	558.2	667.4	-4.65	
Jan 23	1	26.948	-62.802	33.75	21	25.7	-259.1	643.6	764.9	-4.98	
Jan 23	2	27.206	-62.578	45	7.5	27.3	-271.2	643.6	764.9	-5.11	
Jan 23	3	27.360	-62.261	67.5	7.5	-36.8	-278.5	643.6	764.9	-5.23	
Jan 24	1	27.729	-61.937	45	11	-76.6	-205.7	682.9	834.3	-5.43	
Jan 24	2	28.016	-61.335	67.5	14	-67.9	-167.2	682.9	834.3	-5.66	
Jan 25	1	28.211	-60.918	67.5	9.5	-85.6	-55.1	718.5	917.7	-5.82	
Jan 25	2	28.273	-60.899	22.5	1.5	-47	-77.3	718.5	917.7	-5.86	
Jan 25	3	28.418	-60.601	67.5	7	-35.9	-93.4	718.5	917.7	-5.97	
Jan 26	1	28.352	-59.915	101.25	14	-76.7	-132.7	754.4	987.8	-6.13	
Jan 26	2	28.288	-59.678	112.5	5	-91.2	-217.6	754.4	987.8	-6.16	
Jan 26	3	28.147	-59.487	135	5	-34.1	-259.8	754.4	987.8	-6.19	
Jan 26	4	28.409	-59.541	0	6	-67.2	-302.9	754.4	987.8	-6.25	
Jan 27	1	29.115	-59.396	18.75	16.5	-114.2	-257.3	817.1	1090.1	-6.47	
Jan 27	2	29.318	-59.214	45	6	-116.2	-119.4	817.1	1090.1	-6.58	
Jan 27	3	29.377	-59.088	67.5	3	-135.8	-154.1	817.1	1090.1	-6.63	
Jan 28	1	29.651	-58.488	67.5	14	-144.3	-91.9	879.4	1189.7	-6.87	
Jan 29	1	29.993	-57.748	67.5	17.5	-197.4	-158.9	926.8	1282	-7.15	
Jan 30	1	30.126	-57.434	67.5	7	-179.3	17.8	960.1	1366.4	-7.27	
Jan 30	2	29.540	-57.213	168.75	13.5	-158.4	20.7	960.1	1366.4	-7.17	
Jan 31	1	29.864	-57.192	11.25	7.5	-173.1	-104.2	986.7	1459.9	-7.25	
Jan 31	2	30.160	-56.919	45	8.75	-208.8	-3	986.7	1459.9	-7.39	
Jan 31	3	30.445	-56.312	67.5	13.5	-156.3	53.9	986.7	1459.9	-7.62	
Feb 1	1	31.446	-54.245	67.5	45.75	-165.1	107.8	1023.8	1587.2	-8.37	

THE EASTWARD VOYAGE: LOG AND TRACK (cont.)

Date	Leg	Lat.	Long.	Course	Lgs.	North current t set (m/hr)	East current t set (m/hr)	N-S current variance total (A) (nmi)	E-W current variance total (A) (nmi)	Magnetic Dec. (degrees)	Notes
Feb 2	1	32.080	-52.950	67.5	29.25	-181.5	-43.5	1070.1	1605.5	-8.83	
Feb 3	1	33.333	-50.404	67.5	56	-282.8	134.2	1125.9	1719.5	-9.61	
Feb 4	1	33.823	-48.772	78.75	32.5	-261.3	120.2	1160.5	1800.2	-9.97	
Feb 4	2	33.955	-47.735	90	19.25	-186.1	203.4	1160.5	1800.2	-10.13	
Feb 5	1	34.230	-45.491	90	41	-232.7	316.9	1202.5	1866.6	-10.37	
Feb 6	1	34.720	-41.529	90	73.75	-493.9	225.4	1676.4	1953	-10.5	
Feb 7	1	35.105	-38.561	90	54.5	-253.5	260.2	1729.5	2041	-10.33	
Feb 8	1	35.103	-37.869	98.65	12	-144.8	290.3	1787.8	2130.3	-10.23	
Feb 8	2	34.599	-37.470	157.5	13	-162.7	164.7	1787.8	2130.3	-10.1	
Feb 9	1	34.481	-37.377	157.5	3	-193.8	185.9	1844.6	2195.3	-10.07	
Feb 9	2	34.641	-36.805	78.75	11	-231.7	199.6	1844.6	2195.3	-10	B
Feb 9	3	34.816	-36.642	45	5	-205.7	179.1	1844.6	2195.3	-9.99	
Feb 9	4	34.870	-36.145	90	9	-207.9	209.5	1844.6	2195.3	-9.92	
Feb 10	1	35.239	-33.026	90	57.25	-268.1	224.5	1921.2	2284.9	-9.31	
Feb 11	1	35.570	-30.004	90	55.5	-237.5	140.3	1991.4	2376.4	-8.47	
Feb 12	1	35.717	-28.366	90	29.75	-192	115.3	2049.9	2456.5	-7.9	
Feb 13	1	35.814	-26.913	90	26.5	-273.3	64.5	2118	2583.4	-7.35	
Feb 14	1	36.152	-26.356	56.25	13	-359.7	133.4	2171.5	2609	-7.14	
Feb 14	2	36.298	-25.986	67.5	7.5	-355	166.9	2171.5	2609	-7.01	
Feb 14	3	36.371	-25.891	45	2.5	-324.6	181.5	2171.5	2609	-6.96	
Feb 15	1	36.618	-25.243	67.5	13	-312.3	155.3	2216.9	2684.6	-6.71	
Feb 15	2	36.725	-24.999	67.5	5	-207.4	246.9	2216.9	2684.6	-6.69	

Total voyage: 1073 leagues

Notes:

A. Currents are given in meters per hour; to get knots, divide by 1,852. Currents are measured once per leg (which is usually less than a whole day), but current variances are only measured once per day, because the underlying data was only collected once per day. Variances always increase during the voyage, but only on the first leg of any given day. Current variances are given in nautical miles per day. To get the standard deviation on any given day, take the square root of the variance. At the end of the voyage, the standard deviations are 47.1 nmi north-south, and 51.8 nmi. east-west. Positions and magnetic declinations are given for the end of each leg's run.

B. The log entry of February 9 has four legs, summarized below:

Course	Leagues
SSE	3
S by E	??
NE	5
E	9

The S by E leg has no recorded distance, leading John McElroy to assume a distance of zero, and Jim Kelley to assume a distance of 3 leagues (although he does allow that this is a guess). But there are several good reasons to suppose that this missing distance should be much greater, more in the range of 9 to 18 leagues.

1) *The Rising Wind Argument.* The previous day's run (Feb. 8) was 25.5 leagues, but the following day's run (Feb. 10) was a phenomenal 54 leagues—the third-best day's run on the whole voyage. In every other case of a day's run of 50 leagues or more, the 50+ league run was preceded by a creditable run of 28 to 35 leagues. If we allow no distance (as does McElroy) the 54-league run of Feb. 10 would be preceded by a measly 17-league run:

perhaps half of what we would otherwise expect. In order to fit the established pattern, the missing distance must be at least 11 leagues, and perhaps as much as 18.

Further, every other 50+ L run was the end of a two-day pattern of increasing distance. To fit this pattern, the run of Feb. 9 must be greater than the 25.5 league run of Feb. 8. This implies that the missing distance must be at least 9 leagues.

2) *The Average Speed Argument.* The average speed of the previous day's run was just over 1 L per hour. The final 9 L leg of Feb. 9 was accomplished in 8 hours, again resulting in an average speed of just over 1 L per hour. If the average speed for the entire day of Feb. 9 were the same as the final leg, that would imply a total day's run of 27 leagues, and a missing distance of 10 leagues.

3) *The Missing Time Argument.* This is really an extension of the previous argument. The last leg of the day started at 10:00 a.m. The times of the other legs are not recorded, but we can make reasonable guesses. At an average speed of about 1 L per hour, the NE (5 L) leg should have taken about 4.5 hours, which would mean starting at about 5:30 a.m. The first leg of the day should have taken about 3 hours, ending about 9:00 p.m. That leaves a gap of 8.5 hours for the missing distance leg, again implying a missing distance of 9 or 10 leagues at the same speed as the final leg.

4) *The Dead Reckoning by Chart Argument.* On February 27, Columbus wrote that he was 125 leagues from Cape San Vicente, 108 leagues from Santa Maria, and 80 leagues from Madeira. This works out to a point very near 37° 11' N, 17° 36' W: a point from which the distances to Cape Saint Vicente, Santa Maria, and Madeira are in a 125:108:80 ratio. The actual distances are 411 nm, 355 nm, and 263 nm, respectively, which is 3.29 nmi. per league.

Question: How did Columbus know he was 80 leagues from Madeira? Or 125 leagues from Cape San Vicente? Or any distance from any point that was beyond the horizon and that he had not visited? Answer: In dead-reckoning navigation, the navigator marks his position on the chart each day (or more frequently, if necessary). The navigator determines distances to other points by direct measurement of the chart, using the scale of leagues printed on the chart. These distances taken from the chart allow us to determine the scale of the chart by comparison to the known distances. On February 27, he simply measured the distances from his pinprick position to Madeira, Cape San Vicente, and Santa Maria using the scale of leagues. So the chart that Columbus was actually using had a scale of leagues that was about 3.3 nm per league, pretty close to the Portuguese Maritime League commonly used throughout Iberia.

On February 7 Columbus recorded that he was 75 leagues south of the latitude of Flores in the Azores, which he must have determined by measuring his chart. Three days later, after making some distance southward, Columbus recorded that he was at the latitude of Nafe (Casablanca) also determined by measuring his chart. Let's assume that the southward components during that time were as follows:

Date	Leagues	Course	Perceived Southing (L)
Feb 8	3	E	0
	9	E by S	1.76
	13.5	SSE	12.47
Feb 9	3	SSE	2.77
	11 ?	S by E	10.79 ?
	5	NE	-3.54
	9	E	0

The total amount of southward distance made during this time was therefore 24.3 leagues. This means that on February 10, when Columbus thought he was at the latitude of Nafe, Columbus also thought he was 75 + 24.3 = 99.3 leagues south of the latitude of Flores, as determined by chart measurement. The southern cape of Flores is at latitude 39° 21', and Nafe is at 33° 39', a difference of 5° 42', or 342 nm. So dividing, we find 342 ÷ 99.3 = 3.4 nm per league on Columbus's chart: not perfect, but a reasonable fit with the February 27 chart scale measurement of 3.3 nm per league. (The fit would be perfect if the missing distance were 16 leagues.) But assuming zero leagues for the missing distance results in a chart scale of about

3.9 nm per league, which is badly out of whack with the Feb. 27 measurement.

In light of all this, I have used 11 leagues for the missing distance here. Although I may be slightly wrong, I believe this is closer to the truth than any previous guess. Keen-eyed critics will notice that this change has moved the end-of-track slightly from the version I put up on my website in 2004. The conclusions of the analysis are unaffected.

Appendix C
Columbus Landfall Scorecard

BY now you probably realize that the accuracy or importance of every one of these clues has been challenged by someone or other. But that doesn't necessarily imply, as Round Robin member Neil Sealy once said, that the exercise is junk. Islands are abbreviated in the columns below as follows: Pla=Plana Cays; May=Mayaguana; Sam=Samana Cay; Con=Conception Island; Cai=Caicos; GrT=Grand Turk Island; Wat=Watlings Island; Egg=Egg Island; Cat=Cat Island.

The scoring system (from 0 to 3):

0 = does not fit the evidence, requires assumption of major error
1 = poor fit to the evidence, requires unusual interpretation
2 = reasonable fit with the evidence
3 = perfect fit with the evidence

COLUMBUS LANDFALL SCORECARD

Clue	Pla	May	Sam	Con	Cai	GrT	Wat	Egg	Cat
Newest model of the geomagnetic field in the fifteenth century, combined with analysis of the transatlantic track, points to a landfall in the south-central Bahamas.	3	3	2	1	2	1	1	0	1
Analysis of the log indicates Columbus could not have been a celestial navigator.	3	3	3	3	3	3	3	0	3
References on seventeenth and eighteenth century maps showing Guanahani.	0	0	0	2	0	0	3	0	3
Juan de la Cosa map shows Guanahani as a multiple island.	3	0	0	0	3	0	0	3	0
Juan de la Cosa map shows that Guanahani islets are small.	3	0	3	3	0	3	1	3	0
Juan de la Cosa map shows Guanahani on an east-west axis.	3	3	3	1	3	0	0	3	0
Juan de la Cosa map shows Guanahani north of Cape Mola, Hispaniola.	3	3	3	1	1	0	2	1	1
Columbus saw a light on the night of October11. Theory has a place for such a light to be.	3	1	1	3	3	1	1	1	3
Columbus does not say that there is more than one island at island I.	0	3	3	3	0	3	3	0	3
There was a large pond in the middle of Island I.	1	2	0	3	0	2	3	3	3
Columbus explored "the other part, which is the eastern part" of Island I by boat on October 14.	3	2	3	3	2	1	1	3	2
The boat trip went "the length of the island."	3	0	2	3	0	0	0	3	0
The boat trip went NNE along Island I.	3	3	0	3	0	3	2	3	0
There was a surrounding reef at Island I.	3	3	3	3	3	3	1	1	0
Between the reef and the island was a large harbor.	2	3	2	2	3	3	3	1	0
Columbus reported entrance through reef was "very narrow."	3	3	3	3	3	?	1	3	0
There was a peninsula with a narrow neck at Island I.	1	3	1	2	1	1	2	2	0
The population of Island I was in the range 500-1,100.	3	1	2	1	1	3	1	1	1

Clue	Pla	May	Sam	Con	Cai	GrT	Wat	Egg	Cat
Many islands were seen at various distances after leaving Island I, some closer than five leagues.	2	0	0	0	3	3	0	3	0
It was 5 to 7 leagues from I to II.	2	0	3	1	0	3	3	1	2
Island II has a coast running north-south.	3	3	3	3	2	3	3	0	0
The N-S coast of II faces Island I.	3	3	0	0	1	3	1	0	0
The N-S coast of II is 5 leagues long.	3	3	3	0	0	3	0	1	0
The E-W coast of II is 10+ leagues long.	3	3	3	0	2	3	0	1	0
The N-S coast of Island II was (by clear implication) not followed.	3	3	3	3	3	3	1	3	0
Columbus reported seeing Island III from Island II.	2	2	2	3	0	0	3	0	3
Columbus sailed on an E-W course from Island II to Island III.	3	3	3	1	3	1	1	3	0
The distance from Island II to Island III was 8 or 9 leagues.	2	2	2	1	0	0	1	2	0
Columbus arrived at a cape where coasts ran NNW-SSE.	3	3	3	1	3	0	1	1	0
Island III had a coastline running NNW-SSE.	3	3	3	2	0	0	2	3	1
Island III was more than 20 leagues long.	3	3	3	3	2	1	3	3	3
A harbor two leagues from the end of Island III.	3	3	3	0	0	3	0	3	0
There was a small island in harbor's mouth.	3	3	3	3	2	0	3	1	1
The two harbor entrances at Island III were "very narrow."	3	3	3	3	1	3	3	0	1
After leaving the harbor at Island III, Columbus sailed NW.	3	3	3	2	0	0	2	1	1
After leaving harbor to the NW, Columbus reported a coast running E-W.	3	3	3	1	3	1	1	3	1
Columbus sailed ESE on the night of October 17.	3	3	3	3	3	3	3	0	3
Columbus continued his attempted circumnavigation of Island III on October 18.	3	3	3	3	1	1	3	0	3

COLUMBUS LANDFALL SCORECARD (cont.)

Clue	Pla	May	Sam	Con	Cai	GrT	Wat	Egg	Cat
After leaving Island III, Columbus "returned" to Island IV, "which had been left behind."	3	3	3	0	2	2	0	0	0
Columbus did not sight Island IV until three hours after leaving Island III.	3	3	3	1	1	1	1	0	1
Columbus sighted Island IV to the east after sailing SE from Island III.	3	3	3	0	0	0	0	2	0
Columbus arrived at Island IV at the northern end.	3	3	3	3	3	3	3	0	3
The coast of Island IV runs west from the northern point.	0	0	0	0	3	3	0	0	0
The coast of Island IV is12 leagues from point of arrival to Cabo Hermoso.	0	0	0	0	3	3	0	1	0
There were many ponds near Cabo del Isleo (at the northern end of Island IV).	3	3	3	1	1	1	1	0	1
There was a large bight northeast from Cabo Hermoso.	3	3	3	3	3	3	3	0	3
From within the bight, there was a way southwest that was "very roundabout."	3	3	3	3	0	0	3	0	3
Columbus departed Island IV from northern end.	3	3	3	3	3	3	3	0	3
Columbus's initial course was WSW from Island IV.	3	3	3	3	2	2	3	0	3
After leaving Island IV, Columbus was seven leagues from Cabo Verde on Island III.	3	3	3	0	0	0	0	0	0
Cabo Verde is "in the western part of the southern part" of Island III.	3	3	3	3	3	3	3	0	3
It is 23 leagues from Cabo Verde Fix to Ragged Islands.	3	3	3	3	0	0	3	1	3
Columbus reports that Island IV is 8 leagues from Island I.	1	1	1	0	3	0	0	0	0
Total Score	136	126	123	96	87	85	85	64	65
Average Score	2.5	2.3	2.3	1.8	1.6	1.6	1.6	1.2	1.2

Bibliography

Associated Press. "Geographer says Columbus didn't land at accepted site." *Lancaster Intelligencer-Journal.* October 16, 1989.

Atlas de Cuba. (Instituto cubano de Geodesia y Cartografia, La Habana, 1978).

Casas, Bartolome de Las. *Historia de las Indias.* (Mexico: Fondo de Cultura Economica, 1951).

Castleman, Bruce A. Cmdr USN. "Navigators in the 1490's." *Proceedings of the U.S. Naval Institute.* 118/12 (December 1992) 39-43.

Colon, Cristobal. *Textos y documentos completes. 2nd edition,* Consuelo Varela. ed., (Madrid: Alianza Editorial, 1992).

Colon, Fernando. *The Life of the Admiral Christopher Columbus.* trans. Benjamin Keen (New Brunswick: Rutgers University Press, 1959).

Constable, C. G., C. L. Johnson, & S. P. Lund. "Global Geomagnetic Field Models for the Past 3000 Years: Transient or Permanent Flux Lobes?" *Philosophical Transactions of the Royal Society of London.* ser. A., 358 (2000) 991-1008.

Cook, Sherburne Friend and Woodrow Wilson Borah. "The aboriginal population of Hispaniola." in *Essays in population history: Mexico and the Caribbean.* vol. 1. (Berkeley: Univ of California Press, 1971).

Craton, Michael and Gail Saunders. *Islanders in the Stream: A History of the Bahamian People.* (Athens and London: University of Georgia Press, 1992).

Davies, Thomas D. "New evidence places Peary at the Pole." *National Geographic* 177:1 (1990) 44.

Didiez Burgos, Ramon J. *Guanahani y Mayaguain.* (Santo Domingo: Editoria Cultural Dominicana, 1974).

Dunn, Oliver and James E. Kelley Jr., trans. *The Diario of Christopher Columbus's First Voyage to America, 1492-1493.* (Norman and London: University of Oklahoma Press, 1989).

Dyson, John. With nautical research by Luis Miguel Coin Cuenca. *Columbus: for gold, God, and glory.* (New York: Simon & Schuster, 1991).

Fox, Gustavus V. "An Attempt to Solve the Problem of the First Landing Place of Columbus in the New World." *Report of the Superintendent of the U. S. Coast and Geodetic Survey Appendix No. 18, June 1880.* (Washington: Government Printing Office, 1882).

Fuson, Robert H. *The Log of Christopher Columbus.* (Camden, Maine: International Marine Publishing, 1987).

Gerace, Donald T., editor. *Columbus and His World: Proceedings of the First San Salvador Conference.* (San Salvador: College Center of the Finger Lakes, 1986).

Goldsmith, Roger A. and Philip L. Richardson. "Reconstructing Columbus's First Transatlantic Track and Landfall Using Climatological Winds and Currents." *Woods Hole Oceanog. Inst. Tech. Rept.* WHOI-87-46 (November 1987).

———. "Numerical Simulations of Columbus' Atlantic Crossings." *Woods Hole Oceanog. Inst. Tech. Rept.* WHOI-92-14 (February 1992).

Gould, R. T. "The landfall of Columbus: An old problem restated." *Geographical Journal.* 49. (1927) 403-429.

Harland, John. *Seamanship in the Age of Sail.* (Annapolis: Naval Institute Press, 1984).

Henige, David. *In Search of Columbus: Sources for the First Voyage.* (Tuscon: The University of Arizona Press, 1992).

———. *Numbers From Nowhere: The American Indian Contact Population debate.* (Norman: University of Oklahoma Press, 1998).

Henige, David and James E. Kelley Jr., editor. *The Working Papers of the Columbus Round Robin.* (Madison: University of Wisconsin Libraries, microfilm, 1993).

Hongre, L., G. Hulot, and A. Khokhlov. "An Analysis of the Geomagnetic Field over the Past 2000 Years." *Physics of the Earth and Planetary Interiors,* 106. (1998) 311-335.

Irving, Washington. *A History of the Life and Voyages of Christopher Columbus.* (New York: G. & C. Carvill, 1828).

Jane, Cecil, editor. *The Four Voyages of Columbus.* (New York: Dover 1988).

Johnson, Allen W. and Timothy Earle *The Evolution of Human Societies: From Foraging Group to Agrarian State* (Stanford: Stanford University Press, 1987).

Judge, Joseph. "Columbus's First Landfall in the New World." *National Geographic,* 170 (November 1986) 589-590.

Karolle, Bruce. *Atlas of Micronesia.* (Honolulu: Bess Press, 1993).

Keegan, William F., Allen Johnson, and Timothy Earle. "Carrying Capacity and Population Regulation: A Comment on Dewar." *American Anthropologist,* 87. (1985) 659-663.

———. *The People Who Discovered Columbus: The Prehistory of the Bahamas.* (Gainesville: University Press of Florida, 1992).

Kelley, James E. Jr. "In the Wake of Columbus on a Portolan Chart." *Terrae Incognitae,* 15. (1983) 77-111.

———. "Epistemology 101 for Landfall Students: An Appreciation of an Important New Book." *Terrae Incognitae,* 24. (1992) 101-110.

Korte, M. and C. Constable. "Continuous global geomagnetic field models for the past 3000 years." *Physics of the Earth and Planetary Interiors,* 140. (2003) 73-89.

Kuhn, Thomas S. *The Structure of Scientific Revolutions.* (Chicago: University of Chicago Press, 1962).

Lardicci, Francesca. *A synoptic edition of the log of Columbus's first voyage.* (Turnhout, Belgium: Â Brepols, 1999).

Lester, C. Edwards. *The life and voyages of Americus Vespucius*. (New Haven: H. Mansfield, 1858).

Marden, Luis. "The First Landfall of Columbus." *National Geographic*, 170. (November 1986) 572-577.

Marvel, Josiah. "Columbus: The Light of 11 October, 1492." *The Islands' Sun*. (March/April 1990) 6.

McArthur, Norma. *Island Peoples of the Pacific*. (Canberra: Australian National University Press, 1967).

McElroy, John W. "The Ocean Navigation of Columbus on His First Voyage." *The American Neptune*, I. (1941) 209-240.

Meeus, Jean and Hermann Mucke. *Canon of Lunar Eclipses -2002 to +2526*. (Vienna: Astronomisches Buro Wein, 1979).

Molander, Arne B. "A New Approach to the Columbus Landfall." *Terrae Incognitae*, 15. (1983) 113-149.

———. "Columbus and the Method of Lunar Distances," *Terrae Incognitae*, 24. (1992) 77-103.

Morison, Samuel Eliot. *Admiral of the Ocean Sea*, (Boston: Little, Brown & Co., 1942).

———. *Journals and Other Documents on the Life of Christopher Columbus*. (New York: Limited Editions, 1963).

Müller, Johann. *Kalendar Maister Johannes Kunisperger*. (Augsperg: Erhart Radolt, 1489).

———. *Ephemerides sive Almanach perpetuum*. (Venice: Petrus Liechtenstein, 1498).

Murdock, J. B. "The Cruise of Columbus in the Bahamas, 1492." *Proceedings of the U.S. Naval Institute* 10. (1884) 449-486.

Nader, Helen and Luciano Formisano, editor. *The book of privileges issued to Christopher Columbus by King Fernando and Queen Isabel, 1492-1502*. (Berkeley: University of California Press, 1996).

National Oceanographic and Atmospheric Administration. "Surface Current (Ship Drift)." (Washington: NOAA, 2 CD-ROMs, undated). https://www.nodc.noaa.gov/access/cdrom.html.

Newton, Robert R. *The Crime of Claudius Ptolemy*. (Baltimore: Johns Hopkins University Press, 1977).

Nordyke, Eleanor C. *The Peopling of Hawaii*. (Honolulu: Published for the East-West Center by the University of Hawaii Press, 1977).

Parker, John. "The Columbus Landfall Problem: A Historical Perspective." *Terrae Incognitae*, 15. (1983) 1-34.

———. *A Great Sign of Land. Columbus and the Sea-Birds: Ornithology and Navigation in 1492*. (Minneapolis: Cleora Press, 1992).

Pastor, Xavier. *The Ships of Christopher Columbus*. (Annapolis: Naval Institute Press, 1992).

Pearl, Raymond. *The Biology of Population Growth*. (New York: Knopf, 1925).

Peck, Douglas T. *Christoforo Colombo, God's Navigator*. (Columbus, WI: Columbian Publishers, 1993).

———. "Re-thinking the Columbus Landfall Problem." *Terrae Incognitae*, 28. (1996) 12-35.

Phillips, Carla Rahn. "The Evolution of Spanish Ship Design from the Fifteenth to the Eighteenth Century." *The American Neptune*, 53. (1993) 229-238.

Phillips, William D., editor & trans. *The Columbian Lawsuits*. (Turnhout, Belgium: Brepols Publishers, 2000).

Pérez, Alejandro R. *Columbus was never in San Salvador*. (Washington, DC: ABBE Publishers, 1988).

Pickering, Keith A. "Columbus's Plana Landfall." *DIO* 4:1. (1994) 14-23.

———. "Columbus's Method of Determining Longitude: An Analytical View." *The Journal of Navigation*, 49:1. (1996) 99-113.

Power, Robert H. "The Discovery of Columbus's Island Passage to Cuba." *Terrae Incognitae*, 15. (1983) 165-167.

Rensberger, Boyce. "Peary's Polar Mystery." *Washington Post*. June 9, 1991, D3.

Richardson, Philip L. and Roger A. Goldsmith. "The Columbus Landfall: Voyage Track Corrected for Winds and Currents." *Oceanus* 30. (1987) 3-10.

Rose, Richard. "Pigeon Creek." *Florida Anthropologist*, 35. (1982) 129-145.

Rose, Richard, Donald T. Gerace, editor. "Lucayan Lifeways." *Columbus and His World: Proceedings of the First San Salvador Conference*. (San Salvador: College Center of the Finger Lakes, 1987).

Rosenblat, Angel. *La Poblacion de America en 1492: Viejos y Nuevos Calculos*. (Mexico: Colegio de Mexico, 1967).

Russell, Jeffrey Burton. *Inventing the flat earth: Columbus and modern historians*. (New York: Praeger, 1991).

Sadler, H. E. *Turks Islands Landfall: A History of the Turks & Caicos Islands*. (Grand Turk: Marjorie E. Sadler, 1997).

Schmitt, Robert C. *Demographic Statistics of Hawaii, 1778-1965*. (Honolulu: University of Hawaii Press, 1968).

Schott, Charles A. "An Inquiry into the Variation of the Compass Off the Bahama Islands, at the Time of the Landfall of Columbus in 1492." *Report of the Superintendent of the U. S. Coast and Geodetic Survey*. (Appendix no. 19, June 1880) (Washington: Government Printing Office, 1882).

Smith, Julian A. "Precursors to Peregrinus: The early history of magnetism and the mariner's compass in Europe." *Journal of Medieval History*, 18:1. (1992) 21-74.

Thacher, John Boyd. *Christopher Columbus: His Life, His Work, His Remains*. (New York and London: G. P. Putnam's Sons, 1903).

Thompson, R. and D. R. Barraclough. "Geomagnetic Secular Variation Based on Spherical Harmonic and Cross Validation Analyses of Historical and Archaeomagnetic Data." *J. Geomag. Geoelectr.*, 34. (1982) 245-263.

Toomer, G. J., editor. *Ptolemy's Almagest*. (New York: Springer-Verlag. 1984).

U.S. Naval Institute. "Where Did Columbus Land? The evidence to date." 118th annual meeting and second Annapolis seminar, Tape 2 (Annapolis: US Naval Institute, VHS, 1992).

Van der Gucht, J. and S. M. Parajon. *Ruta de Cristobal Colon por la Costa Norte de Cuba.* (Habana: P. Fernandez, 1943).

Verhoog, Pieter H. G. "Columbus Landed on Caicos." *Proceedings of the U.S. Naval Institute,* 80. (1947) 1101-1111.

Vorsey, Louis De Jr. and John Parker, editor. *In the Wake of Columbus: Islands and Controversy.* (Detroit: Wayne State University Press, 1985).

Wadsworth, James E. *Columbus and His First Voyage: A History in Documents.* (London: Bloomsbury Academic, 2016).

Wallich, Paul. "Polar heat: The argument continues over an explorer's good name." *Scientific American,* 262:3. (March 1990) 22.

West, Delno and August Kling. *The Libro de las profecías of Christopher Columbus.* (Gainesville: University of Florida Press, 1991).

Wilford, John Noble. *The Mysterious History of Columbus.* (New York: Vintage, 1991).

Wilson, Curtis. "Hipparchus and Spherical Trigonometry," *Dio* 7.1. (February 1997) 14-15.

Wilson, Samuel M. "Taino and Carib Strategies for Survival." Paper presented at the conference "Non-Imperial Polities in the Lands Visited by Christopher Columbus During His Four Voyages to the New World." (Panama: Smithsonian Tropical Research Institute, 1990).

Zamora, Margarita, Stephen Greenblatt, editor. "Christopher Columbus's Letter: Announcing the Discovery." *New World Encounters.* (Berkeley: University of California Press, 1993).

Index

About the Author

KEITH A. PICKERING is a retired systems analyst and software engineer living in Watertown, Minnesota. He has published academic works in astrophysics, the history of astronomy, navigation, and exploration, and is co-author of *First to the Pole*, the story of the Plaisted North Pole expedition of 1968. He is also a former editor of *DIO: The International Journal of Scientific History*.

Between 1992 and its demise in 1996, Pickering was a member of the Columbus Landfall Round Robin, a committee of correspondence that tasked itself with discovering the true first landfall of Christopher Columbus in the New World. Pickering was a featured interviewee on the History Channel's 2007 documentary *Columbus: The Lost Voyage*. He lives in Watertown, Minnesota.

www.ingramcontent.com/pod-product-compliance
Lightning Source LLC
Chambersburg PA
CBHW021400090426
42742CB00009B/944